The Making of Europe

Series Editor: Jacques Le Goff

The *Making of Europe* series is the result of a unique collaboration between five European publishers – Beck in Germany, Blackwell in Great Britain and the United States, Critica in Spain, Laterza in Italy and le Seuil in France. Each book will be published in all five languages. The scope of the series is broad, encompassing the history of ideas as well as of societies, nations, and states to produce informative, readable, and provocative treatments of central themes in the history of the European peoples and their cultures.

The First European Revolution, c. 970–1215

R. I. Moore

BLACKWELL
Publishers

ABK 9786
10/05/2001
GBC
$ 27.95

First published in English by Blackwell Publishers Ltd 2000, and by four other publishers: © 2000 Beck, Munich (German); © 2000 Critica, Barcelona (Spanish); © 2000 Editions du Seuil, Paris (French); © 2000 Laterza, Rome and Bari (Italian).

2 4 6 8 10 9 7 5 3 1

Blackwell Publishers Ltd
108 Cowley Road
Oxford OX4 1JF
UK

Blackwell Publishers Inc.
350 Main Street
Malden, Massachusetts 02148
USA

British Library Cataloguing in Publication Data

A CIP catalogue record for this book is available from the British Library.

Library of Congress Cataloging-in-Publication Data is available for this book.

Hardcover ISBN 0–631–18479–1
Paperback ISBN 0–631–22277–4

Typeset in 10.5 on 12pt Sabon
by Kolam Information Services Private Ltd., Pondicherry, India
Printed and bound in Great Britain by Biddles Ltd
www.biddles.co.uk

This book is printed on acid-free paper

For Olivia, Richard and Gerald

Contents

Maps and Figures

Maps

Figures

Series Editor's Preface

Europe is in the making. This is both a great challenge and one that can be met only by taking the past into account – a Europe without history would be orphaned and unhappy. Yesterday conditions today; today's actions will be felt tomorrow. The memory of the past should not paralyze the present: when based on understanding it can help us to forge new friendships, and guide us towards progress.

Europe is bordered by the Atlantic, Asia, and Africa, its history and geography inextricably entwined, and its past comprehensible only within the context of the world at large. The territory retains the name given it by the ancient Greeks, and the roots of its heritage may be traced far into prehistory. It is on this foundation – rich and creative, united yet diverse – that Europe's future will be built.

The Making of Europe is the joint initiative of five publishers of different languages and nationalities: Beck in Munich; Blackwell in Oxford; Critica in Barcelona; Laterza in Rome; and le Seuil in Paris. Its aim is to describe the evolution of Europe, presenting the triumphs but not concealing the difficulties. In their efforts to achieve accord and unity the nations of Europe have faced discord, division, and conflict. It is no purpose of this series to conceal these problems: those committed to the European enterprise will not succeed if their view of the future is unencumbered by an understanding of the past.

The title of the series is thus an active one: the time is yet to come when a synthetic history of Europe will be possible. The books we shall publish will be the work of leading historians, by no means all European. They will address crucial aspects of European history in every field – political, economic, social, religious, and cultural. They will draw on that long historiographical tradition which stretches back to Herodotus, as well as on those conceptions and ideas which have transformed historical enquiry in the recent decades of the twentieth century. They will write readably for a wide public.

Our aim is to consider the key questions confronting those involved in Europe's making, and at the same time to satisfy the curiosity of the world at large: in short, who are the Europeans? where have they come from? whither are they bound?

Jacques Le Goff

Preface

Like almost everything I have written since, this book has its origin in the most unexpected conclusion of my early work on popular heresy in the twelfth century, that many of those accused of deviating from the traditional teachings and practices of the church were in fact clinging tenaciously to what they had always been used to. Conversely, their accusers, though they believed themselves the staunch defenders of tradition against 'novelties' in faith or worship propounded by their often puzzled adversaries, were in reality radical and dynamic innovators in these as in so many other aspects of social and cultural life. The translation of this paradox into intelligible questions, of the questions into a coherent inquiry, and of the inquiry into a long-delayed book, has depended at every stage on the ideas, enthusiasms and curiosities of far more colleagues, friends and pupils than I can list. To all who have organized visits and meetings, who have lavished hospitality, who have given me offprints and even books, who have answered innumerable queries directly and indirectly, who have talked and who have listened, I am more grateful than I can say. A few especially heavy debts must be acknowledged in the place of all, and four friends in particular must accept a large share of responsibility for this book's existence, though not for its flaws. The train of thought which became its central argument began in Barbara Rosenwein's office at Loyola, at our first meeting, as I began dimly to sense some of the enormous implications of what she was explaining about the conclusions of her study of Cluny's property, *To Be the Neighbor of St. Peter* (Ithaca and London, 1989). Soon afterwards Richard Landes showed me that I must think more seriously about the early eleventh century, as he has continued, with the most passionate and fruitful of disagreements, to goad me to do ever since. Another brilliantly original study of tenth-and eleventh-century Cluny, this time of its spirituality, Dominique Iogna-Prat's *Agni immaculati*, prompted the connection from which the rest has followed, whose consequences I was encouraged to tease out by the sympathetic and learned imagination of an ideal colleague, Conrad Leyser. The resulting synthesis would have been a great deal shallower and narrower but for Chris Wickham's searching comments on an early outline and for the gentle, relentless curiosity of Jinty Nelson; if I had managed in the intervening years to answer half their questions this would be a very good book indeed.

Meeting Rosenwein and Landes was one of the indirect benefits which flowed from an invitation to teach for two quarters in the History Department of the University of Chicago. The direct ones included membership of a uniquely vigorous and stimulating community of scholars, and a weekly savaging by a class of graduate students of exhilarating intelligence, energy and enthusiasm. Constantin Fasolt, on behalf of the former, and Valerie Ramseyer of the latter, have continued to monitor the transformation of my views on higher education, as well as on eleventh- and twelfth-century history, which resulted. In the last year of writing, however, Sophie Coulson, Jeremy Currie, Joanna Huntington, Fleur Selwyn-Sharpe and Tom Simon reminded me week in and week out that it is still occasionally possible in the British system for an undergraduate class to reach a startling and inspiring level of erudition and creativity.

It has taken far too long to finish this book. I doubt whether I would have had the temerity to start it if I had dreamt that it would go through the press almost simultaneously with the second volume of Sir Richard Southern's *Scholastic Humanism and the Unification of Europe*, which must treat many of the same issues and personalities as those discussed here, especially in the last two chapters. It is not a coincidence that Southern was one of the first pupils, as I was one of the last, of V. H. Galbraith, from whose tutorials, as well as from Southern's own lectures, and from his pupil and my much loved tutor R. H. C. Davis, I have retained a lasting astonishment at the boldness, energy and ingenuity of Anglo-Norman and Angevin clerks, and at the harshness of the world which they inhabited and rebuilt. Jacques Le Goff, John Davey, and his successor Tessa Harvey have borne the delays and excuses with endless patience and support, colleagues in Sheffield and Newcastle (and especially Bernard Porter), have minimized them by accepting the additional burdens consequent on granting me study leave, and at the last Ann Rooke has drawn the maps and Tony Grahame has edited the copy with exemplary speed and skill. Any cogency or clarity that the result may possess is very largely owed to A. E. Redgate's patient and acute criticism of its drafts. The errors and confusions are all my own.

R. I. Moore
Newcastle, 25 January 2000

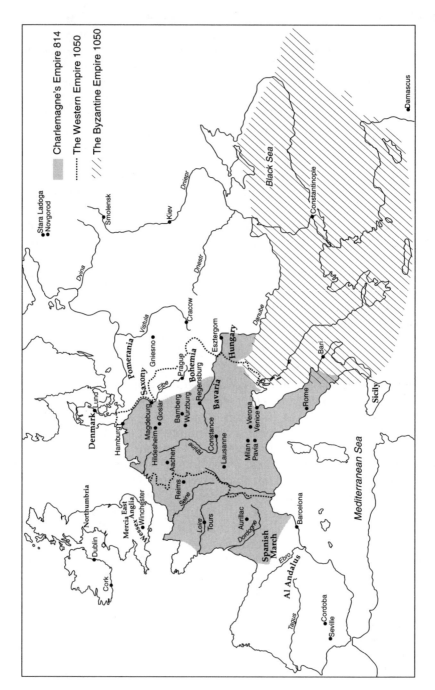

Map 1 The former Carolingian Empire and its neighbours

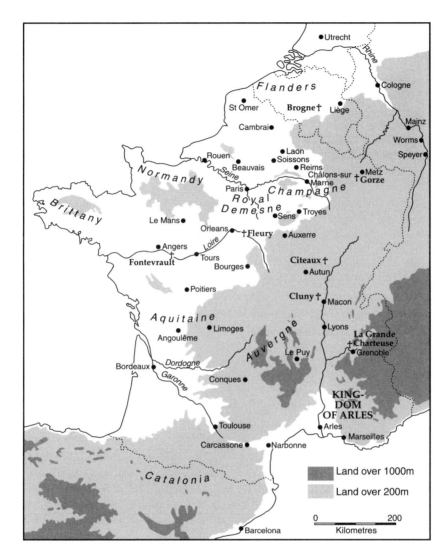

Map 2 Eleventh-century Francia

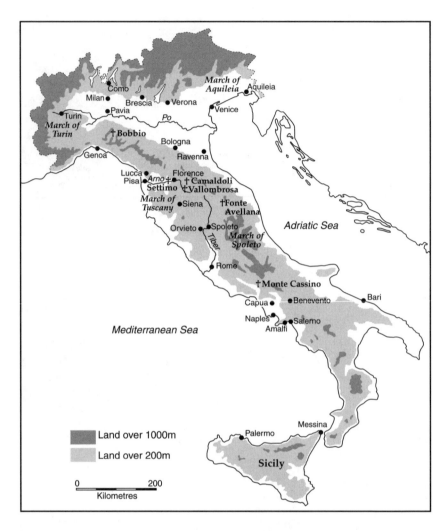

Map 3 Eleventh-century Italy

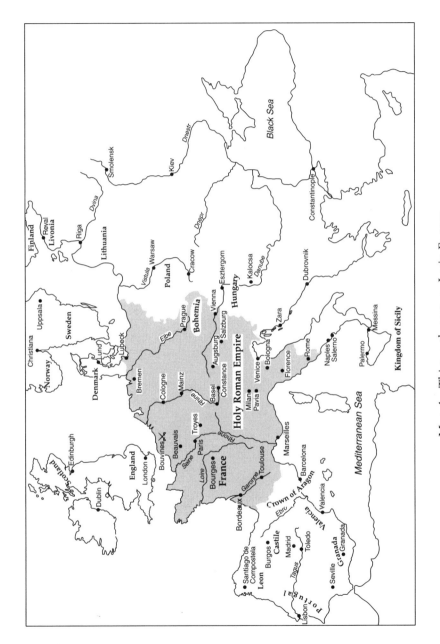

Map 4 Thirteenth-century Latin Europe

Introduction

Bernard of Chartres used to compare us to puny dwarfs perched on the shoulders of giants. He pointed out that we see more and farther than our predecessors, not because we have keener vision or greater height, but because we are lifted up and borne aloft on their gigantic stature.

John of Salisbury, Metalogicon

Europeans, for as long as they have been Europeans (Bernard of Chartres was teaching in the 1120s), have cherished the belief that they are the heirs – the special and particular heirs – of the classical civilizations of the Mediterranean world, and that their civilization is the product of the fusion of the rational and humanistic civilization of Greece and Rome with the spiritual insights and moral strengths of the Judaeo-Christian religious tradition. This belief, like much else that is characteristic of European civilization, is a product of the eleventh and twelfth centuries, when northwestern Europe, which had long been a peripheral region of the cited civilization (a clumsy but expressive phrase coined by the American Islamist G. Marshall Hodgson) based on the Mediterranean, became for the first time the seat of such a civilization in its own right.

Certainly the new civilization owed a great deal to both the Graeco-Roman and the Judaeo-Christian pasts, and especially to the texts which had been handed down from those civilizations and the intellectual and technical skills associated with their transmission and use. The argument of this book, that Europe was born in the second millennium of the Common Era, not the first, is far from seeking to minimize or devalue the achievements of the classical and the patristic eras, or to deny their indispensability to our Europe. But that is not the same thing as saying that they were European achievements, or that their history was European history. Above all, it is not the same thing as saying, what is often said, that these legacies shaped or formed Europe. They did not. They provided an essential stock of materials, certainly – social, economic and institutional as well as cultural and intellectual – but from that stock, as we shall see repeatedly, the men and women of the eleventh and twelfth centuries took what they wanted for their own intricate and highly idiosyncratic construction, and discarded what they did not want. 'Not only is it proper for the new to change the old,' wrote Arnold of Regensburg around 1030, 'but if the old is disordered it should be entirely thrown away, or if it conforms to the proper order of things but is of less use it should be buried with reverence'[1]. His contemporaries and successors more commonly deprecated innovation as dangerous and disreputable, and modestly insisted that they themselves were doing nothing more than restoring broken and tarnished heirlooms to something approaching their pristine glory. The truth is that when they did not find what they needed among the relics of the past, whether it was a collar to enable their few and precious horses to draw heavy loads without throttling themselves, or a harsher but more efficient principle to govern the inheritance of landed property, they did not hesitate to invent it.

The example of the horse collar, which seems to have appeared in the ninth century and was essential to the agrarian and transport revolutions of the eleventh and twelfth, is a reminder of the remarkable achievements of the Carolingian centuries. By the same token the emergence of inheritance by primogeniture, no less essential to the articulation of the characteristic and unique social structure of ancien régime Europe, confirms that the decisive developments and the decisive choices which made Europe came after, not before, the millennium. The map of Charlemagne's Empire (Map 1) anticipates that of the European Economic Community as it was established in 1956, and the European Union which has now extended far beyond those frontiers honours its most distinguished servants with a prize that bears his name. Nevertheless, the Carolingian Empire was a successor state, the greatest of many in the crumbling peripheries of the Roman Empire. It had yet to develop permanent or characteristic forms of its own. In particular, it lacked the urban life, with its need and capacity to organize the life of the countryside around it, which is and which defines civilization. The seeds of the future were there, of course, as they always are, and had begun to germinate; but they did not grow and bear fruit until the eleventh and twelfth centuries, and then not by unaided nature, but because they were arduously and skilfully cultivated.

The construction of a new civilization required profound changes in the economic and political organization of the countryside, amounting to a permanent transformation in the division of labour, social relations, and the distribution of power and wealth. In bringing about those changes, and still more in sustaining them and their effects, the culture of the cities played an indispensable part, equipping its bearers with the vision, the technical sophistication, and the unity and consistency of purpose necessary to bring about these sweeping changes. Because the scale and depth of the changes which accompany the appearance of citied civilization is so great – because, quite literally, nothing would ever be the same again – archaeologists commonly describe these changes in their totality as 'the urban revolution', implying a transformation in the pace and quality of human life comparable with those associated with the invention and dissemination of agriculture (the 'neolithic revolution') and of manufacturing for mass markets with power derived from mineral rather than human or animal energy (the 'industrial revolution'). The phrase was given wide currency by V. Gordon Childe, and his description of 'The Urban Revolution' in Mesopotamia of *c.*3000 BCE, in the fifth chapter of *What Happened in History*,[2] together with its prelude in 'The Higher Barbarism of the Copper Age' – for 'Copper' read 'Carolingian', will strike many echoes for a reader familiar with the history of northwestern Europe between the ninth and twelfth centuries, although Childe's explanatory framework now seems somewhat crude in itself (his Marxist ideology apart), and in obvious respects inapplicable to the later context. Hence my claim that there was a revolution in the eleventh and twelfth centuries, and that since it brought Europe into being it was, by definition, The First European Revolution. The argument of this book is that the character and consequences of that revolution were profoundly influenced by the nature of the political processes which brought it about, though not necessarily, as I shall be compelled to insist repeatedly, through the conscious intentions of the people involved in them.

'Revolution' has been a dangerous word for historians, both in general and in particular contexts. Each of the classic revolutions of the modern world – the Protestant Reformation, the English, American, French and Russian Revolutions, and the 'Industrial Revolution' – possesses an immense and bitterly controversial literature, stretching over several generations and engaging the most brilliant scholars in each, which rages around such questions as whether the revolution may be properly said to have taken place at all, and if so, in what it consisted and what, if anything, it achieved. In the last few years the idea of a 'feudal mutation' in the early decades of the eleventh century, which generalizes the 'feudal revolution' associated above all with the name of Georges Duby, has begun to acquire a distinguished polemical literature of this kind, inspired and led by the powerful and increasingly comprehensive assaults of Dominique Barthélemy on what had certainly begun to show signs of subsiding into a sterile orthodoxy.[3] This controversy seems set to continue, and to broaden its scope, for some time. Until Barthélemy blew his whistle, however, it had not been at all unusual to speak with impunity of revolution in the eleventh and twelfth centuries. The papal revolution (itself, for Karl Leyser, the First European Revolution[4]) is one of our oldest orthodoxies. The commercial revolution and the legal revolution provide titles of familiar textbooks; the agrarian revolution and the revolution in government feature in innumerable articles and papers; there is talk occasionally of eleventh-century revolutions in transport and technology and increasingly of scientific, and of military revolutions; a cognitive revolution has been proclaimed,[5] and a gender revolution cannot be far away. But while these particular revolutions and the controversy they stimulate multiply by the year there has been relatively little serious discussion of the question whether it is appropriate to speak of the period as one of revolution *tout court*. As Berengar of Tours or Peter Abelard might have put it, are we to be nominalists or realists? Are we confronted by a series of spectacular but discrete developments in different areas of thought and activity which we perceive as 'revolutionary' in their own domains and label accordingly, or was there a revolutionary essence of the period, of which these were separate but none the less ultimately related manifestations?

In arguing for revolution I follow in the footsteps of some of the most respected, and most respectable, of modern medievalists. In the preface to one of the most influential books ever written on the European middle ages Sir Richard Southern, identifying a development which almost everybody agrees in seeing as central, specifically characterized 'the slow emergence of a knightly aristocracy' as a social revolution, which unlike other social revolutions contained 'no great events or clearly decisive moments'. For that reason he described it, with other associated developments, as a 'secret revolution',[6] though he also shows, with a vivid quotation from Chrétien de Troyes, how conscious it was possible to be by *c*.1176 that a great historical transformation had taken place in the not very distant past:

> Our books have informed us that the preeminence in chivalry and learning once belonged to Greece. Then chivalry passed to Rome together with that highest learning which now has come to France. God grant that it may be cherished here, that the honour which has taken refuge with us may never depart from France. God has awarded it as another's share, but of Greeks and Romans no more is heard; their fame is passed and their glowing ash is dead.[7]

Though we might be tempted to suspect him of chauvinism, Chrétien was essentially correct in identifying France (that is, what is now northern France) as the home of the new civilization. The 'knightly revolution', like the clerical revolution of which it was part, began there, and throughout our period the most resonant innovations and the greatest energy for change emanated from the lands between the Rhine and the Gironde, or from those like England and Sicily which were colonized from them. Those who warn against the tendency for debate on this period to be conducted entirely in terms of French evidence and French circumstances, as though France was the whole of Europe (which is also a tribute to the brilliance of modern French historiography) are, of course, quite right.[8] Nevertheless, it is inescapable that we shall be very largely preoccupied with the regions where the crucial developments with which this book is concerned occurred, and which, it is contended, transformed the future of Europe.

Some of the implications of calling this transformation a social revolution may be conveyed by borrowing the opening sentences of Theda Skocpol's *States and Social Revolutions*, with the omission of only half a dozen words which limited her application to the period since the French Revolution:

> Social revolutions have been rare and momentous occurrences in [modern] world history. [From France in the 1790s to Vietnam in the 1970s] these revolutions have transformed state organizations, class structures and dominant ideologies. They have given birth to nations whose power and autonomy markedly surpassed their own prevolutionary pasts and outstripped other countries in similar circumstances.[9]

Allowing for a little harmless pedantry in respect of the phrases 'state organizations' and 'class structures' it would be hard to disagree with this as a short description of what happened in northwestern Europe in the eleventh and twelfth centuries. What is more, it will be argued in the pages which follow, the changes which brought this transformation about were accompanied by the threat and sometimes the reality of popular force, and probably could not have been accomplished otherwise. Whether there was, as the classical (marxist) understanding of revolution would require, a transfer of power to a new dominant class is a more complex question. As we shall see, the people who exercised power in the eleventh and twelfth centuries were overwhelmingly the biological descendants of those who had held it since the eighth. There was no moment at which, and no single or simple process by which, power was transferred from one group to another. There was no individual or group of individuals who foresaw or consciously pursued all the transformations which took place. On the other hand, among those transformations the most momentous were in the sources and nature of power itself. In order to secure the rewards which became available in consequence the descendants of the Carolingian aristocracy found it necessary to reorganize themselves into a new social order, and to distribute power and authority among its branches by means of new techniques, and according to new definitions. The greatest beneficiaries of the redistribution, the *clerici* who became the power elite of the new Europe, themselves constituted a class in all but name, and one which was new in all but blood. If this was not a revolution it is difficult to suggest another name for it.

1
The Approach of the Millennium

1   Glad Confident Morning

'When evil doers had sprung up like weeds, and wicked men ravaged the vineyard of the lord like thorn bushes and briars choking the harvest, the abbots and bishops and other holy men decided to call a council at which confiscations (*praeda*) would be forbidden, what had been taken unjustly from the churches would be restored, and other blemishes on the face of the holy church of God scraped away with the sharp blade of anathema. The council was summoned to the monastery of Charroux and great crowds of people went from Poitou, the Limousin and neighbouring regions. The bodies of many saints were brought along to reinforce the pious by their presence and dull the threats of the wicked. The divine will, moved as we believe by the presence of the saints, illuminated that council by frequent miracles.'[1]

In this spirit, according to Letaldus of Micy, on 1 June 989 the monks of Nouaillé bore the most precious possession of their monastery, the relics of its patron saint Jouin, to a great meeting at Charroux, fifty kilometres south of Poitiers. Monks, and lay people of both sexes, summoned by Archbishop Gunbald of Bordeaux and other clerics, including the bishops of Poitiers, Périgueux, Limoges and Angoulême, came to demand the help of God and the saints against the evils of the times. They resolved that (unless the judgement of a bishop was being enforced) three classes of wrongdoers should be excommunicated: anyone who infringed the sanctuary of a church, or took anything from one by force; anyone who took from a farmer, or any other poor person, an ox, a cow, a calf, a goat of either sex or a pig; and anyone who assaulted or carried off an unarmed clerk, or forcibly entered his house.[2] The source of the evils against which these measures are necessary is precisely identified by the fact that the arms whose absence gave title to this protection were specified as those of a trained knight: shield, sword, breastplate, mailcoat.

The following year the Archbishop of Narbonne called together the bishops of his province, and a number of leading laymen, including the vicomtes of Carcassonne, Béziers and Narbonne, to condemn the 'noblemen who not only seized the lands of churches, but behaved in them with the utmost brutality'.[3] In 994 the Archbishop of Lyons presided over a council at Anse in Burgundy at which an even more imposing list of lay and ecclesiastical dignitaries placed a long list of properties of the great abbey of Cluny under the protection of anathema, prohibited clerks from hunting, priests from marrying, and those who were married already from celebrating mass, forbade buying and selling on Sundays (except as much as might be eaten on the day itself), and prescribed appropriate abstinence for laymen on various fast days.[4]

This was the beginning of the movement now called the Peace of God. During the next forty years similar councils were held in the lands south of the Loire, spreading north later in the eleventh century, and into Normandy, the Empire and Catalonia. Its character changed as it spread, and in the change as well as here, in its earliest and most overtly radical phase, it epitomised many of the problems which brought about the reconstruction of European society in the next two centuries, and the responses to them. In the early middle ages Peace had belonged to the king. The powers and responsibilities to enforce the peace assumed by these late tenth- and eleventh-century councils were royal prerogatives, and had been exercised for almost three centuries past by the kings of the Carolingian house and their officers. It was not coincidental that the Peace Councils began a few years after the Carolingian dynasty had been supplanted by the coronation of Hugh Capet at Reims in 987, for Hugh's title was not widely recognized in southern Francia. Conversely, those who supported him in the north looked upon the peace movement as an unwarrantable usurpation of the royal prerogative. When royal and princely power began to be reasserted in the later eleventh century responsibility for enforcing the Peace of God, together with the Truce of God (a set of constraints on private warfare which had come to be associated with the Peace), was again assumed by secular princes. The most forceful of them, William of Normandy, proclaimed it at the Councils of Caen in 1047 and Lillebonne in 1080, thus reintegrating it into the array of prerogatives which he wielded so vigorously as Duke of Normandy and King of England. Thus the history of the Peace of God represents, in one of its many aspects, the central theme of this book – how in the eleventh century power which had leaked away from the established institutions of an old world was used by a bizarre but temporarily effective alliance of church and people to construct a new one, before being brought once more under control, to uphold the newly established social and political order of western Europe for many centuries to come.

The evidence for what happened at the Peace assemblies is so fragmentary that sometimes we scarcely know that they took place at all. Among the miracles of St Vivian of Figeac, for example, apparently compiled at the end of the tenth century, are some which occurred at a meeting at Coler in the Auvergne of bishops gathered to establish the peace and uphold the decrees of the fathers of the church.[5] We have no other knowledge of this Council, but the reference, hopelessly imprecise in itself, serves to confirm a famous assertion of the Cluniac chronicler Radulfus Glaber that 'the bishops and abbots and other devout men of Aquitaine summoned great councils of the whole people, to which were borne the bodies of many saints and innumerable caskets of holy relics. The movement spread to Arles and Lyons, then across all Burgundy into the furthest corners of the Frankish realm. It was decreed that in fixed places the bishops and magnates should convene councils for re-establishing peace and consolidating the holy faith. When the people heard this, great middling and poor, they came rejoicing and ready, one and all, to obey the commands of the clergy no less than if they had been given by a voice from heaven speaking to men on earth.'[6]

We have references to twenty-six such councils between 989 and 1038, most of them in Poitou, the Limousin and the Berry.[7] Their purpose is unambiguously asserted by the description of the meeting at Héry, in 1025. 'Crowds of common people without number, of every age and both genders, hurried there. In order that the devotion of these lay people might be increased on their journey men of faith began to bring the bodies of many saints as well. Along with such venerable relics [the monks of Montier en Die] did not neglect to bring along the relics of the holy body of our patron Bercharius, which were fittingly placed for their journey on a litter. This was done, moreover, so that our leaders could make a proclamation about a certain count, Landric by name, concerning the booty he had stolen from our blessed protector.'[8]

As Radulfus presents them, the novel character of the Peace Councils was that they were convened by clerics but attended by persons of all classes, and especially the humble, who swore on the relics to defend each other, the church and the poor, 'so that all men, lay and religious, whatever threats had hung over them before could now go about their business without fear and unarmed'. 'The robber and the man who seized another's domains were to suffer the whole rigour of the law', Radulfus continues; the sanctuary of the church was to be respected and the safety of clerics and those who travelled in their company guaranteed. Divine approval was signified by the miracles which abounded on these occasions. 'Bent legs and arms were straightened and returned to their normal state, skin was broken, flesh was torn and blood ran freely.' Small wonder that 'such enthusiasm was generated that the bishops raised their croziers to the heavens, and all cried out with one voice to God, their hands stretched out, 'Pax! Pax! Pax!''[9]

As these quotations illustrate, the sources are perfectly explicit about the reason for this great eruption of passionate activity. The peace movement, as it is depicted here, was a response to social collapse, in which the monasteries led the poor in concerted defence against the anarchic conduct of the 'evil men who had sprung up like weeds', seizing the goods and animals of the poor, holding them to ransom and forcing them to work, especially on building the castles from which the usurpers imposed this reign of terror on the countryside. *Pauperes* (the poor) in the vocabulary of this age meant those who lacked power, rather than money. Monasteries and small landowners had a common vulnerability to unrestrained power, and a common interest in restraining it. But for the organizers of the Peace of God lawlessness on earth was only one manifestation of a greater disorder, a breach of the grand harmony of the universe on whose tranquillity, Augustine had said, the peace of all things depended.[10] That is why in his account of the Peace movements Radulfus Glaber particularly stresses the agreement that everybody should abstain from wine on the sixth day of the week and from meat on the seventh: in this way each was individually committed to controlling his or her personal appetites in a manner that paralleled the restraint which, by collective action, they intended to impose upon the world and the evil-doers.

The resolutions for moral and religious reform were preserved in the lists of canons which in most cases are all the record of these councils that remains. The prescriptions of the earliest, like those from Charroux quoted above, appear somewhat arbitrary, though that may represent only the hazard of the record. Later they became increasingly elaborate, until they laid down a comprehensive programme which foreshadowed in all essentials and many details the much more famous programme of reform associated later in the eleventh century with the revival of the Roman papacy and the establishment and dissemination of new religious orders. Thus the council at Bourges in 1031, in addition to providing for the celebration of the mass in the churches every Sunday, ordained 'that no gift should be accepted by the bishop or his ministers in return for holy orders,' that 'laymen should not place priests in their churches except through the bishop,' and that 'no priest, deacon or subdeacon should have a wife or concubine', anticipating the fundamental prohibitions of simony, lay investiture and clerical marriage.[11]

Those provisions of the Council of Bourges will seem very natural to anyone familiar with the general character of Catholic christianity and its place in second-millennium European history. The celibacy of the priesthood has been considered by Catholics since the thirteenth century as indispensable to its sacramental and pastoral functions alike, and in modern times, though frequently controversial, has been widely respected by others as an essential attribute of European Catholicism. The bestowal of ecclesiastical office by laymen upon dependants or relatives has perhaps been too general a custom until modern times to evoke the same universal reprobation as the marriage of clergy vowed to celibacy, but irreligious historians as well as religious ones have almost always regarded the trading of benefices and office in the church, including ordination itself, as a self-evident spiritual and social evil, an 'abuse' of which a healthy and vigorous society would obviously wish to rid itself. Consequently, the extirpation of clerical marriage (nicolaitism) and of improper traffic in clerical office (simony) have usually appeared to later generations as manifestly and unambiguously desirable goals which would naturally attract widespread support.

These were the main objectives of the movement often described, after the greatest publicist and most controversial figure among its leaders, Pope Gregory VII (1073–85, previously Cardinal Hildebrand), as the Gregorian or Hildebrandine reform. They were placed firmly at the head of the political agenda during the pontificate of Leo IX (1049–54), and remained there until they were definitively entrenched as the framework of medieval Catholicism in the decrees of the Fourth Lateran Council of 1215. By that time they had secured at least the acquiescence, and generally the vigorous support, of Europe's secular rulers as well as its clerical intelligentsia. The 'reform' which was embodied in the Gregorian programme was nothing less than a project to divide the world, both people and property, into two distinct and autonomous realms, not geographically but socially. In principle and increasingly in practice every community, from Christendom itself to the remotest hamlet, was to contain an independent clerical domain, with its own powers and functions, its own properties and incomes, its own laws, customs and jurisdiction, and its own membership, separated from others by a distinctive manner of life based on the rule of celibacy.

This meant reversing great changes which had taken place during the ninth and tenth centuries, both in expectations about rights in landed property and in actual possession and control over it. In Charlemagne's time as much as a third of land had belonged to the churches, and he had converted the payment of tithe from a spiritual duty to a legal obligation on all his subjects. In the century and a half following Charlemagne's death in 814 both land and tithes fell on a massive scale under the control of laymen. To recover these lands and revenues for the church was central to the endeavours of the reformers of the eleventh and twelfth centuries. They met with very different degrees of success in different places, but their greatest success was in the areas which will most often be the focus of attention in this book, and especially in northern France. By the time of Lateran IV about one-fifth of Europe's cultivated land belonged to churches, and the church also claimed the right to one-tenth – a tithe – of every legitimate source of income. Distribution of both was uneven. The findings of the Domesday commissioners suggest that in 1086, 26 per cent of revenue from land in England was received by the monasteries, priories and cathedral churches, a good deal more than they had had in 1066.[12] A great deal more still would follow in the following century, as many hundreds of new monasteries, canonries and hospitals were founded and the process of returning or augmenting the revenues of cathedral and parish churches continued. At the end of the twelfth century the churches held perhaps one-third of the cultivated land of northern France, and probably about half as much in southern France and Italy.[13] Even though in many places tithes were paid to lay proprietors, whose right to them was accepted by the church to varying degrees and on varying terms,[14] this represented a massive, ostensibly voluntary and historically unparalleled surrender of power and resources by the lay nobility.

Such a division and redefinition of ecclesiastical property and rights on the scale suggested even by the lowest estimates obviously could not have taken place without equally profound and sweeping consequences on the other side. Lay society was and must have been redefined and reorganized to the same, revolutionary, degree. It is therefore impossible to describe or explain the changes which took place in the church without accounting for those that occurred in the world, and vice versa, though history – itself for long divided by the same events between the secular and the ecclesiastical – has frequently attempted to do so. (The distinction between secular and ecclesiastical history, like that between clergy and laity, is of course much older than the eleventh century: it begins in the fourth, with Constantine and Eusebius, as everybody knows. The argument here is not that the eleventh century invented these distinctions, but that it made them fundamental to European society and culture, for the first time and permanently.) Since this was the foundation upon which European civilization has been constructed it is not easy for Europe's children to remember that it might have been otherwise. Our history has been written by the victors in the struggle to bring this social order into being, in the certainty that their victory was right, and because it was right inevitable. By the middle of the twelfth century they dominated the record almost entirely, and their spiritual descendants occupied the commanding heights of European historiography until the enlightenment, and of much of European education, including higher education, until well into the twentieth century. Consequently, the surrender of extensive territories, abundant incomes and the power which rested on them was recorded and has been widely accepted as the slow and painful recognition of the divine will by men and women persuaded by faith and the desire to conquer their own sin, of which their consciousness had been relentlessly and unceasingly raised by two hundred years of inspired evangelism and instruction. So understood it is indeed a remarkable story, of how a world of savagery, violence and greed was converted to altruism, idealism and service – a fitting birthright for a civilization destined to transform the globe. Without denying the sincerity with which such aspirations were cherished by many individuals, however, it will be necessary to consider the possibility that it was more complicated than that suggests.

2   The Faithful People

History seldom has much time for losers, but there were many at the time who did not think that all that this transformation entailed was right, in theory or in practice, and who did not see the replacement of the old world, in which the combination of secular and spiritual office and its rewards provided a secure and frequently harmonious basis for regional and local hegemonies, as either desirable or virtuous, much less inevitable. As the biographer of the hermit reformer Romuald of Ravenna remarked, 'throughout the whole region up to Romuald's time [the last decades of the tenth century] the custom of simony was so widespread that hardly anyone knew this heresy to be a sin'.[15] More than a century later, after the Investiture Contest had been fought and won, Norbert of Xanten would agree to accept the provostship of St Martin at Laon only if he could maintain his vow 'to live a fully evangelical and apostolic life', which would forbid, among other things, recourse to secular justice, or to the use of anathema, in defence of the church's property. 'I do not refuse the charge, provided that the canons who occupy that church are willing to abide by such a way of living.' The canons were appalled. 'We do not want this man over us, for neither our customs nor those of our predecessors would recognize such a master. May we be allowed to live as we do now: God wishes to castigate, not to mortify.'[16] Resistance to 'reform' was long, desperate and bitter not only because the material interests of the resisters were threatened but because many of them believed just as sincerely as their opponents that justice was on their side, and that they were fighting to sustain an ancient and honourable traditional order against anarchy and confusion. Whether or not the outcome of the long struggle was in itself a triumph of virtue it was, and must have been, also a triumph of force.

To those who brought about the reforms, one essential point was never in doubt. At every stage their demands were supported by 'the faithful people' – in other words the force of popular opinion backed by the threat, and sometimes the reality, of popular action.[17] The crowd which flocked to Charroux was for the next century and a half a regular actor on the stage of European affairs. The Council of Reims, in 1049, when Leo IX used the occasion of the consecration of the new basilica of St Remigius to demand, with spectacular results, that the assembled prelates swear on the relics that they had not paid for their offices is often taken as the opening of the Papal reform movement. It was attended by great crowds who flocked from far and wide to cheer on the reformers, and bring pressure to bear on the unfortunate prelates whom they targetted. In May 1057 a sermon preached at the translation of the relics of St Nazzarro precipitated a rising in Milan, and opened a period of almost twenty years for which the city was dominated (though not controlled) by the Patareni, who installed their own priests in many churches in place of those whom they considered corrupt, held the Archbishop at defiance, and generally acted as trail-blazers of the Gregorian reform.[18] At Florence in 1068 an immense crowd watched a Vallombrosan monk named Peter – thenceforth, Petrus Igneus – walk through the flames to vindicate the relentless campaign which his abbot, Giovanni Gualberti, had waged for many years against the bishop of Florence.[19]

Nothing more clearly expresses the revolutionary character of the pontificate of Gregory VII than his willingness to invoke popular opinion and pressure against the hierarchy over which he himself presided:

> We have heard that certain of the bishops who dwell in your parts either condone or fail to take notice of the keeping of women by priests, deacons and sub-deacons. We charge you in no way to obey these bishops or to follow their precepts...
>
> those who have been promoted by the simoniac heresy... may no longer exercise any ministry in holy church... Those who obtain churches by the gift of money must utterly forfeit them... Nor may those who are guilty of the crime of fornication celebrate masses or minister at the altar in lesser orders.... If they disregard our rulings, or rather those of the holy fathers, the people may in no wise receive their ministrations, so that those who are not corrected from the love of God and the honour of their office may be brought to their senses by the shame of the world and the reproof of the people.[20]

These phrases do not in themselves imply that Gregory VII called the masses to revolt. When he addressed 'the people' of a diocese he had in mind the local aristocracy, and *fideles* in the context of these letters is generally taken in the secular sense to mean landholders, who represented respectable society rather than the population at large. Nonetheless, it was clear enough what such appeals might lead to, and that the Patarenes also called themselves *fideles* does imply at the very least a degree of carelessness on Gregory's part, for he was certainly familiar with the language of such circles, and can hardly have been indifferent to the implications of using it. When, at Cambrai in 1076, a priest named Ramihrdus whose anticlerical preaching had incited popular unrest was examined for heresy his answers were theologically impeccable, but he refused to confirm them by receiving the sacrament 'from any of the abbots or priests or even the bishop himself, because they were up to their necks in simony and other avarice'.[21] Whether or not Ramihrdus actually had Gregory's licence (like Wederic of Ghent, who was also preaching in Flanders, with similar effect[22]), he certainly echoed Gregory's commands, and the Pope reacted with fury when he heard that the bishop's servants had burned Ramihrdus alive in the hut to which he had been confined after his examination. As for the people, 'many of those who had been his followers took away some of his bones and ashes for themselves. In some towns there are many members of his sect to this day [c.1133], and it is thought that some of those who make their living by weaving belong to it.'

The tactics which Gregory VII and his associates used both in their deliberate and organized encouragement of the Patarene movement in Lombardy and Tuscany and in attacks on the old ecclesiastical order elsewhere were revolutionary in the classical sense that they called upon underlings, clerical and lay, to sit in judgement on their superiors, and to withdraw obedience if they found them wanting. Such judgements were generally arrived at not through formal legal process, but by traditional tests of popular reputation and standing in the community. Petrus Igneus survived the flames at Florence; in Cambrai Ramihrdus did not – and both, in consequence, were vindicated in popular esteem as men of outstanding holiness. If Petrus had been burned and Ramihrdus survived the results would have been the same. The significance of the judgement of the flames was not in the 'objective' issue of whether the flesh could withstand them, but in the fact that the outcome was capable of being interpreted in such a way as to express and sustain the verdict of the community.[23]

In this light insistence on clerical celibacy was particularly apt to throw power into the community, since chastity is almost invariably incapable of proof, and therefore must be almost always a matter of reputation. How else could it be decided, and by whom, whether the woman who looked after the daily needs of the priest was his housekeeper or his concubine? That is the judgement which Gregory in effect called upon communities everywhere to make, and why his pontificate was remembered as a time when all Europe was astir, when public affairs were the gossip of street corner and market place, and when 'those who are called the leaders of Christendom' incited 'sudden unrest among the populace, new treacheries of servants against their masters and masters' mistrust of their servants, abject breaches of faith among equals, conspiracies against the power ordained by God'.[24]

The enlistment of popular enthusiasm in the cause of reform had not begun in the pontificate of Gregory VII, and did not end with it. For some decades to come preachers like Wederic and Ramihrdus continued to appear in various parts of Europe, excoriating the sins of the clergy and rousing the people against them. In the 1090s two of the fieriest, Robert of Arbrissel and Vitalis of Mortain, were commissioned by Pope Urban II to preach the crusade in the Loire valley. This access of respectability did nothing to moderate the vigour of their assaults on married and simoniacal priests, whose effect, Bishop Marbod of Rennes complained, was 'not to preach but to undermine'.[25]

Such enthusiasm could easily overstep the bounds of doctrinal orthodoxy, or appear to do so. The blacksmith Manasses of Ghent, who as the Patarenes had done in Milan led a crowd to expel a married priest from his church and take it over for worship in the style approved by the reformers, was said to be associated with another talented assailant of the greed and corruption of the unreformed clergy, Tanchelm of Antwerp, who attracted such crowds and such enthusiastic support that for some years before his death in 1115 nobody dared to arrest him. Tanchelm is generally described as one of the most notorious heretics of the early middle ages, on the basis of a letter in which the Canons of Utrecht urged their archbishop not to release him from captivity. But Tanchelm had been respectable enough, and accomplished enough, to represent the Count of Flanders on a diplomatic mission to the papal court, by whose cynicism and venality impeccably Catholic observers were regularly appalled, and the Canons of Utrecht were among the targets of his rhetoric. Their account of how Tanchelm celebrated his own marriage to a wooden figure of the Virgin is calculated to arouse scandal and dismay, but their letter contains nothing precise to sustain the charge of heresy against him.[26]

Tanchelm is often coupled with another famous rabble rouser, Henry of Lausanne, who led a popular revolt against the clergy of Le Mans in 1116, and presided for some weeks over a communal regime there.[27] Henry became one of the most effective and articulate heretical preachers of his generation. Thirty years after he left Le Mans it needed the best efforts of Bernard of Clairvaux, supported by a string of miracles, to loosen support for him in the Périgord and Toulousain, where for many years he had spread his message to such effect that he left 'churches without people, people without priests, priests without the deference due to them', holy days uncelebrated, children unbaptized and the dead unshriven.[28] A monk named William, otherwise unknown and unidentified, has left an account of a debate (most probably conducted in public) which he had with Henry during this period. It reveals Henry as indeed a radical and a heretical theologian, who denied with articulate vigour the need for the intercession of the church, its clergy or its sacraments between people and their God, and had set out his views in a book from which William quoted several times in the course of the dispute.[29]

That is not to say, however, that Henry was an avowed heretic in 1116. If he had been it is unlikely that he would have sent emissaries before him to ask the permission of Bishop Hildebert of Lavardin to preach in Le Mans – in itself an acknowledgement of the episcopal authority whose denial was the acid test of heresy – and inconceivable that Hildebert would have granted it. Hildebert too was a reformer, a friend and patron of Robert of Arbrissel, and found himself, like many another, frustrated by the recalcitrance of his cathedral chapter, men placed in their comfortable stalls by family patronage, and little disposed to give up their comforts for the sake of a distant pope or a vulgar enthusiasm for spiritual athleticism. One of them, Guillaume, was nicknamed '*qui non bibit aquam*' – 'who doesn't drink water'. Some such tension within the chapter is at any rate hinted at by the fact that some of the younger canons of Le Mans greeted Henry with delight, built a platform for him to speak from, and sat weeping by his feet as he denounced their sins and those of their older brethren, 'his speech resounding as though legions of demons spoke from his open mouth'. He spoke with such effect that the people rose against the clergy, their lords, and for several weeks Henry came and went as he pleased, holding meetings and promulgating his fearsome teachings while the clergy were afraid to act against him.[30] Two of these young clerks left the city with him, later to be received back and forgiven by the bishop, after Hildebert, on his return from Rome, had succeeded in reasserting his control and driving Henry out. It may be difficult to envisage a bishop encouraging such an assault on his own chapter, but it now seems that as much as sixty years later almost exactly the same combination of circumstances led to the emergence of a heretical movement and reputation far greater than Henry's when Valdès of Lyons (another city still backward in its commercial development at the time) was encouraged by Archbishop Guichard of Pontigny to raise popular pressure against the sustained resistance to reform of the cathedral canons, only to be disowned and forbidden to preach by Guichard's successor.[31]

Ironically enough, when Bernard of Clairvaux travelled to the Péri-gord in 1145 to undo Henry's work one of his preliminary tasks was to settle a similar and long running dispute between the Archbishop of Bordeaux and the canons of the cathedral of St André, whom the Archbishop had tried to persuade to embrace the common life – that is to say, to give up their wives and their individual shares of the cathedral's income. 'They had resisted it to the point of being excommunicated for seven years. Because of this the Archbishop had been exiled from his see for five years, leaving the church empty, and they had resisted his return violently.' Here, in contrast to Le Mans, the town supported the chapter – 'The hatred of the people for the Archbishop was so great,' says Bernard's secretary Geoffrey of Auxerre 'that when we entered the town they reviled us all, because we were his supporters. . . . ' There could be no more eloquent testimony of the stubbornness of these pro-vincial grandees in clinging to their positions than the fact that the most eloquent persuader in Christendom had to settle for a 'compromise' by which the canons kept their stalls, which fell into the common pool only when they died – and was glad enough to have done so for his secretary to describe it as a triumph 'worthy to be called a miracle'.[32]

Behind all of these struggles one issue predominated. In the tenth century the wealth of a cathedral church, often the greatest landowner of its region, appeared to the nobles of the locality as one of their most important resources. The arrangement made at Milan in 983 was replic-ated with varying degrees of completeness and formality throughout Latin Europe: the Archbishop bestowed the lands of his cathedral as fiefs upon the greatest families – the *capitanei* – of the region, from whose sons were drawn the upper clergy of the diocese, including the canons of the cathedral, who in turn elected the Archbishop himself – usually, of course, from among their own number. What was to them, as it would have been to the neighbours of an Indian temple or an Egyptian mosque of their time, a perfectly ordinary and elegantly self-sustaining system of elite support, appeared to reformers, led from the middle of the eleventh century by an increasingly articulate, energetic and prestigi-ous papacy, as a scandalous and spiritually devastating depredation of the church, the root of a corruption so profound, as Cardinal Humbert of Silva Candida proved with corruscating passion in his *Books against the Simoniacs* (c.1058) that it threatened to rob Christendom of validly ordained priests, and with them all hope of salvation. The business of reform was by no means so rapidly completed as the reformers demanded – it never is – or as the almost universal acceptance of their case within a generation or so (in the sources which now survive) is apt to suggest. Throughout the twelfth century, in one diocese after another, the moment arrived when a new bishop infected with the idealism of the new age – a Hildebert, a Gumbald or a Guichard of Pontigny – confronted a chapter still wedded (all too literally perhaps) to the ways, and worse still the values, of the old.

An even more famous and complicated affair which was nevertheless rooted in the same problems led in 1155 to the execution of Arnold of Brescia, a preacher of legendary eloquence, austerity and purity of life whose ferocious and devastating analysis of the corruption of the papacy placed him at the head of a civic revolution in Rome which was inevitably, and ruthlessly, suppressed by the Emperor Frederick Barbarossa. Where Arnold differed from Henry of Lausanne and Valdès was not so much that his intervention (like that of the Patarenes at Milan) was uninvited, as that he continued to lead the Roman people in revolt after a compromise had been reached between the Pope and the noble families on the division of wealth and office between the two from which, as happens on these occasions, the people who had supplied the muscle of the commune were excluded.[33]

In this respect as in others the Peace of God had foreshadowed the papal reform movement. From the Patarene rising in Milan through the pontificate of Gregory VII and locally in many parts of Europe right up to the 1140s and beyond, popular pressure under religious leadership was repeatedly and essentially brought to bear on secular magnates who failed to surrender lands and tithes to the church, and on bishops and clergy who failed to acknowledge or implement the new prohibitions on simony, clerical marriage and personal wealth. After the middle of the twelfth century enlisting the people in the cause of reform was no longer a regular or acknowledged strategy, though as we have seen it was by no means abandoned. Up to that point it had been indispensable, though except in Gregory VII's time generally disowned, or at least disguised, after the event. That did not mean that there was no price to pay for it, or for abandoning it.

3   The Gifts of the Saints

In taking the relics from their crypts and parading them through the countryside the abbots and bishops who led the Peace of God entrusted their cause to its surest protectors. 'Under the awesome shadows of the long dead heroes of the faith' the clergy of Roman Gaul had rallied their flocks against the dangers of a lawless age, and buttressed an authority more precarious than it looks in retrospect to implant their faith and the new values it stood for in a backward and recalcitrant countryside.[34] When a sixth-century archdeacon went to clear himself of adultery by swearing his innocence at the tomb of St Maximin at Trier, but confessed his guilt at the last moment because he dared not enter the presence of the saint with the intention of perjuring himself, he showed very well that for some purposes at least waning public authority, formerly embodied in imperial codes and officials, might be effectively replaced by public witness and well founded terror of the consequences of wanton defiance of public opinion.[35] He also felt the sharpest of the weapons that would in the eleventh and twelfth centuries banish clerical marriage (if not altogether clerical concubineage) from the Latin west.

Every fragment of the saint – a shin bone, a finger nail, a hair of his beard – contained his whole being, and guaranteed the presence which had become indispensable to Christian worship. Charlemagne laid it down that churches which had relics should build special oratories to contain them, and Louis the Pious that every church must have one if the mass were to be celebrated there.[36] The enthusiastic pressing of old bones on every gullible northerner who visited Rome that resulted, and the fortuitous discoveries of forgotten saintly graves in increasingly improbable locations, culminating in that of the head of St John the Baptist at Angély, near Poitiers, in 1010, have provided abundant material for the gibes of the irreverent since Guibert of Nogent remarked that since there was also a head of the Baptist at Constantinople at least one of them must be a fraud, unless he had two heads.[37] But a more substantial significance had been revealed by Einhard two hundred years earlier when, after recounting the dubious manoeuvres by which he secured the relics of Saints Peter and Marcellinus for his abbey of Seligenstadt, he described their reception in the various churches to which he sent them, and especially the effect of the miracles which they brought about. 'While the accounts of these and many other workings of God's miraculous power were spreading through the towns and districts [near Aachen] a woman from the land of the Ripuarians who had been blind for a long time . . . asked to be taken to that chapel', and others came from nearby Jülich, Eschweiler, and Gangelt; after a miracle at Hesbaye, 'a great crowd of people poured into that meadow and a throng from the surrounding area gathered to give thanks on behalf of the man who had been cured . . . they kept watch all night long, and the whole area resonated with the praise of God'; at St Bavo (Gent) invalids in search of cure from fourteen named villages came or were brought to the relics; when they reached Maastricht, 'a vast crowd of people had gathered to receive them. They came out from the town blessing and praising God for his vast and ineffable mercy in deigning to visit through such great patron [saints] a people who believed and depend upon him', to be rewarded by a string of cures; and so on.[38] In all this, it is easy to see how the relics drew people into the Christian community and helped to translate, as it were, Charlemagne's lofty ideal of presiding over a community of the baptized into a practical reality. 'As is quite clearly evident in the preceding pages,' says the *Book of Ste. Foy* at Conques, 'St. Foy's power was traversing the farthest regions of the universe and was leaving behind no-one untouched by her gifts.'[39]

Above all the saint was the special protector of his (or her) people, who paraded his relics in the fields to ward off flood or drought, or around the walls of Paris or Tours as their last hope of escaping Viking pillage. When the monks of St Philibert of Tournus quarrelled with the Count of Autun in the 940s and left, taking the relics with them, catastrophe followed in the form of bad harvests, high prices and epidemics, until a great public meeting implored the monks to come back.[40] The power of relics to draw people from far and wide – 'crowds of innumerable people from all directions', 'invalids and sick from great distances as well as from the neighbourhood', 'great numbers of both sexes from the dioceses of Lyon, Autun, Vienne and Macon', 'many people from various regions' and so on[41] – was not at odds with this passionate identification with particular communities. On the contrary, it shows why the relics were put more to use as the power of kings declined. To carry the saint to a newly donated property and march in solemn procession around its boundaries as she received it formally into her care, to bear her solemnly to a farm or building that had been violated by some marauding grandee, and to perform these ceremonies before crowds of witnesses from far and wide, was the best possible way to claim possession, and sometimes the only hope of defending it. Once again Bernard of Angers explains, in the *Book of Ste. Foy*:

> It is a deeply rooted practice and firmly established custom that if land given to Ste. Foy is unjustly appropriated by a usurper for any reason the reliquary of the holy virgin is carried out to that land as a witness in regaining the right to her property. The monks announce that there will be a solemn procession of clergy and laity, who move forward with great formality carrying candles and lamps. A processional cross goes in front of the holy relics embellished all round with enamels and gold, and studded with a variety of gems flashing like stars. The novices serve by carrying a gospel book, holy water, clashing cymbals, and even trumpets made of ivory that were donated by noble pilgrims to adorn the monastery.[42]

No wonder that 'the report of this procession had spread far and wide'. The creation of order which lay at the heart of the church's role in the world was inescapably a theatrical affair. The procession's direct and immediate objective was to secure the interests of Ste Foy, but in doing so it also offered a dramatic representation of the triumph of the saint and her united, precisely ranked and brilliantly arrayed entourage over the dark forces of anarchy and usurpation. In and through this drama the monks did their work in the world as well as securing their own precarious place in it.

Hence the cult of relics is, among other things, a sharp reminder that the Abbot of a great Benedictine house in the tenth century, however much he might long for the *vita angelica* or the *vita contemplativa* prescribed by his rule and demanded by his critics, had about as much chance of achieving it as the Rector or Vice-Chancellor of a modern university has of devoting himself to a life of scholarship. The abbot found himself at the intersection of a series of frontiers – between the monastery and the world, between the powerful and the poor, between heaven and earth, between the living and the dead – which demanded constant policing, intercession and interpretation. He was always on stage. When in 1067 Abbot Hugh of Cluny confronted Count Geoffrey the Bearded of Anjou to secure the return of property seized from the monks of Marmoutier 'words availed him nothing, nor was he ashamed to go on bended knees, or grovel at his feet. He assumed every form of supplication by which mercy might be wrung from cruel power...' – and his warning that Geoffrey should not dare to leave the palace while deaf to Hugh's pleas was awesomely fulfilled when on doing so Geoffrey lost his throne to the revolt of his brother, Fulk Rechin – an event widely regarded as a turning point in the history of the Angevin dynasty.[43]

Hugh resorted on this occasion to a particularly impressive version of one of the most valuable and flexible items in the repertoire of political gesture, the *clamor*. Having recently been the subject of particularly sensitive and wide-ranging studies this rite illuminates several corners of our stage.[44] In late antiquity and Carolingian times the *clamor* was recognized as the way in which the poor – those who did not enjoy the protection of powerful men, specifically including widows, orphans and monks – could bring their tribulations to the attention of the public official, magistrate or Count, who was held to have special responsibility to protect them. Its use by the mighty Abbot of Cluny, one of the most powerful men in Europe, constituted a paradox similar to that in which, in another version, monks would lay the relic of their patron saint on the floor of the church, surrounded by thorns, and hurl execrations upon him for failing to protect them in their calamity. A few years after overthrowing his brother, Count Fulk Rechin was shamed in his turn, this time into compelling one of his knights, Odo of Blazon, to make restitution to the monks of St Trinité of Vendôme for the crops he had stolen from them, after the monks had prostrated themselves in prayer, day after day, before the crucifix laid among thorns on the floor of their church.[45]

These are examples of the liturgical virtuosity which the great monasteries had developed by their dedication to the *opus dei* that patterned the lives of their monks and in the eleventh century inspired the renaissance of church building that, in Radulfus Glaber's famous words, clad Europe in a white cloak of churches. The same elements were blended in the Peace of God, in this respect a particularly dramatic example of a familiar and traditional means of enlisting popular support for monastic objectives, and against the enemies of the church, especially and most regularly those who tried to seize its lands or revenues. The novelty of the Peace of God lay not in its individual elements, but in the co-ordinated participation of so many people from different regions and dioceses, often brought together from considerable distances, and repeated on many occasions over a period of several decades. On every occasion the exercise depended for its effect on presenting the monks as *pauperes* against the *potentes*, appealing to the solidarity of the former and the shame of the latter. The public appeal to the relics, in the fields as in the *clamor*, was the ultimate expression of the alliance between the church and the poor.

4 An Age of Miracles

'This is not an age of miracles' remarked the biographer of Gilbert of Sempringham in the late 1190s.[46] It may seem an odd thing to have said at a moment when the pursuit of miraculous cures, at countless local shrines as well as Canterbury and Compostela, was soaring to new heights of popularity, but Gilbert's biographer was implicitly and somewhat apologetically comparing his master's modest achievements while alive with those of the many spiritual heroes of the previous two and a half centuries, from Gerald of Aurillac (d. 909) to Bernard of Clairvaux (d. 1153). In doing so he acknowledged the distinction between miracles performed after the death and in the lifetime (*in vita*) of the saint, for the lives of many of these earlier heroes describe an impressive repertoire of miracles not merely recorded at their tombs, but performed before enthusiastic or terrified crowds in the full vigour of their maturity.

Miracles abounded, as we have already heard from Radulfus Glaber, when the relics of the saints rallied the faithful to the Peace of God. They were, indeed, eagerly anticipated in these turbulent years not only on great public occasions when church and people came together to defend their liberties against the arbitrary violence of the powerful, but whenever the distress of the poor was to be relieved, the sick to be cured, the helpless to be helped, in whatever ways might display the power of God, and confirm the legitimacy of His earthly representatives. As Bernard of Angers said, 'people hungered for banquets of miraculous and renowned deeds'.[47] If the brothers of Vallombrosa received a gift of bread when through the steadfastness of their refusal to eat meat they were on the verge of starvation, it was a miracle; if the peasant girl whose clear skin threatens to overwhelm Gerald of Aurillac's devotion to chastity appears ugly and deformed in his eyes at the very moment when she is at his mercy, it is a miracle; if a bear which had been killing cattle showed itself at the command of Giovanni Gualberti so that it could be killed it was a miracle; if a tree which Romuald against all advice ordered to be felled refrained from toppling on to his cell, and his hungry disciples found fish in a part of the river where fish rarely appeared, these were miracles; if a monk who had lost his voice recovered it in time for the Christmas services it was a miracle; if, in fact, any success or good fortune fell upon anyone at any time, and in relation to the manifold activities of his or her life, it might have been due to a miracle.[48]

That list echoes Edward Evans-Pritchard's classic evocation of witch-craft belief among the Azande of the Sudan in order to show how if good fortune is substituted for ill, popular belief in the miraculous worked in very much the same way and served very much the same purposes in the early medieval west as the beliefs in witchcraft and sorcery which have been so widely observed in more recent face-to-face societies.[49] This does not mean that the people with whom we are concerned had no such beliefs of their own. Although as Christian writers they did not care to dwell on them, the authors of our sources from the time of Gregory of Tours and Bede up to Burchard of Worms at the beginning of the eleventh century and beyond contain many references both to popular belief in charms and spells, bewitchment and malevolent magic, and to individuals who were credited with magical powers – magicians, sooth-sayers, rainmakers, necromancers and so on.[50] The examples above show how easy it would often be to read the standard repertoire of miracles as reversing or undoing precisely the sorts of misfortune that might be attributed to witchcraft, though (as far as I know) no such suggestion is made explicit in the sources. The idea of the miraculous provided a counterpart to that of witchcraft, and in doing so made it possible to distinguish clearly between holy power that was legitimately possessed and exercised, and fraudulent or illicit alternatives.[51]

The daily expectation of miracles was not peculiar to the Christian west, or to this period. The problems of everyday life – the sickness of children and animals and the accidents that befell them, the threats to precarious subsistence from the failure of crops or the vagaries of fire, storm and flood – and their beneficent counterparts in cure and relief, or the unexpected bounty of nature – were common to all agrarian societies, though they may have been even more than usually pressing anxieties in a world which was, as we shall see, undergoing a profound transformation in its means of subsistence. Nor was there anything new or particularly unusual in the attribution of supernatural powers, for good or evil, to particular individuals. These have been and still are commonplace in peasant societies the world over. What has varied considerably is the extent to which and the manner in which such beliefs are recorded. That may tell us a great deal, since it is directly connected with the attitude adopted to them by religious and political authorities as well as by the cultural elite, which controls what reaches the written record.

Unlike their predecessors in the age of Gregory of Tours and Bede, Carolingian churchmen were little disposed to take much notice of what they regarded as popular superstition, and wrote their saints' lives without adding the miracles which became almost universal in the tenth and eleventh centuries.[52] Odo of Cluny was anxious to minimize this aspect of the reputation of Gerald of Aurillac (d. 909), and was clearly uneasy about the cult which had grown up at Gerald's tomb. 'I have put my faith in the words of witnesses who have recorded not many of the miracles, which ordinary men (*vulgus*) think of great moment, but rather a disciplined way of life and not a few works of mercy pleasing to God.'[53] Or as Odo's own biographer, John of Salerno, put it, 'let those who like to do so praise exorcists, raisers of the dead and all the other people famous for miracles. I will praise patience as the first virtue of Odo'.[54] Nevertheless, on the basis of Odo's *Life*, Gerald must be considered as inaugurating the new age of miracles *in vita* of which Odo himself, like all his successors as Abbots of Cluny down to Hugh the Great (d. 1109) emerges as a powerful exponent.

John's reference to exorcists and raisers of the dead and Odo's to the *vulgus* show what was at stake. To define sanctity in terms of the christian virtues – patience, a disciplined way of life, works of mercy – was to retain the power of definition securely in the hands of men like Odo and Gerald themselves. Their obvious embarrassment at the miracles associated with their heroes is a decisive argument against dismissing such stories in this and the next four or five generations as literary conventions which reflect no real events. On the contrary, Odo would have been delighted and relieved if the careful inquiries which he made of those who had known Gerald in his lifetime had enabled him to shrug off these tales as mere superstition, just as Gregory of Tours and his brother bishops in the sixth century had dealt swiftly with the pretensions of the displaced holy men from the Byzantine world who occasionally turned up in their well-ordered western dioceses. As Bernard of Angers says, addressing his *Book of Ste. Foy* to his master Fulbert of Chartres – a stout champion of episcopal authority in difficult times – 'Partly because it seemed to be the common people who promulgated these miracles of Ste. Foy and partly because they were regarded as new and unusual, we put no faith in them and regarded them as so much worthless fiction.'[55]

Sometimes, however, the enthusiasm of the people was not so easily dismissed. Bernard later explains why during vigils in the church of Ste Foy the illiterate who could not join in the chanting of the psalms were allowed to 'relieve the weariness of the long night with little peasant songs and other frivolities' which might seem, at first sight, to derogate from the decency and dignity of the holy vigil. When Bernard, as a visitor from the sober north, asked in chapter why this was allowed the Abbot told how in his youth the monks decided to forbid 'the unsuitable commotion made by the wild outcries of the peasants and their unruly singing'. Finding that they were unable to enforce silence during services they ordered the doors of the church to be closed at night, and the swarms of peasants to be refused admission to the vigils, until one night a crowd of pilgrims larger than usual appeared 'shouting and demanding that they should be allowed to come inside the walls of the monastery'. Then, 'suddenly while we were sleeping the bars of the doors were spontaneously unfastened' and 'when we rose in the middle of the night for matins we found the church so full of people keeping the vigil that each one of us had difficulty forcing his way forward to his own station'.[56]

We may doubt whether the bars were really unfastened of their own accord, but some of the monks suggested that perhaps the opening of the doors had been a miracle. On reflection others saw the strength of their case. As the Abbot put it, 'If I reassess my own attitude carefully in the light of what you have told me I am satisfied that on account of the simplicity of these people an innocent little song, even a peasant song, can be tolerated somehow. For it may be that if this custom were abolished the crowds that frequent the sanctuary would also disappear. Nevertheless, we should not believe that God rejoices over a little song; it is the hardship of keeping vigil and the good will of simple people that please Him.'

This story illustrates not only how the decision to acknowledge a miracle – here, to account for the bursting open of the barred door – might assist a community to reconcile disagreement or difficulty without loss of face to those who lost the argument, but also how wise leaders adjust themselves to the realities of social power. Similarly, Odo of Cluny stylized the miracles told about Gerald of Aurillac to make them conform to the standard repertory which echoed the life of Christ not as an embellishment to bring his subject up to an expected standard of sainthood, but on the contrary to domesticate, even sanitize, and legitimate a burgeoning local reputation – a reputation among the common people – that wasn't going to go away. The implication of

Odo's embarrassment, therefore, is that what is new in the prominence of miracles in the hagiography of the post-Carolingian period is not so much the activity which they reflect as the fact of their reception into the written record, by which they are conceded, albeit with visible reluctance, a place in the world of high culture.

So far as the miracles associated with shrines and relics are concerned such reluctance was shortlived. Everybody knows with what flair and vigour the medieval church encouraged, or exploited, popular enthusiasm for them, to the point where it seemed, in the words of Achille Luchaire, that the worship of relics, sustained by the miracles associated with them, was the true religion of the middle ages.[57] This was by no means the case of miracles *in vita*, whose prominence in the record, as we have seen, occupies a relatively short and clearly defined period. They do not disappear entirely after the middle of the twelfth century but, as Gilbert's biographer told us, they are few, unspectacular, and above all marginal to the activity of the saint in his lifetime, and, compared with the miracles recorded at his tomb, to his posthumous reputation.

On this reading of tenth-and eleventh-century saints' lives, however, we must suspect that the popularly acknowledged miracle-worker enjoyed a much greater degree of continuity in fact between late antiquity and the high middle ages than the Latin sources care to record. Odo of Cluny's ambivalence towards the living miracle worker is the same which his predecessors as leaders of the church in Gaul had long felt towards a power which could be neither ignored nor acknowledged – the power of the community expressed through its chosen leaders, for its chosen purposes.[58] The bishops of the twelfth century, like their predecessors of the ninth, would seize their opportunity to lock away in the shrines the mana of the saints which had been released by the crumbling of ancient structures of authority. Meanwhile it had a necessary but hazardous role to play in laying the foundations of new ones.

Both the necessity and the hazard are made manifest in the qualities which were attributed to the holy men by the actions and events which those around them chose to acclaim as miracles, and which proclaimed their worker not only as a holy man, but as possessing powers and qualities which have an altogether more precise significance. Though careless of his own safety and well-being, the living saint enjoys a wide immunity from misfortune against both human and natural calamity, which is extended also to his possessions and his followers. He feeds and if need be clothes his followers, and protects them from danger. His benevolence and protection are extended also to the poor and helpless, whose quarrels and conflicts he resolves, and on whose behalf he intervenes against the arbitrary and extortionate behaviour of the mighty and their officials. His ordinary demeanour is gentle and unassuming, but his wrath is quickly aroused against those who contest his authority or defy his judgement, and his curse terrible in its consequences, as to the 'certain proud and haughty Count' who, scorning Romuald's instruction to return the cow which he had seized from a poor farmer, choked to death on its meat. On another occasion a bailiff takes the cow from a *muliercula* (poor woman) who goes to the church and prays to Romuald; the bailiff is struck by an arrow (!), lets the cow go, but dies when he gets home. In the context of the period the portrait thus painted is unmistakable.[59] These are the qualities and powers of lordship. And what underlies the saint's ability to protect his people and punish their enemies is that he himself, like other lords, enjoys the favour of a still greater lord, of whose power and splendour he is the representative and mediator in the community.

The assistance which the ability to rally popular sentiment in such fashion afforded in the short term to churchmen struggling to preserve their property and their values in the face of naked and unabashed power, and the threat which it carried in the long run to the institutions which they established in doing so, sprang from the same source. A miracle *in vita* was established as such not by spiritual or ecclesiastical authority or process, but by the onlookers who decided that the event which they had witnessed was a miracle, not a coincidence, and that it had been performed by virtue of holy, not diabolic power. The miracle worker, in short, exercised social and political power by popular acclaim.

The geography of miracle working is almost as revealing as the chronology. The force of popular indignation under religious leadership was most dramatically harnessed in the cause of ecclesiastical reform in northern and central Italy and southwestern France from the second half of the tenth century onwards, spreading to northwestern France by the end of the eleventh century, and still liable to erupt wherever local conflict became intense for much of the twelfth. Charismatic leadership and the power associated with it are much less evident, on the other hand, in the French royal demesne, the English and Sicilian kingdoms (except for the special case of the influence of Anglo-Saxon hermits in Norman England) and the German Reich[60] – in short, wherever the ecclesiastical hierarchy could expect to call upon the support of well established secular authority. In other words, the capacity to enlist popular support through conspicuous personal holiness, most dramatically acclaimed in acknowledgement as a miracle worker, reflects a leakage of power from established institutions. It was one of the manifestations of what Georges Duby called an age of disorder between the two ages of order which were the Carolingian era and the high middle ages. It underlines the revolutionary nature of the changes with which we are concerned, for it shows that Gregory VII was far from being alone in his willingness to invoke popular enthusiasm to subvert the existing hierarchy and the existing distribution of wealth and power, though he was almost alone in doing it so explicitly. And it immediately raises the question why such popular enthusiasm should have been so readily available in these two and a half centuries to those who had the ability to inspire it.

2

The Powerful and the Poor

1   The Urban Revolution

Intense and widespread religious fervour overflowing the established channels for its expression is often associated with sudden and profound social change. So it was in our period. The nature of the crisis which was so widely perceived at the eve of the millennium is easy to describe in principle, but difficult to discern with clarity. In a sentence, the prevailing mode of production was found lacking, and to make up for the shortfall the more powerful members of society began to quarrel intensely among themselves over the proprietorship of land, while pressing upon the less powerful for greater profits from its cultivation. The resulting increase in the surplus of production, and hence of the size and density of the population which could be sustained, was a necessary condition for the creation of a citied civilization in northwestern Europe.

According to the estimates of J. C. Russell, widely accepted as the best approximation we have, the population of Europe doubled from around 38.5 million in 1000 to around 73.5 million in 1340. But whereas, on his reckoning, the population of Italy, Spain and the Balkans grew by around 50 per cent from 17 to 25 million, that of northern Europe trebled, from 12 to 35.5 million, and therefore from less than one-third to almost half of the total.[1] This was not, by modern standards, a rapid rate of growth, and for just that reason was sufficient to sustain not only quantitative but qualitative change, for it meant that the increase of production was not outpaced by that of people. Consequently, the 'sustained increase in real income per head' which economists regard as the condition necessary for the transformation of social structure, and even as the defining characteristic of industrial revolution, was present more or less continuously in western Europe for some three centuries, from about the middle of the tenth century to the middle of the thirteenth. Yet it was a close run thing: the eleventh century, when the increase of population was apparently gathering pace, was also one of the most famine-struck centuries in European history.

Because the increase was in 'real income per head', and not simply in numbers, social relations not only could change, but were bound to do so. The key to the transformation lay in the increasingly rapid extension of the area devoted to the cultivation of cereal crops, making it possible to support a very much larger number of people per hectare. An increase in the surplus which each worker produces beyond what is necessary to keep him alive and enable him to reproduce successfully, such as Europe experienced with cerealization in our period and again with industrialization in the nineteenth and twentieth centuries (but which has actually been characteristic of its most dynamic regions during almost the whole of their history), makes it possible to support a growing proportion of non-agricultural workers. That in turn permits a much more complex and constantly changing division of labour, and correspondingly richer cultural diversity; greater diversity of skills leads in turn to more precise differentiation of rank and greater differences of wealth and power. The bourgeoisie and the intelligentsia of Europe, with their councils and corporations, their gilds and universities, their law and learning, their pomp and their politics, were the fruit of such growth.

We shall have to return to the meaning and significance of the assertion that a citied civilization was created in northwestern Europe at this time, and for the first time. At the level of the obvious, however – and there is something to be said for starting there – a simple map will suffice to make the point. Map 5 is derived from a data base which assembles population estimates for some 2,300 European cities whose population reached 5,000 at some time between 500 CE and 1850.[2] Of these, 29 are said to have reached 5000 before 1000 CE, and 127 by 1200. For many purposes these estimates would be of little use. The notorious treachery of statistical information is always to be multiplied in dealing with the middle ages, and multiplied again when it relates to population. Even when we have an apparently reliable basis for an estimate in a particular case, which is rare enough, it can hardly ever be extended to others in a way that permits valid comparison. Here, however, though it may be misleading in many individual instances the very variety of the data and the techniques by which it has been arrived at makes it unlikely that all the mistakes are in the same direction.

Accordingly, Map 5 offers a useful bird's eye view of the nature and geography of the first European revolution – that is, of Europe's first authentic and autonomous urbanization – perhaps not least because at first sight it appears to suggest the opposite. It shows that if civilizations

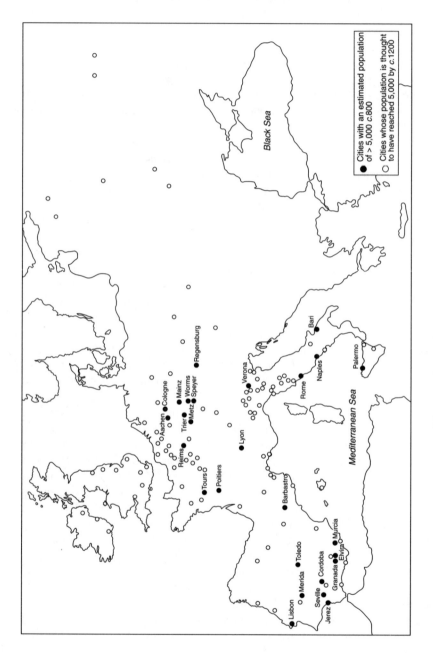

Map 5 European cities, 800–1200

Cities with an estimated population of > 5,000 c.800

Cities whose population is thought to have reached 5,000 by c.1200

Black Sea

Mediterranean Sea

Cologne
Aachen
Mainz
Worms
Speyer
Regensburg
Trier
Metz
Reims
Lyon
Verona
Bari
Tours
Poitiers
Rome
Naples
Palermo
Barbastro
Merida
Toledo
Murcia
Lisbon
Seville
Cordoba
Granada
Elvira
Jerez

are defined by cities then there is no real continuity between our Europe and classical antiquity. In the Mediterranean region the urban character of the brilliant and expanding civilization of the Islamic world after the Abbasid revolution (750 CE) contrasts dramatically with the backwardness of Christendom, though our map does not bring out the scale of the contrast, for most of the Islamic cities shown ran not merely to five thousand, but to several tens of thousands: the population of Cordoba *c.*1000 is estimated at 450,000. In Spain, most of which had been fully integrated into the Islamic world for three centuries, the northern cities grew rapidly in the wake of the Christian Reconquest of the twelfth and thirteenth centuries, while those of Andalusia shrivelled; of fourteen which may have had more than 10,000 in 1000 all declined except Granada and Seville, most of them very sharply, after the reconquest, which gathered momentum from the late eleventh century. Of the great Christian cities of the Iberian peninsula in the thirteenth century, Lisbon, Valencia and Barcelona, the largest and most powerful of them all, had been insignificant in the Roman period. In Italy and Sicily too cities which had flourished under Muslim rule, or in its proximity, declined at least relatively, and most absolutely, after the eleventh century, while most of those which prospered later had been of little or no importance in the ancient world. Twelfth-century Palermo was enormous by Christian standards (150,000), but had already declined sharply since reaching 350,000 under Muslim rule, around 1000, and continued to do so. Proximity to the commercial vigour of the Islamic world doubtless delayed the decay of Naples and Salerno, but like the Greek city of Bari, Rome itself, and Verona, they were still shrinking well into the twelfth century nonetheless: this is still the end of the ancient world, not the beginning of the middle ages. By contrast, of the cities which led the twelfth-century expansion, only Milan (which was the imperial capital in the fourth century CE, but seems to have declined very quickly in the fifth and sixth), had been of much importance in the late Roman world; Florence, Genoa and Pisa were of little account, and Venice was founded according to legend by fugitives from the invading Ostrogoths in the fifth century, and in truth probably rather later. All of these remained very modest in size until the end of the tenth century (though Milan was then probably the largest city in Europe nonetheless), and grew by leaps and bounds in the next three hundred years.

It can certainly be argued that the Romans created no durable cities north of the Alps.[3] The places where Roman populations and institutions lingered longest were not those which showed early signs of urban renewal. Poitiers seems to have had an active school of Roman origin right up to the tenth century, but it had no important urban future; Lyons showed little sign of commercial development until the end of the twelfth century. The Franks established agricultural settlements within the Roman walls of the Rhine cities, Trier, Metz, Cologne, Worms and Speyer. At such places the medieval cities emerged in the eleventh century from the much smaller episcopal and monastic centres, in most cases outside the Roman walls and with little or no continuity of population. Certainly, our map shows several substantial populations proposed for 800, but all of those north of the Alps are exceptions which prove – that is, test – our rule: they are either monastic centres, such as Tours and Regensburg, or royal headquarters like Aachen and Winchester. The underlying pattern was the same in England as on the mainland, but the revival of urban life began earlier. In Wessex Alfred not only organized his resistance to the Vikings around carefully planned fortified burhs but took active measures to stimulate and supervise their markets, while in the tenth century the Danelaw towns benefited (like Rouen) from their incorporation into the trading world of the Vikings. There is certainly a strong case for arguing that Anglo-Saxon England's urban revolution starts here, and that even though it suffered heavily from the second period of Viking invasion and conquest (*c.*980–1016) England, with as much as 10 per cent of its population living in towns by 1066, was the most advanced urban region in Europe before its distinctive and sophisticated civilization was in part extinguished and in part absorbed by the Normans.[4]

The exceptions prove the rule in another sense also, for the great monastic and palace complexes of the early middle ages conformed to a classic definition of the city, as a centre of population which cannot feed itself. To say so is not merely to play games with words. The city represents a necessary and radical division of labour. It is a city by virtue of containing among its inhabitants a number of specialists who having been freed from the production of food are able to develop higher levels of skill in their specialized functions; it can exist only so long as these specialists can by persuasion or compulsion, and through the exercise of their skills, make good the deficiency of food (and of other essential primary products, such as fibres, fuel or minerals) which has been created by the withdrawal of their labour. Some such division usually exists in much simpler communities, of course: the gifts of his followers enable the chief to improve his weapons and attend to the movements of animals or other tribes which may impinge upon the concerns of his people; the man who is handy with his tools may mend his clumsier neighbour's fence in return for half a dozen eggs. But if the chief decides to be nothing but a chief and ceases to tend his animals and land (which may, however, remain 'his' in the sense that those who now look after them are said to do so on his behalf, or to 'hold the land from him' in return for a portion of the produce) he crosses a divide over which he cannot easily return: henceforth he must ensure that his services, as judge or priest or warrior, or all three, are indispensable, or at any rate inescapable. The handyman may spend most of his time mending fences if enough of his neighbours would rather till their fields, but if he deserts his holding to do so (perhaps so that he can travel to other villages, and offer his services more widely) his livelihood will depend on others continuing to have work for him, and being able to pay for it: like the chief, he accepts a radical, and probably irreversible change in his and his family's way of life. If a village, under the persuasion of its chiefs or handymen may be, undertakes to support more of them than its own surplus will sustain, or some project which will require wealth beyond its ordinary means, such as the construction of a great church perhaps, then it too, as a community, finds itself inevitably drawn into relations with the wider world, to which it must look, in one way or another for the additional surplus which the project requires. In deciding to transform itself it commits itself also to the transformation of the countryside around it.[5]

Only in this sense and for this reason can be it said, as it often is, that the cities of medieval Europe 'grew out of' the countryside. Barcelona's first vigorous urban development, around the end of the tenth century, was accompanied by no visible sign of the commercial or industrial growth that came later. But the founder of its comital dynasty, Guifré the Hairy, had participated in the establishment of six great monasteries in the region during the 870s, '80s and '90s, and the cathedral, which had had only six canons in 974, was supporting seventeen in 1005 – and supporting them in style enough to build their own houses and, if they were so inclined, become known as collectors of books. It is to the ecclesiastical communities, together with the entourage of the Counts, settled there since Guifré's time and considerably swollen by the need for defence and the opportunity of profitable revenge which followed Al Mansur's sacking of the city in 985, that we must look for the impetus to the proliferation of crafts and the growth of markets which become increasingly evident during the following century. 'Take-off' is signalled by the minting of gold coins in the city from 1018, by the building of the Romanesque cathedral from 1058, with all that it implies about investment, employment, and the quality and variety of craft specialisms available in the city and now attracted to it, and by a sharp increase in the cost of both land and houses in the city in the following years.[6]

One of the earliest indications of a burgeoning urban community at Barcelona is evidence of a rise in the price of vineyards around the beginning of the eleventh century. The descendants of Llorenc (d. 987), who worked his own land at Provençals, just to the north, made their fortune by supplying the same market with fruit and vegetables.

Llorenc's son Vivas bought out his brother's share of the land, and acquired other property in and around the city, including a shed in the marketplace; his sons, who went as pilgrims to Compostela, expanded further by buying space under the Roman aquaduct, and his grandson married a daughter of the master of the cathedral school, made the pilgrimage to Jerusalem, and in 1046 was one of the *proceres* of the city appointed as arbitrators in a dispute between the bishop and the widow of one of the leading magnates. The same intimate connection between the economic development of the city and its hinterland saw Ricardo Guillermo buying up orchards in the 1060s and 1070s, not for the fruit, it seems, but to grow textile plants for processing in the fulling mills that he acquired in the 1080s and 1090s, together with the wool brought in from the land he was buying in the countryside at the same time.[7]

Another case in which recent investigation has connected the emergence of the city not with long-distance commerce but with the intensification of local exchange and the response of agricultural communities (or rather their lords) to increased demand, is that of St Omer.[8] Allowing for the continuing need for wood and waste, the fact that 60 per cent of its land had already been cleared by 1000 suggests a possible trigger for a series of interacting improvements which from the early eleventh century onwards greatly increased productivity in the region. Better fodder, in the form of vetch, assisted the replacement of oxen, last mentioned in 1120, by horses, which not only increased the efficiency of ploughing but contributed handsomely to the systematic enrichment of the soil, and to the improvement of transportation. The construction of new roads and water ways connected several well developed local markets and stimulated trade in a greater variety of goods from increasingly distant places, including, as in Barcelona, a marked increase in the consumption of wine. From the middle of the eleventh century these developments helped to provide the capital and the labour, as well as the incentive, for the purposeful exploitation of the marshes, the reclamation of land from the sea, and the systematic removal of obstacles to navigation.

These were the foundations of the far-flung and lucrative cloth trade of the twelfth century whose profits enabled a man like William Cade of St Omer to become one of the great financiers and moneylenders of his time. When he died in 1174, probably in London, William held the farm of Dover (the right to collect the king's revenues) as security for £5,468 sterling which he had lent the English kings since 1150. William was one of the grandees emerging all over Europe, but especially here in Flanders and in Tuscany, as the leaders of newly-confident urban communities which were discovering that their wealth could bring freedom – their town air could make them free – and not only freedom but power, to establish their own laws, conduct their own affairs, and establish their own dynasties, in the thirteenth century as proud and as privileged as all but the greatest nobles, and sometimes far richer. They have often been hailed as revolutionaries, and certainly they were the foremost harbingers and representatives of a new world, and a new way of life which grew and flourished but remained in its foundations and essentials unchanged until the nineteenth century. But even when they had to fight for their new liberties – and sometimes they did, though it was usually easier to buy them, for every lord had his price – they did not make the revolution. William Cade was the result, not the cause, of a long and at first very slow, but steady growth of an increasingly complex and effective local economy which had begun with the foundation of the monastery of St Bertin c.648, perhaps a century or so before that of the neighbouring church of St Omer.

If William Cade is one great symbol of our revolution, the rebuilding of Barcelona cathedral which began in 1058 was another. 'The white cloak of churches' with which Radulfus Glaber had boasted that his contemporaries covered the world was by 1300 a far grander cloak than even he had dreamed of, covering a far larger Europe. From Kirkwall on Orkney to Monreale in Sicily, from Lisbon on the Atlantic to Riga on the Baltic or Esztergom by the Danube, the great Romanesque and Gothic cathedrals and the parish churches remain our most familiar and universal legacy from the middle ages. In some areas as many as 80 per cent of today's parish churches have eleventh- and twelfth-century work in their fabric. In France alone some eighty cathedrals, five hundred other large churches and several thousand parish churches were built and rebuilt during the eleventh, twelfth and thirteenth centuries.[9] Church building played very much the same part in the transformation of Europe in this period as did the construction of railways in the industrial revolution of the nineteenth century. Everywhere the churches were both the symbols and the agents of the new age, drawing the remotest villages into a society larger and more closely integrated than ever before, and eventually transforming not only economic but social and cultural life. The building work itself (irrespective of the motives of the builders, which since they were human were extremely varied) demanded skills and resources on an economically revolutionary scale. At first stone could be taken, ready shaped, from the Roman remains which were to be found almost everywhere, but soon quarries had to be discovered and opened up, and forests explored for timber large and straight enough to serve the dreams of architects. Labour was mobilized on an astonishing scale in a world still acutely short of manpower, and new levels of skill and accuracy attained in everything from stone-carving and glass-making to supporting hundreds of tons of masonry on slender columns and soaring vaults. The finest exponents of these techniques were as famous in their day as the railway builders, and like them travelled Europe from one end to the other to place their talents at the disposal of the most thrusting and ambitious employers. In doing so they helped to create a common European culture, common expectations and standards, common designs and techniques, a common language in stone and glass to express the most abstract and the most ethereal anxieties and aspirations.

The spin-offs of advanced technology were pervasive. The ingenuity of the builders, the activity which they generated, and the resources at their disposal, contributed immensely to great improvements in transport and communication by land and water, to the gradual spread of building in stone and brick to non-religious purposes, including storage and dwelling, and what has been called (perhaps with some exaggeration) an 'industrial revolution' in the variety and diffusion of metal tools and implements, and of mills and other machines driven by water power, in both town and countryside. All this represented not only greater production and wealth in the present, but a greater capacity to increase it in the future, and a less exclusive dependence on unaided human toil which brought greater resilience and adaptability in the face of disaster, crucial when the threat of war, famine and disease were ever-present.

All of this could be made possible only by reshaping the countryside into a cereal-growing, market-oriented agrarian economy, taming it to match and support the demands of a more complex civilization. The face of Europe was transformed as wood and scrub were cleared, marsh drained and polder reclaimed from the sea. 'Monks and clerks bear witness to this,' the early twelfth-century Norman chronicler Orderic Vitalis tells us, 'for they cut down dense woods, and now give praise in high-roofed monasteries and spiritual palaces built there, chanting to God with peace of mind in places where formerly robber outlaws used to lurk to perform evil deeds.'[10] His account was quite literally true in the case of the monastery at Afflighem, which was founded around 1100 by a band of reformed bandits at the spot by the road where they had previously lain in wait for their prey.[11] Their story provides a nice illustration of the ways in which religious conversion (here, as usually in medieval usage, to a new way of life rather than to a new religion) might broaden the social base of the church by offering legitimation and enhanced social standing in return for the acceptance of religious authority: after all, though at first they lived in great poverty, alms from passers-by still contributed substantially to the support of the monks of Afflighem.

The village of the children's storybook, grouped around its castle or manor house and its parish church, now began to take shape. Archaeologists have uncovered many examples of settlements becoming permanent at this time, at Wharram Percy in Yorkshire and Gladbach in Westphalia, for example,[12] as communities ceased to shift every few years, though within a fixed territory, to allow the roughly cleared land to recover from the effort of supporting their meagre crops. How and why they were enabled or compelled to do so, and with what results for their patterns of life and thought, are questions which take us to the heart of the social revolution which it entailed. The descendants of lawless warriors who controlled such places slowly became seigneurs and justices of the peace, supported by the labour of an industrious peasantry, and supporting in their turn the courts, the cathedrals, the crusades of a cosmopolitan aristocracy. The new secular and ecclesiastical elite (not new in blood, as we shall see, but in just about every other way possible), attended the courts of many monarchs but (with relatively minor local variations) lived within a common framework of increasingly bureaucratic lordship made articulate by the precepts of Roman law, guided by the lights of Latin culture, and united in devotion to a Catholic faith. Shortly after the middle of the thirteenth century the architects of Beauvais had raised the vault of their cathedral 48 metres above its floor, and Thomas Aquinas synthesized the teachings and authority of the Church with the precepts of Aristotle. Neither vision could have been realized if at the same moment the grain fields had not stretched higher up the hillsides than they had ever done before, or ever would again.

2   The Crisis of the Carolingian Regime

The transformation of the countryside in the eleventh and twelfth centuries was itself the result not of evolutionary but of revolutionary change. Despite the show farms so impressively described in the imposing estate surveys, or polyptiques, which were compiled in the ninth century for a number of royal properties and great churches in Francia, Carolingian agriculture was not truly cereal-based or market-oriented. The forests which had advanced as the Roman world declined continued to dominate the landscapes. Most people supported themselves by a combination of hunting, foraging and cottage gardening, supplementing the produce of the intensely cultivated patch around the homestead from the woodland, pasture, marsh and scrub to which the Roman arable had succumbed, and which provided a smaller population with essential ingredients of a mixed and nutritious diet. Many – though *ex hypothesi* we cannot guess how many – lived in the forests, wastes and mountains, outside the bounds of organized, governed society. The marshes, woods and streams were still indispensable to the diet and economy of those who lived within it. The immemorial peasant community so firmly rooted in our imaginations is an illusion. Beyond the great estates, which constituted only a small and unrepresentative part of the Carolingian countryside, farming communities frequently did not occupy settled and fixed sites, but moved within a limited territory, to remain close to fields which were cultivated for a few years at a time, and then left to recover their vitality while the cultivators attacked some other patch. The bounded and continuously inhabited village with its surrounding fields was a product of the regrouping of the later tenth and eleventh centuries. Bread was not yet the staff of life, and did not become so until much later.[13] Even in the twelfth century the regime of vines and cereals, the foundation crops of European civilization, was not universal in the eyes of the Parisian master Hugh of St Victor: 'In antiquity men used to eat merely by hunting, as they still do in certain regions where the use of bread is extremely rare, where flesh is the only food, and water and mead the drink.'[14] It was no accident that bread and wine were the symbolic as well as the material staples of the new world which Hugh inhabited.

The chronology of cerealization, both uneven in itself and unevenly recorded, and hence of the wider transformation with which it was inextricably interconnected, remains controversial. Both the population and the amount of land under cultivation had been increasing slowly since the seventh century, particularly on the fertile western and northern plains from the Garonne to the Weser. On the whole, despite the terrified chroniclers' lurid descriptions of Viking and Magyar raids and the local devastation which they undoubtedly caused, there are no persuasive grounds for seeing the ninth and tenth centuries as marked by general economic decline. But the steady growth of population, very slow though it was, in itself created pressure in some areas to clear land for grain, which could support a much greater concentration of people than the traditional mixed economy. When the monks of Bobbio had forest cleared for thirty-two new farms between 862 and 883 they did it 'out of necessity', uneasily conscious that with the woodland they destroyed a source of pasture, nourishment and fuel which underpinned the life of the countryside.[15] The ten general famines recorded in Francia in the tenth century and the twenty-six in the eleventh stand grim witness that the old methods of feeding the population would not sustain the demands it made on them. The success of the agrarian revolution with whose negative consequences we shall be much preoccupied is just as plainly confirmed by the same test. There were only two general famines in the twelfth century, and none in the thirteenth, but a steady increase in each successive century thereafter, from six in the fourteenth to sixteen in the eighteenth, again reflected increasing strain on the land

and its users (exacerbated by many ill turns of climate, disease and disorder), until in the nineteenth and twentieth centuries industrial society demanded another transformation of the agrarian system.

The role of the church in bringing the population within the sway of organized society was indispensable. The spread of Christianity, and especially of monasticism, had always brought both increased demands on the land and more sophisticated techniques of social organization to enable them to be met. A crucial instance was the payment of tithes, demanded as a Christian duty by the Frankish church since the seventh century, but made a civic one – that is, compulsory – by Charlemagne and Louis the Pious. If everyone had to pay it was necessary to specify the church to which the payment was due, so *c.*810 it was decreed that 'each church shall have boundaries (to determine) from which villas it receives the tithes'.[16] The resulting profits, already a powerful incentive for the widespread secularisation of church land in the ninth century, became ever greater as productivity increased and new land was brought under cultivation. The *(decimae) novales* figure prominently in eleventh- and twelfth-century charters both as donations and as sources of conflict, which they continued to provoke to such an extent that the Third Lateran Council of 1179 decided that the boundaries of every parish must be defined by written deeds and witnesses.

More frequent calls for payments of dues and taxes in cash, further increased by the demands of the Norsemen for geld, and by the recoinage carried out by Charles the Bald in 864, also helped to press the working population in many areas towards the expanding markets and the more habitual use of coin which in the long run proved a powerful means of bringing people within the reach of government and the sway of lordship. The most specific evidence for the changes comes from the polyptiques. These fascinating documents show (if they are to be taken at face value, as depicting actual practice rather than idealized theory), that the estates which they describe were organized not only to secure labour services and shares of the crops from the peasants who worked the land, but increasingly to take dues in the form of cash, sending the peasants into the burgeoning local markets to raise it, like the *rusticus* who attended an annual fair in the Ardennes in the 870s 'to acquire the wherewithal to pay what I owe to my lord'.[17] In such regions, and especially in the heart of the west Frankish kingdom between the Seine and the Rhine, trade was growing, markets were being established, a greater range of crafts was being practised and higher levels of skill attained, notably in building and metal working.

These developments, and especially the institution of the tithe, undoubtedly helped to bring the potential for profit from agricultural revenues to the attention of the secular nobility. Nevertheless, its transition from living on the profits of plunder to living on those of agriculture, from booty to tax and rent, was a gradual one. There was considerable progress in that direction in the reigns of Charlemagne and his son and grandsons, but the rewards of conquest, and perhaps still more the expectation of them, remained an essential though increasingly irregular buttress of royal authority. The erosion of that authority, and the consequent passing into private hands of the public prerogatives and responsibilities which the Emperor had entrusted to his officials, including above all the power of doing justice, have traditionally been represented as the root cause of the desperate struggle for control over landed property which is increasingly evident in the sources from the last decades of the tenth century and shaped the social revolution of the following two hundred years.

It is long past time to discard the tradition of attributing the eventual decline of Charlemagne's empire to the personal incompetence of his successors, who for the most part battled energetically enough against forces which they could do little to control. The cliché that the death of Charlemagne himself, in 814, quickly followed by prolonged and intensifying rivalry between his successors and their followers, led in Francia to two centuries of intermittent, frequently savage and increasingly localized civil warfare and the destruction of the Carolingian Empire, is now substantially discredited. The formal unity of the Empire was not radically inconsistent with a division of kingly power and wealth such as the sons of Louis the Pious agreed upon in 843, and recorded in the Treaty of Verdun. Charles the Bald (d. 877), who under its terms ruled the western parts of the Frankish empire, exercised formidable political authority, and a splendid ecclesiastical culture flourished under his patronage. The Carolingians would retain the crown for barely a century after his death, but Charlemagne's innovations in local government remained effective (though quite how effective they were at any time in their history will always be controversial) for some generations yet in much of his former Empire; his cultural patronage and policy laid the foundation for the renaissance of the twelfth century; and the aristocracy created from his friends and relations became, though reshaped and reformed in the eleventh and twelfth centuries, the privileged elite of Europe's ancien régime. Nevertheless, although their blood was still held uniquely to confer legitimacy on political authority, and courts held in their names by their appointed officers continued in some areas to offer a measure of protection to the weak even into the eleventh century, it was apparent by the end of the ninth that the descendants of Charlemagne no longer had the means to enforce their will at the highest levels, and therefore could not maintain order among the magnates of their kingdoms or organize effective defence against its external enemies.

Their difficulties can no longer be attributed primarily to the irregular though certainly terrifying raids of Vikings, Saracens and Magyars, which were not so much the cause as the symptom of social disruption and political disarray. In 859–60 the longboats of the Vikings sailed round the Iberian peninsula to enter the Mediterranean and sack Narbonne, Marseille and Pisa, but they never troubled the Caliphate of Cordoba, as far superior to the Christian territories of the west in government as in wealth. At the frontiers of the Carolingian world Alfred of Wessex (871–899) and his successors took advantage of the Viking destruction of the Mercian, East Anglian and Northumbrian kingdoms to lay the foundations of a single, centrally governed English state. Henry I (919–936) and Otto I (936–62) of Saxony showed that they had mastered the same lesson, that crisis offered opportunity to the able and fortunate, by placing themselves at the head of the eastern Franks against the Magyar invaders. Otto's victory over the Magyars at the Lechfeld in 955 enabled him to claim the title of Roman Emperor in his turn, and in doing so to inaugurate the tradition of aspiration to unified dominion over the German lands which created the largest and most impressive political structure of the medieval period, though by no means the stablest or most cohesive.

The triumphs of the West Saxon and Ottonian monarchs of the tenth century rested on the continuing flow of booty from their frontiers with, respectively, Danish settlers and Slavs. Similarly, in Leon-Castile the profits and opportunities of frontier warfare helped the monarchy to remain strong until the death of Alfonso VI in 1109, whereas in Catalonia the Counts of Barcelona were on peaceful terms with the Islamic kingdoms, but suffered violent and persistent internal revolts from the 1040s onwards.[18] The troubles of west Francia in the tenth century flowed from the same cause as the success of the West Saxons and Ottonians. It is obvious (with hindsight) from the beginning of real dispute over the succession to the Carolingian Empire, in the reign of Louis the Pious, and very much more seriously after the death of Charles the Bald, but it is already visible almost from Charlemagne's assumption of the imperial crown in 800. This was a conquest empire. The enormous power and prestige of Charlemagne, as of his father and grandfather before him, had depended very largely on there being booty and land to distribute among his followers at the end of each summer's campaign. There were intermissions, of course, and even occasional failures, but for almost the whole of the eighth century nobody had reason to doubt that the path to fortune was through the favour of the king (or, until 751, the mayor of the palace), or that the place for an ambitious man was by his side. Even if Charlemagne had been immortal territorial conquest could hardly have been sustained indefinitely. The year 803, when Charlemagne 'marched into Bavaria, and after settling the affairs of Pannonia returned to Aachen in the month of December and celebrated Christmas',[19] marks the end of an era. Such expeditions continued to provide quite frequent opportunities, and sometimes substantial winnings, for most of the ninth century,[20] but the setbacks and reverses of Charlemagne's last decade in the short run, and the increasingly obvious difficulties of his successors in the long, quickly changed the political rules. It remained the case, as it always had been among the Franks, that a man's hopes must lie in following a lord whose lord was a winner, but by the end of the ninth century it was no longer a safe bet, or even a very good one, that that winner was most likely to be the king. So for those who wished to retain their own following it became increasingly necessary to seek an alternative source not only of protection, but of reward. Since the most obvious means of doing so was to follow a likelier leader localized conflict and political fragmentation wrote the headlines of the age. Behind them the reliability of warfare itself as the basis of power, status and ambition was increasingly uncertain.

In west Francia, therefore, where there was no longer an open frontier, the very success with which the kings and the great churches compensated for its loss by developing the economic resources of their estates became a source of weakness. It showed what could be done with land and its cultivators, and encouraged the nobility to turn inwards upon their own territories in search of the riches no longer assured by the summer campaign. The prospect was the more enticing since (it was ever thus) the appetite for wealth did not diminish as its source dried up. On the contrary, the perceived needs of the privileged were enlarged as the revival of Mediterranean commerce brought eastern fabrics and spices once more within the reach of those who could pay for them, while the rising cost of weaponry and up-to-date military training and equipment increased the price of remaining within the circle of the powerful, and with it the desperation of those who competed to do so. For the churches competition was no less intense than among the laity, and even more expensive, since everywhere it took the form, pre-eminently, of the building and rebuilding on an ever more splendid scale which provided Europe, in its first revolution, with its first truly European architecture – which historians, ever loyal to meretricious tradition, have chosen to call Romanesque. But for laity and churches alike increasing expenditure looks less like the cause of increasing competitiveness than its result, for these were mainly developments of the eleventh century, whereas the escalation of dispute and disorder arising from conflict over the control of landed property which lay at the heart of the crisis was well under way in many regions by the middle of the tenth.

3   The End of Affluence

In a famous essay on 'the original affluent society' Marshall Sahlins described the equilibrium which hunter-gatherers achieved with their environment. He called them affluent in the sense of having secured their material requirements, which were limited by the imperative of portability: as nomads they could not afford to become dependent on anything which could not accompany them on their annual round of habitats and harvesting places.[21] In that perspective, Sahlins suggested, the coming of agriculture could scarcely be viewed as a blessing, except for the few who were able to gain from the consequent differentiation of power and wealth by securing control of the surplus produced by the rest. Carolingian peasants were not hunter-gatherers, but they did resemble them, as we have already seen, in depending vitally on their ability to draw sustenance from a variety of natural resources, and to maintain a delicate ecological balance with their environment. Like Sahlin's 'affluent society', Carolingian society was much less sharply differentiated than that to which it gave way. Disparities of wealth and status were very great, but they were not always clearly or precisely marked, and the gradations of wealth did not correspond consistently to those of either rank or freedom. The most generally used social distinction was that between *potentes*, the powerful, and *pauperes* – literally, the poor, but better translated as powerless. The latter included not only the slaves who in many regions were still to be found working quite modest estates and even small farms, but often their masters, lacking power in the sense that they could not command other free men or brave the wrath of a great warrior, but landowners in their own right nonetheless, free to claim the protection of the public courts, and to obey the summons to the royal host.

This form of society, in retrospect most easily visible at the margins of Frankish society, in Brittany or southern Italy for example, was a good deal more resilient than the familiar narratives of invasion and internecine warfare suggest. But, as we have seen, it possessed neither an economy which could sustain long-term population growth nor social and political structures which could contain the appetites and ambitions of a warrior aristocracy starved of the prospect of continuing conquest. Both deficiencies pointed implacably to the same solution: more must be produced from the land, and more of the product taken from the producers. That in turn meant, among other things, bringing the land under systematic and continuous management, and therefore concentrating its ownership in many fewer hands. As usual, the churches led the way. 'Although this field had been rendered destitute by the number of its owners and their quarrels, our Abbot Jarento saw that it was most promising for harvests of all types. He went to each of the owners of the place in each of the towns and villages they inhabited. Although many owners refused and many were reluctant...still, with God's help he brought it about that all gave up their land'.[22] The cartulary of the Abbey of Chamalières-sur-Loire is unusual in the frankness with which it describes what is usually recorded as spontaneous piety, prompted by the consciousness of sin in this world and its consequences in the next. Indeed we need scarcely doubt that such donations were among the forms which God's help to Chamalières assumed. Piety apart, the religious houses accumulated both land and people almost involuntarily simply because they were able to come to the help of those who needed it in emergencies, from the poor man for whom the only way to survive a hard winter or a bad baron was to give himself and his descendants to the monastery as serfs to the great noble who pledged land in return for cash to cover his crusading expenses. But if the churches took the lead the nobles were not slow to follow, and since they lacked the mask of piety when building lordships on their own account the nature of their operations is more starkly portrayed by the (ecclesiastical) sources. In truth, however, both were engaged in the same enterprise, 'to command your serfs and your plough teams to serve them', as Count Otto of Nordheim, rallying the Saxon nobility against Henry IV at Hötensleben in 1073, complained of the castles which the Emperor had recently built, 'and even compel you to bear filthy burdens on your own free shoulders'.[23]

Pierre Toubert has described precisely and vividly how the farmers of Latium (to the south and east of Rome), until the mid-tenth century still loosely dispersed in villas and homesteads in the ancient manner, were thereafter marshalled into new centres, compact, fortified and enclosed, with stone houses intended from the outset for permanent habitation, not a passing emergency.[24] His account has become the leading model of how European society now began to be reconstructed from its foundations. Here, in the most ancient city-supporting region in western Europe, the corn lands were old and the remaining wood and pasture too precious to be further eroded except on the rarest and most pressing occasions, so increased productivity was achieved through the creation of an intensely cultivated area of garden and vineyard around the new village. This was in part a response to the same pressure of growing population on limited resources that had driven the monks of Bobbio to clearance, but it also enabled that population to be much more closely directed and the fruits of its labour more efficiently tapped.

Two hundred years later chroniclers remembered the *incastellamentum*, as this process was called, as marking the end of a golden age of plenty and freedom – an end which they attributed not to the menace of Saracen pirates, but to the greed of the local aristocracy. The people of Casciavolo blamed the same passion when, around 1100, they complained to the cathedral and consuls of Pisa about the behaviour of their neighbouring lords of Casciano – and, luckier than many, secured a measure of protection by doing so: 'When all power lost its strength and justice was dead and perished in our land, they began to do us all evil, as though they were pagans or Saracens. They began to attack our houses, to assault our wives as they lay in bed and beat them, to take all our goods from our houses, to strike our children and roll them in water and mire, to take all our animals, to devastate our fields, to despoil our gardens of all their fruits and to take all our possibilities of life.'[25]

Proprietorship of land meant nothing without control over the men and women who worked it. Whether the ultimate beneficiary of these depredations was the castle or the church, their target was not the goods, services or animals which were complained of, but through them the land itself and the people who worked it. For a smallholder the loss of a beast or the destruction of a crop might mean the difference between being able to remain solvent and free or being driven to hand over his land to the local big man in return for the means to survive another winter, in effect selling himself into servitude. That is why Romuald of Ravenna, like many another saint, had come to the rescue of a poor farmer whose cow had been seized by a 'certain proud and cruel count' – and why the count had condescended to steal the cow;[26] it is why the restraint of the parents of Ariald, the leader of the Milanese Patarenes, in forbidding their servants to ride down their neighbours' crops, even though they had plenty both of servants and horses, showed the saintliness of their characters, and why Odo of Cluny presented Gerald of Aurillac's greatest achievement, after his chastity, as the conquest of avarice, so that he increased his property without doing injury to anyone.[27]

Beyond the Alps the principle and the process were the same, whether to push forward the clearing of new land or secure more intensive cultivation of the old. Around Cluny – a telling example, since it relates to the greatest ecclesiastical lordship at the time of its most decisive expansion – a population which was still dispersed on villas in the Roman manner in the time of Abbot Maiolus (942–994) was gathered into substantial villages in that of his successor Odilo.[28] Such concentration was not necessarily imposed on people against their will. In the neighbourhood of Béziers people who for centuries had lived on widely scattered farmsteads gathered themselves during the eleventh and twelfth centuries into fortified settlements called *castra*, and retained

enough freedom in the thirteenth to have set up self-governing con-
sulates like those that were appearing in the larger towns of the region
at the same time.[29] But coercion was very widespread, advertised and
achieved everywhere by the building of castles. The addition of archaeological to literary evidence has shown that castles were very much more
numerous than used to be supposed, and that the period of their greatest
proliferation was the later part of the tenth century and the greater part
of the eleventh.[30] In other words, it had little directly to do with the raids
of Vikings, Saracens or Magyars, though a good deal – at least if
chronological coincidence is anything to go by – with the diminishing
capacity of the Carolingian kings and their leading representatives to
exercise their powers and defend their prerogatives, to which the raids
had certainly contributed. 'Although he was on other occasions a most
Christian and just man,' as Bernard of Angers remarked of Count
Raymond II of Rouergue, 'it seemed that he was going to erect that
structure in order to subjugate violently those who refused to offer the
allegiance owed to him, and to subject them to his dominion.'[31] In
Provence less than a dozen castles in the middle of the tenth century
had become several times that number by 1000, and perhaps one
hundred by 1030; in the Auvergne nine appeared in the tenth century,
forty-one in the first half of the eleventh; in Catalonia civil war between
1020 and 1060 allowed newly constructed castles to provide the bases
for the enserfment of the peasantry, and in the Charentais sixty-one
castles were added by 1050 to the dozen there had been in 1000; in
the Chartrain, and Burgundy too, most of the castles that existed in 1050
were of quite recent construction.[32] Thereafter, as expansion to the
north, east and south from the springboard of the Frankish and Rhenish
heartlands began to gather pace, castle building was always the first
priority of the conquering knights.

'When and how ancient slavery came to an end', in the words of a
question famously posed by Marc Bloch, remains a complex and vigorously disputed issue. The institution of slavery continued long after the
formal fabric of Roman government had disappeared, although it was
shaken by the successive upheavals of the fifth, seventh and ninth
centuries. Reinvigorated and brutally sustained by the lawcodes of the
Germanic successor states, in this case reflecting common practice rather
than mere aspiration, slavery was in the tenth century still widespread
throughout the former Carolingian empire. Yet by the twelfth century it
had apparently disappeared, to be replaced by the characteristic medieval institution of serfdom, which embraced a far larger proportion of the
population, in effect amounting in many parts of lowland Europe to the
entire productive population. So, at least, many scholars maintain, and
much controversial erudition has been expended in elaborating and

explaining a distinction between two institutions habitually described by the same word (*servus*). From the present perspective, however, the transition from 'slavery' to 'serfdom' was important not so much because of whatever modifications it may have implied in the circumstances of individuals so described, as because it became the condition of almost the entire rural population rather than of a relatively small proportion of it. The *servi* or *mancipii* of the ninth century were descended, for the most part, from the slaves of antiquity, their numbers topped up by capture in war and legal punishment, but still (in the view of most scholars) amounting to no more than a small minority of the agricultural work force. The *servi, colliberti, villani, homines* and so forth who in the lowland regions constituted the great majority of the twelfth-century population were the descendants, for the most part, of free men and women. That may be why they sometimes attached great importance to differences of status and nomenclature that signified no real advantage in their material condition, since they shared a uniform subjection to the uses and demands of the masters to whose lands they were firmly tied.

The essence of the condition to which so many were reduced is conveyed by the long lists of 'customs' (*consuetudines*) that form the substance of hundreds of monastic charters from around 1030 onwards, and conferred upon the beneficiaries the right to demand an immense and miscellaneous variety of services and renders from the occupants of the land being transferred. They must work in the monastery's fields and render it tithes, pasture its animals, grind their flour in its mills, bake their bread in its ovens, billet its men, mend its roads, build its bridges and pay tolls for using them, – and so on, almost ad infinitum. Above all, they must attend its court, where these customs would be promulgated and enforced, and profitable fines levied upon those who infringed them, as well as on the petty crimes and misdemeanours of everyday life. Some of these were dues and services ordinarily taken by landlords from their tenants. Others, like road mending and bridge building, or giving lodging to armed men, were derived from the power of the ban (*bannum*) which the Carolingian kings had conferred on their counts and other officers to command or constrain the goods and services of free men in the interests of defence or public safety, but were now being exercised by castellans on their own account. Many more (having to use the lord's mill and oven for instance, or to pay tolls at this place or that) were simply invented by the ingenuity of the moment and demanded by right of the ban, 'custom' being (contrary to the cliché) precisely what was not sanctioned by law. Hence the form of lordship which they created is now known as the banal seigneurie.

The detail becomes finer and richer with each new regional mono-graph or archaeological survey, but the picture remains essentially the same. From around the end of the tenth century, and somewhat sooner in the south than in the north, European society was reorganized from and around rapidly multiplying castles. Their purpose was less military than economic, to act as centres from which communications could be commanded, rents and tolls collected, and the countryside controlled.[33] The apparent exceptions prove the rule. The absence of castles from England before the Norman conquest of 1066 was a striking sign of the continuity and comprehensiveness of royal authority – and the same authority enabled the wealth of the countryside to be more efficiently tapped through a network of well supervised markets in the royal burhs. In Muslim Spain castles not only became more numerous in the tenth century, but began to assume functions that went distinctly beyond the military, being used as centres from which surrounding villages could be organized, and taxes well in excess of the tenth that was customary in Muslim lands could be collected.[34] Both examples underline how gen-eral a characteristic of our period was a closer, more intensive exploita-tion of the countryside, whether or not it was accompanied, as it generally was in the heartlands of the former Carolingian Empire, by the undermining of central authority and the dispersal of governmental powers.

By these means, as well as by mere force, legions of the *pauperes*, the *miserabiles personae* who had been entitled to the protection of the Carolingian courts, and sometimes at least received it, were reduced to servitude. Particularly revealing is the observation of André Debord that the proliferation of mottes in the Charentais was most evident not in the areas controlled by the relatively few castles which had been constructed earlier in the tenth century, under royal or princely authority, but remote from them, in the places where clearance was being pushed forward most rapidly at the time.[35] The knights were assisted in their work by the famines which killed so many, but reduced many more to penury and therefore dependence. The process has been tracked with precision through the records of pious donation to the cathedral at Chartres. 80 per cent of the gifts between 980 and 1040 were of alodial (freehold) land; the proportion fell to 45 per cent between 1030 and 1060 and 38 per cent between 1060 and 1090. By 1090–1130 it was 8 per cent. Land sales in Catalonia tell a similar story: in the last decade of the tenth century 65 per cent of them involved alodial land, between 1120 and 1130, only 10 per cent.[36]

In the eyes of many observers this change took place more universally, more suddenly, and within a much shorter time, than Marc Bloch had supposed. From the vallies of the Rhine to the Ebro and of the Seine to the Tiber the indications continue to mount that rural populations substantially free in the last years of the tenth century were experiencing rapid and ruthless enserfment in the early decades of the eleventh. Not until then did the tripartite society of lords, free peasants and slaves, still in the tenth century approximating much more to the social structure typical of the ancient world, give way to that of the 'feudal' middle ages, in which the division between the free and the unfree was both stark and universal. Hence the audacious claim, which also gains plausibility from other points of view, that it was in the eleventh century, and not until then, that Europe experienced the transition from antiquity to feudalism.

Whether slavery was swept away by revolutionary upheavals which from the closing years of the tenth century reconstructed the society of western Europe, as Pierre Bonnassie in particular has argued with great force and eloquence, or was continuously modified by a much longer, more gradual and regionally differentiated movement towards a serfdom characterized essentially though variously and often vaguely by dependence on a particular master rather than by strictly defined legal status, as Dominique Barthélemy maintains with no less learning and cogency, remains intensely controversial.[37] In either case, one does not make a mythical 'golden age' of the Carolingian past (though many twelfth-century memories did) by insisting that the universal and systematic subordination of the cultivators of the soil in the eleventh and twelfth centuries provided the basis of a new social order and supported the construction of a citied civilization. Since its powers, originating in royal authority, were exercised not over serfs or tenants but over free men precisely in that capacity, the *ban* was a great leveller. It dissolved the myriad gradations of freedom and unfreedom into a single and universal chasm which divided European society from this time onwards, between those who were subject to the ban and those who enforced it and lived off it. Even if the 'disappearance' of old-fashioned serfdom, or slavery, in many regions in the early decades of the eleventh century was a real phenomenon, and not, as Barthélemy maintains, a mirage produced by the irregularities of the records, it means only that slavery was absorbed into a far more comprehensive structure of exploitation in which out of date distinctions of personal freedom and dignity – though still fiercely cherished by those affected – counted for very little. The crucial fact was that by 1100 many who had once been free were free no longer. In principle the gradations of personal status and obligation were so complicated and entangled that, as one historian has said, nobody was either wholly free or wholly unfree.[38] In practice there were two worlds, absolutely divided, and nobody but a saint, or a heretic, had any doubt as to which he belonged.

4   The Shaping of an Agrarian Economy

As the establishment of a more intensive agriculture became the object of policy rather than an expedient reluctantly adopted, lords understood quite clearly that the destruction of the 'affluent society' was a prerequisite. People must be compelled not only to surrender their lands and themselves into servitude, but to adopt the rhythms of life which the new system of production demanded. Extension of the arable was accompanied by the cutting off of alternative sources of nutrition. When the Norman peasants appealed to their Count in 996 to restore their traditional freedom of access to the woods and streams he ordered the hands and feet of their emissaries to be cut off, and told them to take that reply back to those who had sent them. Throughout the eleventh century the relentless reservation of hunting rights emphasized the growing social gulf between those who enjoyed them and those who did not. The process not only made hunting a clear and potent emblem of the aristocratic lifestyle but forced the peasantry into exclusive dependence on the grain fields for their sustenance. As the forest came to stand for the hunt, and for the freedom which only lords and outlaws enjoyed, the seignurial system was equally famously symbolized by the mill to which the peasant was compelled to bring his corn for grinding, so that he could not avoid handing over the share that his lord demanded. The spread of the water mill – rapidly from around the middle of the tenth century in Catalonia and the Chartrain, the middle of the eleventh in Provence and Picardy – was accompanied by the widespread prohibition of handmills, so that the right to use them became a valued liberty, secured in their charter in the reign of Henry I by the citizens of Newcastle upon Tyne.[39] The opposition between meat-eaters and grain-eaters, elementary in so many of the cultures of Eurasia, was increasingly emphasized in the spirituality of the period. That monks should not eat meat was taken for granted by everybody – though the legitimacy of exceptions, for example in illness, was often an important point of difference between the more and less rigorous observances – but beyond that, abstention from meat was a regular feature of the piety of movements of religious enthusiasm among the laity, and therefore increasingly regarded with suspicion as a sign of heresy until, by the end of the twelfth century, it had become, with abstention from marriage, the most fundamental and most notorious teaching of the Cathars. A man of noble birth who refused meat abjured the prerogatives of his class, as those who aspired to embrace the new monasticism with Romuald of Ravenna or Giovanni Gualberti were expected to do; conversely, at Goslar in 1051 the Emperor Henry III ordered the hanging of people accused of Manicheeism when they refused to kill a chicken.[40]

Whereas in the tenth and eleventh centuries the holy men had often come to the aid of the poor against their oppressors, in the eleventh and twelfth the powers of the shrine were increasingly used to enforce the needs of the new order. Runaway serfs might be the victims of the relics' fierce defence of their houses. A famous story from Fleury (St Benoit-sur-Loire) in the 1060s tells how Stabilis ran away, prospered and set himself up as a knight in Burgundy, but was recognized and challenged by a visitor from Fleury. He denied the accusation and undertook to confirm his oath by battle (the prerogative of a free man), but was exposed when the coins in his sleeves, representing the poll tax to which as a serf he was liable, became so heavy at the crucial moment that he could not defend himself. Fleury's patron, St Benedict (usually represented in other contexts as one of the gentlest of saints), crippled the hand of another of its serfs for life when he dared so much as to think of running away, and a serf of Notre Dame de Paris was struck dumb for claiming his freedom.[41] Mutilation was the routine punishment which lay lords inflicted on runaway serfs.

The relics were also used to enforce the new, more disciplined habits and patterns of work which collective cultivation demanded. The savage punishments inflicted by the saints on those who neglected to observe the religious calendar – a hand paralyzed for grinding corn at Easter, a house burned down when beer was brewed on a saint's day, a woman crippled for baking bread on Sunday night[42] – asserted the priority of a man-made division of time over the looser rhythms of nature by fitting the life of the countryside to the patterns of the Christian day, the Christian week and the Christian year. The ruthless discipline which had a fourteen-year-old girl struck dumb by her father for working on St Cecilia's day, and another returned by Ste Foy to the crippled state from which she had been cured because she refused to stop weaving for the procession of the relics ('working to pay for her food, because she was poor'[43]), supported the drive for sweeping and often unwelcome change.

These stories, which though they have yet to be systematically collected and analysed are abundant among the miracles of the eleventh and twelfth centuries, show a very different face of the supernatural from that which we encountered in the previous chapter. Stabilis might well have envied the *ruricoli* who two hundred years earlier had been intercepted by Gerald of Aurillac as they were leaving their holdings (*colonia*) to move to another province – that is, out of his lordship. 'When he recognised them and asked where they were going with their belongings they replied that they had been wronged by him when he put them on their holdings (*beneficiaverat eos*). The soldiers who were with him urged that he should have them beaten and made to go back . . . but he would not do so, because he knew that he and they had one Lord in heaven . . . He therefore allowed them to go away, to where they thought they would do better, and gave them permission to make the change (*ei dedit licentiam conversandi*).'[44] Almost as interesting as Gerald's action is the fact that Odo of Cluny reports it, and that he does so in language which, though it stresses as little as possible the servile status of the people concerned, does not attempt to conceal it. *Ruricoli* – 'country-folk' – suggests humble, but not necessarily unfree status, but a *colonia* was certainly an unfree tenure, and though a 'benefice' might in other circumstances suggest a return for military service it is hard to see here what wrong Gerald might have done in 'granting' it unless it were against the will of those involved; finally, the long-winded phrase about giving the fugitives licence to change their way of life avoids saying bluntly that Gerald set them free. So it looks very much as though these were people who had been forced into servitude by Gerald's bailiffs or managers, in order to bring land under cultivation. Gerald's willingness to release them disappointed and doubtless humiliated his retainers, who expected him to support their colleagues by punishing the runaways and sending them back. Odo recognizes the Christian virtue of Gerald's action (as he did again in recounting how Gerald gave presents and kind words to another runaway whom his retainers had captured and dragged before him[45]), but he is not altogether comfortable about its practical implications. Saints can be difficult.

The use of the relics to enforce a new way of life on the countryside was not novel. In a brilliant analysis of the sixth-century cult of relics so voluminously documented by Gregory of Tours, Raymond Van Dam has shown how profound were the implications, beyond simply enforcing a new rhythm and pattern of work, of insisting (through miracles of punishment by physical injury which were the prototypes of those described above) on strict observance of the holy days and festivals of the church.[46] The general and familiar congruity between the agrarian and the liturgical year, he points out, is nothing like so important as their incongruity in detail. Nature does not respect the liturgical calendar: animals which have broken through a fence to graze on the crops or a thunder storm which threatens to ruin the harvest will not wait until the saint's day has passed. Unlike the rich man, the poor farmer cannot ignore the problem; unlike the merchant or the craftsman he cannot adjust his work to suit the church's timetable. So pressing the priority of liturgical time over agrarian time means drawing new lines of social difference, between those who can and those who cannot afford to observe it, and between those who follow the occupations of the town (including the full-time ritual observance which was the monk's raison d'être) and of the countryside. In each case only the former, by implication, are capable of living as Christians. This is one of the implications of finding the peasantry characterized as a distinct social order (*agricolae*, a classical word quite outside the tenth-century lexicon) for the first time since antiquity, in the canons of the Council of Charroux in 994, instead of being included among the *pauperes* in the Carolingian fashion.[47] It is the beginning of a new and more brutal habit of classification which over the following two centuries increasingly lumped together as *rustici, pagani, illiterati, heretici*, all of those who lacked the privilege and culture of the elites which they supported with their labour, while the *laboratores* of the traditional three-fold classification of society re-emerged as the triumphant, and legally privileged, bourgeoisie of the thirteenth-century city, and the ancien régime.

In these ways the power of the saints was mobilized to invigorate the mode of production which sustained the new social order, and to police and defend the frontiers which defined it. From the middle of the twelfth century the task of subordinating the countryside to the town was taken over with increasing efficiency by the spreading markets, (including the market in labour for the many crafts that could be 'put out', of which weaving was the most universal), and by the parish system, which was effectively completed in most parts of Europe in those decades, and brought under increasingly uniform and efficient discipline by the bishops, especially after the Fourth Lateran Council of 1215. The cult of relics declined into the correspondingly controlled and sanitized institution, largely dealing in miraculous cures, of the familiar, patronizing accounts of popular piety in the middle ages, though also, most certainly, with more varied uses to those who sought them than have yet been detected. The new regime was not, of course, universal. Its dominance, and the social forms associated with it – most notably, chivalry – created a new division between feudal and non-feudal Europe. And, as Bishop Jacques Fournier's dealings with the people of Montaillou, which Emmanuel Leroy Ladurie's brilliant monograph has made the most familiar of all medieval communities, would show at the beginning of the fourteenth century, the authority of lord and bishop never stretched securely into the mountain regions.

5   The Little Community

The prominence of 'the people' in the great events of the eleventh and twelfth centuries was not, in the main, a consequence of the growth of towns. The previous chapter suggested that the power of the holy men whom they acclaimed as their leaders, the regular resort to ritual cursing and to the *clamor*, was derived from an ancient tradition of appeal to collective opinion against the abuses of the mighty, and that the acclamation of miracles confirmed popular endorsement of leaders whose authority was rooted in the community. The influence of such leaders between the late ninth and the early twelfth century, and the fact that the powerful frequently felt themselves obliged to negotiate or compromise with them and the forces which they represented, reflected the fragmentation of power and the diminishing capacity of the Carolingian state to assert, or appear to assert, local authority. There is room for widely differing assessments of the practical effectiveness of the high ambitions of Carolingian government to enforce royal rights and protect the *miserabiles personae* who appear so frequently in its proclamations. Yet even on the most sceptical view, that it was very largely for show, the show itself nourished and reinforced a sense of community and of collective responsibility. Ninth-century free men were accustomed to participate in public business, attending courts and assemblies, bearing witness, explaining their law and customs to royal officers, hearing royal decrees read and the king's will pronounced to his subjects. The great explosion of the use of documents in governmental business under the Carolingians meant, at the least, that the immediate forebears of those who lost their lands and freedom to the seigneurie in the tenth and eleventh centuries were familiar with public reference to written documents as a source of authority and legitimacy.[48] When the people who were accused of heresy at Arras in 1024/5 were called upon by Bishop Gerard of Cambrai to confirm their acceptance of the confession of faith which he had dictated they refused on the ground that they didn't understand Latin, and asked for it to be translated before solemnly putting their crosses to it. In this they were doing exactly what royal government had taught them to do, and following the procedure familiarized by the regular actions of Carolingian officials when the king's orders were being promulgated, or public acts committed to charter form.

These were the people who during the next two and a half centuries lost their land and freedom to the *seigneurie*, who found themselves inexorably reduced to servitude, and with it to the rhythms of village life in which the parish church articulated the vision and enforced the discipline of the new regime. The parish system of northern Europe as it emerged in the eleventh and twelfth centuries constituted a radical departure from the social and institutional structures of the previous thousand years. In the ninth century Christians owed their tithes to the church in which they had been baptized and were expected to be buried – that is, the cathedral church itself or a baptismal (minster) church, to which the rights and duties later to be associated with the parish had been deputed. The extent to which dioceses were sub-divided varied greatly – Auxerre had thirty-five baptismal churches in the seventh century, and the East Frankish dominions perhaps some 3,500 in the ninth, amounting perhaps to an average of one for every seven or eight villages[49] – but with its concentration of authority and function in the diocesan church or one of its handful of satellites, the structure of the Carolingian church remained a reflection and a relic of the subjection of the countryside to the city and its institutions upon which the Roman Empire had been founded.

From the middle of the tenth century the restructuring of old communities and the creation of new ones was hastened almost everywhere by the concentration and consolidation of settlement described above, and by the clearing of new land for cultivation. The focus of the new settlements was often provided by a village church or castle chapel. The requirement for tithe in effect defined the community dependent on each church, and endowed it with clear, universal, and universally known boundaries. The acquisition of the tithe gave the lord, often for the first time, a claim on the produce of everyone who lived within those boundaries, free and unfree alike – which wove another thread of community among those who had to pay. If the alienation of tithes into the hands of the laity in the ninth and tenth centuries constituted in this way the first step in the creation of the parish system, their recovery in the eleventh and twelfth was the basis of the second. Already by the middle of the tenth century bishops like Atto of Vercelli and Ratherius of Verona were deploring the quality and discipline of the parish priests, and the lack of decorum with which services were conducted and the sacraments administered. Charging fees for the sacraments, including burial, the appointment of unfit priests by lay proprietors, the irregularity of services and the inadequate maintenance of churches were attacked by the Peace Councils and everywhere became prime targets of reform, providing a growing incentive for lords to lay in spiritual capital by restoring to the church parochial rights (*parochiales*) which because of these attacks represented a diminishing material asset.

In Italy, however, the centralization of parochial rights remained normal. Many dioceses were too small, and too poor, for delegation to be necessary or practicable. In the larger dioceses, especially in the centre and north, it became usual for a collegiate church (*pieve*) under the direction of an archpriest to collect the tithes and provide the sacraments for several villages and their hinterlands: by the thirteenth century Verona had fifty-five rural *pievi* and Lucca fifty-nine. In northern Europe the dioceses were generally much bigger: in the thirteenth century

England and Wales had twenty-one dioceses, while Calabria, one-tenth the size, had twenty-two.[50] The restoration of parochial rights, accompanied by the creation of many hundreds of new communities as land was cleared and brought under cultivation, provided a basis for the social organisation of the countryside which remained familiar well into industrial times. From around 1100 the word *parrochia*, formerly meaning diocese, began to signify the unit to whose church parochial rights had been transferred. By 1200, at least along the Atlantic seaboard and in England, northern France, the Rhineland, the Low Countries and Scandinavia, the parish was firmly established as the primary unit of social life. The parish church stood at the centre of every village. Men and women were baptized, married and confessed their sins in it, attended its services regularly throughout their lives, and (unless they were important enough to find a place in a monastic church of which their family was an established patron) were buried in the church or its churchyard, precisely disposed, each in their families, and each family allocated to a niche or plot whose location and splendour reflected its worldly rank and wealth with great exactness – the rich man near the altar, the poor man by the gate, as it were – bearing perpetual witness to a clearly and precisely articulated social order.

In retrospect the parish appears as the natural, almost the inevitable complement to the *seigneurie* in the process of subordination which it eventually completed. Yet such an outcome was very far from inevitable. On the contrary, the close and direct relationship between the spread of parishes in the eleventh and early twelfth centuries, the clearing of new land for cultivation, and the formation of new communities made the parish the focus and framework of new communal loyalties and solidarities, which were often expressed with vigour and independence. In areas of new cultivation the parish of this period strongly resembled the 'land shrines' which Max Gluckman and others observed in new settlements in central and southern Africa.[51] These shrines, together with their accompanying ritual, were maintained by those whose common bond lay in their joint involvement in the exploitation of a particular piece of land; the rituals drew out and reinforced the principles of cooperation which its cultivation required. Land shrines were often associated also with ritual declarations that peace would be observed at particular places and particular times, very much like those proclaimed by the Peace Councils of the eleventh century, and were often specifically linked with the first settlers on the land in question, just as so many of the place-names in the regions where great stretches of forest were cleared in our period are derived from personal names – signified, for example by the names ending in *erie* or *ière* which are so common in northwestern France.

The regular connection between the establishment of land shrines and the veneration of prophets originally from outside the community is reminiscent of the role of hermits or holy men who might act as leaders and counsellors in founding new communities. When the Breton hermit William Firmatus died *c*.1095 the men of three townships fought for his remains, and his biographer attributed the victory of Mortain to 'its entire clergy and an innumerable force of its people', acting on the orders of the Count. The monks of Savigny had to use their fists to prevent the men of Telleuil from seizing the corpse of their founder, Vitalis, during its last journey.[52] The body of Vitalis's companion in many preaching missions in northwestern France, Robert of Arbrissel, was at the centre of an even more impassioned dispute in 1116, which began when he entered on his last illness and died not at Fontevrault, the great and already famous double monastery which he had founded some fifteen years earlier, but at one of its priories, Orsan, in the Berry. Alardus, the lord of Orsan, whose wife was prioress, was anxious to keep Robert's body there, and threatened that any attempt to move it would be prevented by the crowd which surrounded the priory at the news of the impending demise. To secure the bones of her founder Petronilla, the redoubtable abbess of Fontevrault, who had made the journey to the death-bed with just such an eventuality in mind, found herself driven to steal Robert's body at the moment of his death, and hide it in the cloister until Archbishop Léger of Bourges, whom she had threatened with all sorts of terrors, including an appeal to Rome, came to her rescue and provided an escort to secure Robert's safe passage to Fontevrault.[53]

Petronilla's reasoning was no doubt similar to that of the people of the area around St Severinus, near Ravenna, a century or so earlier, when 'hearing that Romuald was about to leave [the monastery], they were greatly perturbed by the news and talked among themselves about how they could frustrate his intentions. The plan that finally seemed best to them was that they should send assassins who with infamous impiety would slay him. Their reasoning was that if they could not keep him alive they would at least have his dead body to protect their lands.'[54] The objective of these passionate manoeuvres amounted to the creation of a shrine (frustrated in Romuald's case, on the occasion mentioned above) by popular acclaim, representing an affirmation of community on the part of those involved. Any corpse was a potential relic, and might become the focus of powerful loyalties, as William the Conqueror knew very well when, after the battle of Hastings he refused to hand over the body of Harold Godwineson to his mother, and Frederick Barbarossa when in 1155 he not only executed Arnold of Brescia, the inspirer of a powerful communal movement in Rome, but had the body burned and the ashes scattered in the Tiber. To venerate a saint or a martyr was to declare an identity – as Englishmen, not Normans, as heretics, not Catholics – or as men of Orsan or Mortain, not of Fontevrault or Mayenne.

The burial ground which therefore provided the permanent focus of communal sentiment and identity was probably older than the church itself in old settlements, and inescapably one of the first common institutions to be established in new ones. One of the earliest and most general demands of the Peace Councils was to confirm and reinforce the right of sanctuary (*salvamentum*) for the unarmed and their goods in the *cimiterium* or *atrium*, the area around the church or burial place whose boundary was marked by crosses, by custom with a radius of thirty paces, which made it roughly similar in size to the castles of the oppressors. From this area armed men were excluded, and with them much that was associated with their power, including the enforcement of the *consuetudines*.[55] Charter after charter recording the foundation of new settlements lays down that the sanctuary and its privileges will be at their heart. In consequence, as Robert Fossier has put it, the churchyard was often 'the first communal possession of the village'.[56] Thus by 1100, for example, the sanctuary of Pierreclos in Burgundy not only protected those within it and their goods from violence, but gave the inhabitants recourse to the church court, exempting them from the justice of the castellan and his provost even in crimes of blood. Not surprisingly, residence within the sanctuary soon became highly prized: in Catalonia the first stone houses were built within the bounds of cemeteries. Similarly, the burg at la Peyratte, in Poitou, was built within the cemetery.[57] The use of the churchyard for the transaction of every kind of business – the holding of courts and markets, the meetings of guilds, the witnessing of important transactions like the manumission of slaves, the claiming of found and stolen property, and more and more often at this time the performance of marriage – reinforced and re-emphasized its place at the heart of the community. During his insurrectionary occupation of the city of Le Mans in 1116 the great heretical preacher Henry of Lausanne called a meeting of the people to denounce the new restrictions on marriage which the church was pressing at the time, and to find husbands for the prostitutes of the town in return for their agreeing to renounce their wicked ways. The meeting was held in the churchyard of St Germain and St Vincent. Nothing could show more clearly that it was regarded as the property not of the church, but of the community.

At most periods in European history the parish priest is a figure as poorly documented as he is obviously influential. In principle he was the representative in the little community of the large, of the bishop and his authority, the city and its culture. In practice he was the heir of traditions of local and communal religious leadership, christian, pre-christian and partly christian, of which we know even less than we do of him. With very rare exceptions (like Coifi, the high priest whose advice to Edwin of Northumbria to convert to Christianity on the ground that its God is manifestly more potent than his own is memorably reported by Bede) we encounter them, or rather their shadows, only as the astrologers, magicians, sorcerers, soothsayers, stormraisers, rainmakers and so forth against whom the councils and bishops of the early medieval church inveighed with great regularity.[58] Yet every community needs such people, and it is a fair guess (but no more) that in general they occupied their positions because they possessed the skill, wisdom and acknowledged capacity to provide necessary arbitration and leadership. Ordericus Vitalis's legend of St Judoc, upon the site of whose supposedly sixth-century hermitage his monastery of St Evroul was founded in the 1040s, probably describes many modest hermits and holy men of his own day who did not reach the ranks of the well known spiritual heroes of the age – the Romualds and Robert of Arbrissels. The early life and miracles by which Judoc demonstrated his indifference to power and wealth and therefore his fitness to exercise holy power, have a very eleventh-century appearance. The qualities themselves, however, or the appearance of them, have a longer history, something of which may be reflected in the aftermath: after Judoc's death two nephews inherited his hermitage and 'regularly shaved and bathed his holy body, which remained uncorrupted'.[59] With the hermitage they would have inherited also the informal but effective local support system which piety afforded, and their scrupulous maintenance of Judoc's corpse maintained also a flow of visitors in search of the consolation, mediation and advice which the hermit had provided in his lifetime, and of the alms with which they expressed their gratitude for them.

These were the services for which the community would also look to the priest, and indeed there are occasional signs of rivalry. Though they later became good friends the first reaction of Brihtric, the priest of Haslebury in Somerset, to the appearance in 1125 of the hermit Wulfric in the cell beside his church was one of resentment.[60] In new communities the priest might play a particularly prominent part: we find him leading his parishoners in demands for further definition of their privileges, and serving as a *bonus homo* among the chosen governors of the community, as well as performing more traditional functions like leading his flock in procession to the episcopal church at Pentecost. Hence the anger when he was subverted, either by one family in the community through marriage, or by the lord through simony, was a measure of his (growing) importance to the community. The reason for popular hostility in the eleventh century to the marriage of priests and to the sale or gift of benefices in the church was not so much that they were thought spiritually objectionable in themselves as because they represented ties which bound the priest to his lord and family at a time when the community more and more felt the need of his services as a free and independent leader and arbitrator. It was not the payments themselves that were at issue but the subjection of the parish clergy to lordship, in breach of a Carolingian requirement that they should be free men.[61] Provided that the priest's integrity was not compromised from the point of view of the community it was not thought objectionable that he should be rewarded, within reason; after all, he had to live. Signs that parish churches might be run, in effect, as hereditary family businesses have been noted in eleventh-century England, where Domesday Book records the testimony of the burgesses of Lincoln that the church of All Saints which its incumbent had tried to give to Peterborough Abbey when he took his vows there could not be given outside the city or the family without royal consent.[62] Priestly dynasties were certainly not unusual in England even much later: Osbern, the son of Brihtric the priest of Haslebury 'succeeded his good father Brihtric in that charge', and the Cistercian abbot John of Ford, writing in the 1170s, mentions the fact more than once without obvious surprise or disappoval.[63] The early tenth-century charters of Redon, in Brittany, show priestly dynasties in their heyday, passing the office and the land that went with it from generation to generation, active in the business of the community, providing witnesses and intermediaries in business transactions, and sometimes in court cases, acting as sureties and money lenders, and in effect as notaries, providing a record of local transactions and settlements. It is easy to see why their independence of lords ecclesiastical and secular should have been valued by their parishioners. It was already being undermined here in Brittany by the late ninth century, when some of these priests began to enter the monastery, handing over their land and presumably their offices as they did so.[64] By the time Robert of Arbrissel, the son of a priest and of a priest's daughter, was conducting his campaign against clerical marriage in the diocese of Rennes, in the 1080s, we may suspect that it had largely disappeared.

From this point of view the campaign for clerical celibacy in the eleventh century must be regarded in part, like so many other aspects of the reform, and like earlier campaigns against sorcery and later ones against heresy, as an attempt to subordinate local hierarchies to central authority. As Mr. Chichely put it, in *Middlemarch*, '"Hang your reforms! you never hear of a reform, but it means some trick to put in new men."' In the short term, however, the circumstances in which the parish system was established very often told against such a design, at least in the two or three generations between the relinquishing of parochial rights by secular lords, a phenomenon by and large of the eleventh and early twelfth centuries, and the establishment of episcopal control over the appointment and discipline of parish priests, which was probably not widely effective until well into the twelfth or even the thirteenth century. Even then and for some time to come, there were regions where the priest continued to be elected by their parishioners – a relic not only of the favourable conditions of the eleventh-century impasse between lord and bishop, but of still more ancient conditions and expectations. That is one of the reasons, if only one, why now and very often for centuries after, the priests were often far closer to their parishioners than to their superiors in outlook and culture, as doubtless in blood. In the middle of the tenth century a priest of the Vermandois was punished by the relics of St Hunegond for agreeing with his parishoners, and working on her festival; in the 1150s Albero of Mercke, near Cologne, offered to put his belief in the inefficacy of sacraments administered by corrupt priests to the test of fire (in itself a method of submitting himself to the judgment of the community rather than his bishop); in the 1160s Lambert le Bègue in Liège was disciplined by his bishop for criticizing to his parishioners the morals and conduct of his fellow priests in the diocese.[65]

The retention of parochial rights by the cathedral churches of Italy, and with them the continued long-term domination of the countryside by urban centres which had by no means generally succeeded in maintaining vigorous market or administrative functions since the end of antiquity, underlines the special character of what happened in northern Europe, where the parish provided the inhabitants of the countryside for the first time with an autonomous framework for their social and political life, and encouraged the formation of rural communities, as distinct from mere clusters of habitation. By the thirteenth century, indeed, it was also becoming more and more a framework which sustained and reinforced the authority and the culture of the city, as represented by the bishop. But this had been by no means a foregone conclusion, or even a natural or necessary consequence of the manner of its formation. Georges Duby described the social history of this period as one of disorder in transition between two ages of order, that of the Carolingian world where a large but loosely defined and structured nobility supported itself with a haphazard combination of plunder and booty, largely sustained by military expansion, and that of the precisely articulated society of orders, sustained by legal and social domination, which settled into place in the closing decades of the twelfth century and remained familiar in western Europe until the age of revolution. Its religious history can be written in very much the same way. Sacred power escaped from Carolingian shrines and relics, to be deployed for a heady moment when the voice of God was the voice of the people, by living holy men and miracle workers, before the bishops and clerks of the twelfth century gradually brought it under control again, in the shrines and at the altars of duly canonized saints. The peace of God itself became another instrument for the preservation of noble hegemony. The parish priest was first the lord's man, then the village's man, and then the bishop's man. And in his churchyard the indiscriminately broadcast corpses of the Carolingian world were brought into the midst of the community and carefully marshalled in their ranks and orders, according to their station, to show that for the dead as for the living these centuries witnessed the foundation of Europe's ancien régime.

3

Sex and the Social Order

I remember reading somewhere the confessions of a Benedictine abbot: my vow of poverty has brought me an income of a hundred thousand crowns a year; my vow of obedience has brought me the power of a sovereign prince. I forget the consequences of his vow of chastity.

Edward Gibbon, The Decline and Fall of the Roman Empire, ch. xxxvii

1 Family, Land and Power

The success with which the powerful increased their control over the poor during the tenth and eleventh centuries by no means diminished the ferocity of competition among themselves. As lordship over land offered ever more opportunity to exploit a growing array of regular and secure revenues it became necessary to do more than maintain general domination over broad stretches of territory. Changing the ways in which land was used so as to increase the productivity of those who worked it and the efficiency with which their surplus could be tapped – by planting a vineyard, or constructing an oven or mill for example – would require continuity of occupation and management from generation to generation. Conversely, winning a larger surplus from fields and villages would reduce the area of land needed to sustain a community which was not self-supporting (for example, of monks or warriors), and therefore allow the size and number of such communities to be increased. Both considerations pointed towards a closer, more intimate and more durable relationship between the land and its lords.

The need to establish long-term control over acknowledged and defined domains which this implied was the same for lay and ecclesiastical proprietors. The means by which they secured it were quite different, but in the long run, and necessarily, complementary. Until both had done so disputes over property, which appear to have multiplied markedly in the generations on either side of the millennium, continued with undiminished vigour. This was the most general underlying cause of the apparently endless and pointless internecine conflict which raged at every level of aristocratic society from the tenth century onwards. It continued everywhere in Latin Europe (though taking a somewhat different form to the east of the Rhine) throughout the eleventh century, and did not subside in most regions until well into the twelfth. The gradual diminution of this anarchy (as it is often called) was both the clearest indication and the crucial success of the re-establishment of royal authority which was the outstanding political achievement of the twelfth and thirteenth centuries, beginning in the English and French kingdoms.

A crisis arising from multiple claims to inheritance was not in itself unusual in agrarian societies. Increasing subdivision of estates was a common cause of the undermining of territorial aristocracies, now and in the future. It had been a problem in Sassanid Persia, and in our period was a source of instability in India and gave rise to concern among officials of the Song dynasty in China; it would do so again in sixteenth-century Russia. It was not the problem which distinguished western Europe, but the solution. The emergence of a new political and social order in the twelfth and thirteenth centuries was not due simply to the energy and determination of kings and their ministers. It was also, and indispensably, the outcome of a gradual acceptance of two principles of social organization which, despite a great deal of local and regional variation, were sufficiently general and sufficiently coherent to endow European civilization with some of its enduring characteristics: that land or revenues once granted to the church would remain in its possession, 'in perpetual alms' as the charters put it, and that land held by right of descent through the paternal line (the patrimony) would constitute the core of a family's possessions, and should be expected to pass undivided from each generation to the next.

Eleventh-century conflicts about property or property rights typically involved either a dispute between the laity and the church or one between a designated or prospective heir to the property in question (often but not necessarily the eldest son) and the uncles or brothers, aunts or sisters (often represented by their husbands) and their children, who maintained that they too were entitled to a share. Title to landed property would always remain a source of endless and bitter contention, governed by infinitely various and complicated combinations of differing legal traditions and local customs and conditions. Nevertheless, by the end of the twelfth century the redefinition of each of the competing groups, and still more the establishment of essential and interlocking relationships between them, had made it possible for land to be divided between the church and the laity, and in the case of the latter for control of the patrimony to be transmitted substantially unimpaired, in a relatively regular and predictable fashion. In the process the distinctions between the ecclesiastical and the secular and between the eldest legitimate son and his siblings became both clearer and more important than they had ever been before. Henceforth these would be, despite great variation between regions and between classes, fundamental organizing categories of European society.

The resolution of the struggle for control of secular land demanded nothing less than the reconstitution of the aristocratic family. Formerly – a caricature will point the contrast – immense tracts of territory had been roamed and ruled over by kin-based bands, defined somewhat differently in different regions and for different purposes, but essentially comprising the male descendants of both paternal and maternal forebears for three or four generations – brothers, uncles and various degrees of cousins in each generation, all more or less on the same footing in relation to each other. Increasingly from around the middle of the tenth century individual leaders sought to carve out of this collectively-claimed territory estates which would support their followers and be inherited by their offspring. Their lives were shaped by these two goals: to secure their land, and by ensuring that it passed directly to their own direct descendants to make it a patrimony. The reward of success was to be remembered – some of them, to this day – as the founders of families.

The simplest way to create and preserve a patrimony, and one which was widely adopted in the eleventh and twelfth centuries, especially in England, northern France and the Low Countries, was through the principle of male primogeniture – the presumption that a man's entire property would pass at his death to his eldest son. For convenience we shall sometimes speak in the following pages as though that were the only mechanism at stake. In fact it was very far from being so. There was no simple relationship between the controls which were exercised over the transmission of property during the eleventh and twelfth centuries and the intricate pattern of European inheritance customs which becomes more or less visible from the thirteenth century onwards. From the latter period, for example, the customs which prevailed in much of northern and western France, including Normandy, maintained the principle of equal shares within the lineage, by contrast not only to the rule of primogeniture in England, and in Germany under *Hofrecht*, but to the practice of much of Mediterranean Europe, where the widespread use of the will enabled fathers to give preference to one child.[1] In Provence *frerèche*, by which a group of men, not necessarily related to each other, held their lands and goods in common, '*ad unum panem et vinum*' (roughly, as a single granary and vineyard), was widely adopted in the eleventh century and still widespread in the sixteenth; similar ways to share among the descendants of common male ancestors property which itself was transmitted intact, recognizing but also limiting their claims, were devised elsewhere, among them the Tuscan *consorteria*.[2] In many areas the practice of passing the family property to the youngest son rather than the eldest was particularly favoured among the peasantry, for whom it often made sense, especially in less fertile regions, to send the elder sons to work in the towns, and keep the youngest at home to support aging parents. The universal element in all these devices was the strengthening of the patriline. This happened even in communal Italy, where the rapidly developing commercial economy made the division of revenues without fragmentation of property much easier, while intense factional rivalry in the cities sustained the primacy of kin-based networks. In Genoa, for example, a few members of the aristocracy still identified themselves through their mothers in the twelfth century, but none did so in the thirteenth. An intimate relationship between commercial success, the physical domination of particular sectors of the city, and participation in its political processes, militated against the rights of mothers, wives and daughters, which were steadily undermined. By the middle of the twelfth century women all over northern Italy were losing their ancient right to inherit one-third of their husband's estate (the *tercia*) – in Genoa it was abolished by consular decree in 1143 – and everywhere the marriage settlement, which tended to lead to the alienation of land from the family which made it, declined, while the dowry, which would revert to the bride's family if the marriage was childless, became increasingly important.[3]

The exclusion of the maternal line was the first step in narrowing the claims upon property of the wider kin group in favour of the children of a particular marriage in each generation – the dynastic principle which gained almost universal predominance during the twelfth century. The essential goal, which was secured in one way or another through most of the former Carolingian lands, was that estates should be transmitted from each generation to the next more or less continuously, without being subjected to the constant fragmentation and reparcelling associated with the older practice of dividing property between all the children in each generation (partible inheritance), which in turn created multiple and often overlapping claims between generations. The interests of a lord, where they were concerned, would often require responsibilities for the performance of particular obligations associated with the tenure of a property or an office to be retained in a single pair of hands. The close connection between the multiplication of castles and the emergence of dynastic lineages in the early eleventh century obviously owed much to the necessity of unified command and economic support, whether demanded by the interests of the lord, where lordship was strong, or of the castellan. We should not, however, exaggerate the role of lordship in these developments: as Duby remarked, the fief 'never played more than a peripheral part in what is generally known as feudal society'.[4] His observation reflects a growing acceptance that most land was held as of right, even if those who owned it also owed services of one kind or another to the crown. As Susan Reynolds has recently demonstrated comprehensively, the idea that all land was ultimately owned by and held of the king which for so long dominated writing about medieval society, was devised and propagated by thirteenth-century lawyers in the service of the newly aggressive monarchies of that epoch, and projected backwards in the search for precedent and legitimation.[5] It was the interests of the families themselves, not those of their lords or kings, which reshaped western society in the eleventh and twelfth centuries.

The victory of the dynastic principle in northern France, and with it, *de facto*, of male primogeniture, is attested by many family histories composed in the twelfth century, which with due attention to the dignity and connections secured by each advantageous marriage recount the fortunes and achievements of its successive lords. Almost invariably these histories trace the ancestry of the family back to the tenth century, if its progenitors had held office as vicomtes or castellans at that time, and to the eleventh if not. They do not go further back. Yet where the origins of these eleventh-century founders of dynasties can still be traced, as Duby demonstrated in a famous paper, most of them turn out to have been descended from a handful of ruling clans of the Carolingian period. Of thirty-four knightly families established in the southern Maconnais around 1100 at least twenty-eight were descended from the six families which had dominated the region in the ninth and tenth centuries.[6] Similar indications have subsequently been found for many other regions throughout the former Carolingian Empire. In other words, as the surnames which they began to adopt during the eleventh century so often reflected, the families had crystallized into dynastic form at the time when one of their members, later remembered as the founder, secured his position as master of a castle, to be succeeded by his son. At this point the fortunes of the family became permanently linked with its possession of the castle and the lands which depended on it. Thenceforth its memory of itself as a family was given form by the line of dynastic heads around and under whom it was organized in each generation. The confusion of ancestry which had previously prevailed is marked, and disguised, by the mythical descent from some valiant, even supernaturally favoured adventurer, to whose skill and luck the inauguration of the family fortune is attributed. One such was the 'Siffredus' from whom the descent of the Counts of Guines was traced by Lambert of Ardres, another the 'Guillaume Taillefer' who was supplied as the founder of their line by the anonymous historian of the Counts of Angoulême, both writing late in the twelfth century.[7]

What justifies the description of this development as being of revolutionary importance in the eleventh century is not so much its intrinsic nature as the level of society at which it took place. A tendency towards primogeniture has been detected in the ninth century and was in effect adopted by the Capetian family, whose practice it became at least from the time of Count Hugh the Great (d.956). The Capetians passed their patrimony intact to the eldest son, making provision for cadets only when the family fortunes had improved to the point where it could be done out of acquisitions and patronage.[8] By the middle of the eleventh century the same strategy was being widely pursued by the lords of the castles which had multiplied so profusely throughout the former Carolingian lands. Upon his accession the eldest son became head of what was now conceived as a dynastic family, capable of being depicted by the diagram or 'tree' in which the European aristocracy has invested its identity ever since. This dynastic family – *genus*, as it began to be called with pride – gradually superseded the more loosely articulated kinship group in much of northwestern Europe for the purpose of controlling and transmitting landed property. But it was never an easy victory, or one which could be taken for granted.

Duby's findings exploded the long-standing belief that the disorders of the tenth century had given rise to a 'new aristocracy' of low-born adventurers who took advantage of troubled times to fight their way to the top. Not only in southern Burgundy but over much of western Francia, including the Isle de France, Normandy, Flanders, Anjou, Touraine, Poitou, Tuscany and Catalonia, the aristocracy of the twelfth century and after can be seen to have been created during the first three or four decades of the eleventh century by the emergence of dynastic families from within the more broadly defined lineages of the Carolingian nobility. It was new only in the sense of being newly organized. With the exception – and it is an important exception[9] – of those who acquired a foothold by marrying the daughter of a nobleman unprovided with sons, its members were still overwhelmingly descended from the small group of closely connected families which had spread out of Neustria under the leadership of Charles Martel and Pepin the Strong in the eighth century to establish their hold over the kingdom of the Franks, and under Charlemagne to add to it Lombardy, Catalonia, Saxony and Bavaria.

The conditions which gave rise to this change, and the circumstances in which it was worked out, can be seen in the family history of an otherwise obscure Norman warrior. Despite the ultimate failure of his line, Giroie is remembered because some of his descendants founded St Evroul, the monastery on the southern frontier of Normandy which was home from his entry at ten years old in 1085 until his death in 1142 or shortly after to one of the great historians of the twelfth century, Ordericus Vitalis. Orderic's *Ecclesiastical History* is famous for the vividness with which it describes the savage and incessant feuding of the Norman aristocracy, often but by no means always dominated by the internal disputes of the most ruthless and ambitious lineage of them all, that of the Norman dukes. It not only records these feuds but is very much a product of them, because the foundation of St Evroul had arisen directly from the rivalries of and between the founders' kin, which continued to reverberate inside the cloister in Orderic's time, as well as bearing heavily upon the relations of the monastery with the world beyond.[10]

Giroie, Orderic tells us, was a (younger?) son of 'great French and Breton nobility', who around 1020 settled on the borders of Normandy and Maine, a region at the margin of ducal power which would be dominated in the coming decades by the rivalries of the lords of Bellême, Mayenne and Brionne. With the support of William of Bellême Giroie was betrothed to the daughter of a minor lord named Helgo. When both Helgo and his daughter died before the marriage could take place Giroie was allowed by Duke Richard to take over Helgo's lands, although Helgo apparently had at least two sons of his own. In this way Giroie secured Montreuil l'Argillé and Échaffour, where he built castles around which the feuds of his children often turned. The children – seven sons and four daughters – were by his marriage to the daughter of another local warrior, Thurstan of Montfort-sur-Risle, through whom he acquired a connection sufficiently extensive to protect his family, after his death, against the ambitions of Gilbert of Brionne, one of the really powerful lords of the region. Giroie's eldest son, Arnaud, died young, and the affairs of the family were mainly managed by the next son, William, in alliance with his brother Robert, to whom he gave or left another castle, at St Céneri in Maine, and in bitter rivalry with another brother, Fulk, who joined the retinue of William's deadliest enemy, Gilbert of Brionne. When Fulk was killed in an ambush in 1035 Robert was one of the attackers. Of the remaining sons of Giroie two were killed by accident, one from a fall at wrestling and one by a lance misdirected during drill, and one, Ralph 'the ill-tonsured', travelled widely and eventually became a monk at Marmoutiers, though he remained much involved in his family's affairs, and particularly in their foundation at St Evroul.

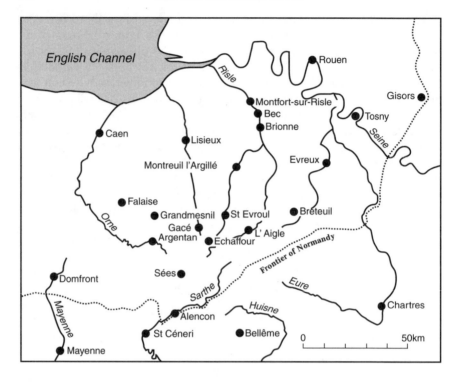

Map 6   The neighbourhood of St Evroul

William Giroie's military career ended prematurely when he was seized at a wedding feast by William Talvas of Bellême, blinded and castrated, forcing him, in effect, to become a monk at Bec. These savage mutilations, so common at this time and so obviously designed to remove their victims from the competition for succession, underline how directly the feuds which inspired them were focused on the control of land and the formation of dynasties. The foundation of St Evroul was the fruit of William's ill luck, and of his careful disposition of his four sisters, of whom (in what seems to have been a typical pattern) two were given to minor lords in the neighbourhood to tie them in to William's following, and two to more distant but grander partners through whom his connections could be advantageously extended. The best of these matches had given Hawise to Robert of Grandmesnil, and it was in conjunction with her sons Hugh and Robert that William Giroie founded St Evroul. On taking his vows William presented the abbey of Bec with a church in the forest of Ouche, served by two aged clerks, to which three monks were sent from Bec to take over the services. Some time later, according to Orderic, he heard that his two Grandmesnil nephews were contemplating a foundation, and persuaded them that this site, where there had been a monastery in Merovingian times, would be a better place for it than the one they had in mind. The brothers agreed, and in 1050 sought the approval of Duke William, 'asking him to give his support to so worthy an undertaking. By common consent they gave the chosen site into his protection, free and quit from all customs and dues which anyone might try to exact from the monks or their men, save only prayers.' Shortly afterwards William and Robert Giroie and Hugh and Robert of Grandmesnil agreed 'that each of them should give himself with all his substance to St Evroul at his death, and that none of them would give, or even sell, any church or tithe or other ecclesiastical property without first offering it for sale to the monks'. They then 'took stock of their wealth and assigned a handsome proportion of it according to their means to the church they had established'. This was done in the presence and with the approval of their sons, kindred and vassals.[11]

Without impugning the piety which Orderic praises so highly we must conclude that William Giroie's concern for family aggrandizement had not ended with his adoption of the monastic life. The foundation of St Evroul linked him and his descendants firmly to their more powerful and illustrious relations the Grandmesnils (whose original plans for a foundation had not included the Giroies), raised their social standing by association with the abbey and its holy relics, and protected a substantial parcel of lands and revenues from the ambitions of feuding kinsfolk and predatory neighbours by placing them directly under the protection of St Evroul, and hence in effect of the Duke himself. As founders' kin, with a plausible basis for guarding and enforcing that protection, the Giroies secured a degree of legitimacy for their exercise of power, and hence a firmer base upon which to build and develop a seignurial *ban*. In short, the foundation was calculated not only to preserve the family's memory through prayer and plainsong, but to enhance and extend its earthly prominence. But not all the family, which as we have noted was by no means a harmonious one. Of the seven sons of Giroie only three had sons of their own; and one of these, Fulk, had been squeezed out by William and Robert: Orderic treats their descendants together with those of the Grandmesnils, as founders' kin, while dismissing Fulk's sons as 'by a concubine'.[12] Orderic mentions the marriages and children of Giroie's other three daughters in friendly enough terms. None of them is mentioned among those who made donations at the time of the foundation, or as witnesses to it.

The might of their enemies, the distrust of the dukes and poor judgement, or bad luck, in matters of rebellion would prove too much for the

Giroies, who were impoverished and dispersed over the next two generations, though one of them, another Robert, succeeded in putting most of the patrimony together again for a short time early in the twelfth century. The memory of the name and abilities of William son of Giroie have been preserved not by his success in welding his turbulent kindred into a dynasty, but by his good fortune that the historian of the quarrels which tore it apart was so very talented. Nevertheless, his ambitions, the difficulties which he faced and the solutions which he devised were all characteristic of his age. One of the most important ways in which this was so cannot easily be conveyed in an abbreviated narrative. For more than a century after the emergence of Giroie his descendants behaved as an extended kin group or clan of the kind which had been familiar in Europe since the Germanic settlements, often warring bitterly and destructively among themselves, but also drawing strength from their numbers, and from the marriage alliances which numerous progeny enabled them to forge. On the other hand, the ablest of them, William, Robert and their sister Hawise of Grandmesnil, whose connections are hardly touched upon here, became the founders of dynasties (though, as it turned out rather short-lived ones), reducing claims on the inheritance by pushing out surplus kin to wander far afield and find favour and fortune where they could – even, if need be, among their traditional enemies, which was another way of ensuring that whatever the outcome some part of the clan would survive. In other words, the Giroies' adoption of the new and revolutionary dynastic principle did not involve a sudden and dramatic jettisoning of the more extended kin group, but a gradual and cautious, even piecemeal adaptation to changing times.

The emergence of male primogeniture as the dominant principle in structuring the aristocratic family was neither novel nor complete in the time of which we write, and in many parts of Europe never happened at all. On the one hand, Patrick Geary and others have pointed to a gradual narrowing of the effective kinship group, accompanied by increasing inequality within it and growing dependence on its leading members, from as early as the ninth century.[13] On the other, the solidarity and rivalries of the wider kin in the defence and pursuit of its interests remained in the twelfth century and for long after a powerful and even predominant element in political life and culture.[14] Indeed, modern studies of the working of kinship in traditional societies point to the division of the kin group to relieve the strain on its existing resources and to take advantage of new ones not as a once-for-all event, but as likely to recur every three or four generations. So it was in traditional Europe. As the sixteenth-century Valencian chronicler Martin de Viciana observed, 'if today someone should, by his courage or fortune, establish

a home for the lineage, those who succeed him will call themselves after
the home where he first settled . . . Some such houses were established in
Aragon around 812, others around 1100, others in Valencia around
1240, and those who go off to India nowadays do the same.'[15] Nevertheless, the widespread division of noble kingroups into separate and
thereafter continuous dynastic lineages in the eleventh century was not
simply the adjustment of a social structure to enable it to survive in the
same form, such as anthropologists usually report and Viciana assumed.
On this occasion the division produced a new and different family
structure (even though the old one also survived and for many purposes
retained its importance), whose particular characteristic was the essential connection which it made and required between the family, defined
by descent from father to eldest son in each generation and not by the
common descent of each generation from more distant ancestors, and
the lands from which it, and it alone, drew its sustenance and standing.
Henceforth, as Duby maintained, aristocratic society in northern Europe
experienced 'a deep fissure that was to become its principal line of
cleavage . . . between those who were elders and those who were not
yet – and in most cases would never be – *seniores*, between the married
men (*conjugati*) and the bachelors – that is, between the eldest and the
younger sons.'[16]

2   Vying in Good Works

The foundation of St Evroul played an essential part in the strategy of
William Giroie both to establish his dynasty and to secure his patrimony.
That is what made his period one of the great ages of monastic foundation. The tide of donation flowed increasingly rapidly throughout the
tenth century, when kings and princes everywhere showed renewed
enthusiasm for the foundation and endowment of monasteries; in the
eleventh century and the first half of the twelfth they were imitated by
lesser lords, and then by lesser still. This is the most elementary reason
for the number and variety of religious houses that covered medieval
Europe. The anxiety of 'new men' like the Giroies to become respectable
made the decades on either side of the millennium a particularly active
period both for founding new houses and adding to the endowments of
existing ones. The pattern of almost three thousand surviving charters
which record gifts and other transfers of land to Cluny between its
foundation in 909 and the death of Abbot Odilo in 1049 would be
typical of most parts of Francia and Italy: just under 374 may be dated
before 942, 546 between 942 and 964, 1,021 between 964 and 994, and
978 between 994 and 1049.[17]

In England as in Francia the ninth century had been a period of widespread secularization of ecclesiastical property. When Alfred of Wessex complained of the ruin into which monastic life had fallen in his kingdom he referred not to the raids of the Vikings but to the aggrandizement of noble families through the alienation of monastic land to relatives of the donors, including the monks and nuns themselves. Conversely, Alfred's attempts to reinvigorate monasticism by establishing communities dedicated afresh to the rule of poverty (that is, community of property), chastity (freedom from family ties) and obedience (to an abbot or abbess appointed by the king himself) may have been part of his vigorous programme to reassert royal authority over the West Saxon thegnage. Certainly, that is now an accepted interpretation of the 'Tenth-century Reformation' in the West Saxon kingdom which was carried out under the aegis of Alfred's great-grandson Edgar the Peaceful.[18] In his reign (959–75) married canons were expelled from Winchester, Canterbury and Worcester cathedrals to restore the communal life and provide incomes for royal officers. Royal authority was bolstered at strategic points, notably in the Fens and East Midlands, by endowing new monastic foundations like those at Ely, Peterborough, Ramsey, and Thorney with extensive 'liberties' or 'sokes'. By the paradoxical method of exempting them from royal jurisdiction (that is, in practice, from the magnates who had appropriated to themselves delegated royal powers) this guaranteed the abbots' independence of their mighty neighbours. In short, the aim of wresting church land and the power that went with it from the control of local magnates and the methods by which it was achieved, both of which were central to 'reform' in the eleventh century, were operative in England, under royal not papal guidance, certainly from the middle of the tenth century and quite possibly from the end of the ninth. Whether it is better to regard that as part of the general monastic movement of the late Carolingian world of which Wessex was certainly a part, or of its own 'First Revolution' which, as we shall see, was overwhelmed and absorbed into our First European Revolution by the Conquest of 1066,[19] may be an interesting question.

Where there was no simple conflict between central and local power the politics of monastic foundation were more complicated, and in some fundamental respects are only beginning to be understood, but in principle the issues were the same. Thus Karl Leyser showed how in tenth-century Saxony the lavish endowment of nunneries protected by royal diplomas of immunity contributed to the stabilization of the kin by inhibiting the fragmentation of property holding, protecting the inheritances of women and providing for the commemoration of the dead – until the scale of the endowments itself became a source of instability.[20]

Perhaps the most famous example of the use of immunity to protect monastic endowments against covetous neighbours – in this case the Bishops and the Counts of Macon – is the foundation charter granted to Cluny by Duke William 'the Pious' of Aquitaine and his wife Ingelberga in 909, which placed it directly under the protection of the papacy.[21] Cluny's property and influence extended rapidly and on a very large scale, not only in its neighbourhood in southern Burgundy, but much further afield, and especially southwestward in the Auvergne and south-eastwards into the Rhone valley. Barbara Rosenwein has shown how each of these accumulations of property (which together amounted to some 60 per cent of donations to Cluny by the end of the tenth century) was due to the benefactions over several generations of interlocking family groups which were closely connected with the founders.[22] In the Auvergne the expansion was led by the friends and relations of the vicomtes of Clermont (including the family of Abbot Odilo, whom we have already encountered as the architect of Cluny's eleventh-century greatness) and the lords of Bourbon. The latter were descended from a follower of William the Pious himself, the former from a follower of his nephew and successor Acfrid, and both represented important and extensive connections in a region of continuing strategic importance to the Dukes. The extension of Cluny's possessions into the Rhone valley was similarly interwoven with the attempts of the kin of Ingelberga's father, Boso of Provence (d.887), the first non-Carolingian to call himself a King, to restore their fortunes in lower Burgundy, Provence and Italy (where their struggle helped to precipitate the developments in Tuscany discussed immediately below[23]) after Boso's defeat at the hands of the Carolingians.

Cluny was the first and greatest example of a new form of monastic organization to which the tenth century gave rise, a chain or network of monasteries spread across a wide area, and linked to each other at least by observation of the same liturgical and disciplinary customs and often by common subjection to the Abbot of the senior house, perhaps through his right to nominate the superior. Estimates of the number of houses involved are bedevilled by difficulties of both definition and evidence. However, the scale of the movement may be suggested by the map of tenth-century monastic reform in the *Grosser Historische Weltatlas*, which shows 70 houses in various categories affiliated to Gorze, in Lotharingia, up to 1150, 607 to Cluny, 121 to Hirsau in Swabia, and 49 to St Victor, Marseille.[24] This excludes the English movement discussed above, and that from Brogne, in Flanders, as well as many individual foundations. For want of a better term these congregations are often called 'orders'. It was a word which meant many things, but in monastic contexts by the twelfth century generally suggests a much closer and more permanent degree of subordination to the mother house than was implied in the tenth.[25] The founder or patron who placed his house under the authority of the Abbot of Cluny usually did so, he said, out of admiration for the care and efficiency with which the rule of St Benedict was observed at Cluny, the beauty of its liturgy and the efficacy of its prayers. The services of the house being handed over would henceforth be conducted in the same manner and according to the same timetable as at Cluny itself, and if the foundation was a new one, in a church built on the same plan and in the same style. The rapid growth of the order is often attributed to a longing for peace and unity in the turbulent and fragmenting world of the tenth century, and the Cluniac ideal was undeniably a powerful one: wherever and whenever a traveller might stop at one of their houses he would find himself, just as though he were at Cluny itself, in a corner of heaven, where the monks in preparation for the *vita angelica* to which they would be called, performed the work of God with the unvarying dignity and splendour that befitted it.[26]

In linking and protecting widely scattered concentrations of territory in some of the areas where the remnants of Carolingian power were most keenly contested through benefactions to Cluny and similar foundations, the monastic 'orders' of the tenth century reflected the wide-ranging and overlapping struggles of great clans for regional hegemony which characterized this stage of the disintegration of the Carolingian Empire. Episcopal power could be defended and reasserted in the same way. For example, George Dameron has shown how the early eleventh-century bishops of Florence laid the foundations of a wealthy and enduring territorial lordship by reasserting their rights of jurisdiction to reclaim and develop the property of their see, provoking some of the most celebrated episodes of the reform movement of the eleventh century.[27] By the end of the tenth century the lords in the Arno valley had profited from the bidding for regional support of the various competitors for the inheritance of the collapsing Carolingian state to accumulate extensive territories, largely from the imperial fisc but also including substantial appropriations from the lands of the bishopric of Florence. They sought to preserve these acquisitions as patrimony by endowing monasteries which were protected against local rivals by imperial immunities. One such was San Salvatore at Settimo, founded in 998 by the Cadolingi, one of four lineages which emerged from the nobility of late Carolingian Tuscany in the tenth century, to consolidate and legitimate their immense territorial acquisitions in the Arno valley, as well as to commemorate their dead and intercede for their sins. Its first abbot was Guarino, a strict disciplinarian who within a few years was to undertake a campaign to eradicate simony and clerical marriage from the diocese of Florence where Bishop Ildebrando had bought the see for cash from the Emperor and shared the episcopal palace with his wife Alberga and four sons. It was Guarino who cursed Alberga as a Jezebel when, sitting beside the bishop in his court, she presumed to answer a question which Guarino had addressed to her husband.[28] The incident is recorded by the late eleventh-century disciple and biographer of Giovanni Gualberti as a dreadful example of the decadence against which his hero had to contend, but it may have seemed less obviously scandalous to Alberga's contemporaries, for a number of women played prominent roles in public life in tenth- and earlier eleventh-century Italy.

Guarino's campaign against Ildebrando and his clergy weakened the bishop's public position and made it more difficult for him to defend disputed lands and rights, thus, no doubt coincidentally, serving the interests of the Cadolingi. In retaliation Bishop Ildebrando himself espoused the cause of reform by promoting the cult of the Florentine martyr Minias, in whose honour he founded in 1014 a new monastery and basilica, enlisting the support of the Emperor Henry II. Henry agreed, but also maintained a judicious balance among his followers in the region by granting Settimo, in the same year, an imperial charter confirming its lands and rights. Undeterred by the tradition that the bones of Minias had been removed by Bishop Dietrich of Mainz sixty years previously, Ildebrando launched a new, and as it turned out successful search for them, and instructed Drogo, the abbot of his new foundation, to write a fresh account of the martyrdom. Drogo's work not only enhanced the reputation of both the saint and his promoter Ildebrando, but pointed the way to the possibility of further relic discoveries by revealing that Minias had not died alone, as the previous tradition had held, but with several others.[29]

As a soldier Minias was a fitting patron to rally the *milites* who occupied the bishop's *castella* in the countryside and constituted a crucial element among his supporters. From his own resources and by securing donations from others Ildebrando was able to endow his new monastery, San Miniato al Monte, with oratories dedicated to the Saint (some forty of them) and estates throughout his diocese, many of them at places where the lineages with which the bishop was mainly in contention, the Cadolingi and the Guidi, already had important interests. In this way he created, in effect, a local network of supporters and patrons of St Minias as well as what amounted to an administrative structure to coordinate the management of his extensive but scattered and miscellaneous territories. These donations included many estates reclaimed from or disputed by the Cadolingi and the Guidi, which were now placed under the protection of the new cult and its numerous and powerful supporters.

Guarino of Settimo's rebuke to Ildebrando and Alberga and the events surrounding the foundation of San Miniato foreshadowed a much more famous dispute. Fifty years later another bishop of Florence, Pietro Mezzabarba, whose father claimed to have bought the job for him at the imperial court, found himself hounded by another abbot of Settimo who was supported by the Cadolingi, Giovanni Gualberti. The bishop tried to turn the tide of public opinion with another magnificent monastic foundation. He failed, and was deposed after Petrus Igneus triumphed in his ordeal by fire in 1068.[30] Having survived chiefly in the lurid and entertaining polemics of Gualberti's generation of reformers Ildebrando has not enjoyed a high reputation among historians – deservedly, it may seem, since one of the main aims of his strategy was to create an ecclesiastical patrimony for his sons. Nevertheless, Dameron has revealed him as a vigorous and inventive protector of the interests of his bishopric, who by rescuing its estates from the acquisitiveness of the rural lords preserved and deepened its influence in the countryside as well as laying the basis of future prosperity and power. He was also, of course, not only a target of reformers, but through St Minias himself a proponent of 'reform', as well as the original patron of one of the most beautiful churches in Europe.

At first sight the tenth and eleventh centuries seem to have experienced simply another rotation in a cycle of generosity and withdrawal which had characterized the relations between church and nobility in Europe, and indeed in much of Eurasia, for several centuries past. Alternation between lavish generosity in the support of religious and charitable institutions and ruthless plundering of the wealth which they accumulated thereby was characteristic not only of early medieval Europe but of all the traditional societies of contemporary Eurasia. In China the dramatic spread and endowment of Buddhism between the fourth and the seventh centuries was followed in the eighth by confiscations and temple closures; in the central Islamic lands the widespread endowments of mosques, madrasehs and other charitable institutions in the ninth-century Golden Age was followed by renewed attempts to control them, and in the tenth century the Byzantine Empire saw a strong reaction against perceivedly over-generous monastic patronage in the ninth.[31] The great age of temple building in India in the eleventh and twelfth centuries which produced magnificent monuments like those at Kjuraho (*c.*1002), Thanjavur (*c.*1012), Udaipur (*c.*1059–80) and Bhubaneshwar (*c.*1060) – a movement in many respects comparable with that of church building in western Europe at the same time in respect of the political context and social impulses which gave rise to it as well as in the splendour of the results – was followed by rebellions against not only the expense of the temples but the strengthening of royal control with which they were associated.[32]

The reason for this alternation between giving land to religious foundations and taking it back again emerges clearly from those examples. The foundation of a holy place, a monastery or a temple, created a concentration of prestige and resources which enhanced the standing and influence of the people associated with it, and through it with each other. It brought land and other economic assets into use, and established a network of new relationships and loyalties in the neighbourhood, and often well beyond, drawing the locality into broader and more regular relations with a wider world. Harnessing local resources more effectively assisted patrons to assert their independence of more distant authorities – emperors, kings or princes – who in turn were compelled to respond with the even greater gifts which their status required, or to reassert their influence by undertaking new and more lavish foundations of their own. In short, religious foundation was part, and in our period an extremely important part, of the intensification of the exploitation of land and people which we have already seen exemplified in castle building and in the creation of the seigneurie. It was therefore also an agent of destabilisation: generosity which increased the power of the giver was bound to become competitive. As Ordericus Vitalis put it, after Duke William's magnificent twin foundations of Holy Trinity and St Etienne at Caen (undertaken in expiation of his incestuous marriage) 'the barons of Normandy were inspired by the piety of their princes to do likewise, and encouraged each other to undertake similar enterprises for the salvation of their souls. They vied with each other in good works, and competed in giving alms generously as befitted their rank.'[33] Towards the end of the eleventh century, as more modest families increasingly aspired to establish their own foundations rather than merely support those of their lords, the houses of the 'new' monasticism, such as the Cistercians, began to compete in austerity, which was easier to fund, rather than in splendour, but the principle was the same.

3   Chastity, Property and Obedience

It is misleading to think of the fluctuations in the balance between monarchs, landlords and religious foundations which lie behind the alternating periods of endowment and depletion of church lands as cyclical. That the means by which patrons strengthened their positions were much the same on each occasion (typically, offering an endowment or gift more lavish than the last and piously guaranteeing the independence of the institution from the officers and agents of rival lords), makes the process appear repetitive. But since the competitive alternation led at each turn to a greater degree of intensification it was spiral rather than cyclical, and cumulative in its effect. Each fresh round of foundations, gifts and counter-gifts tended to bring more land into cultivation, increase the complexity and differentiation of local society, and integrate it more closely, culturally, economically and politically, with the wider world. The importance of the new turn which was given to the spiral in tenth- and eleventh-century Europe went even further than this, however. The terms upon which the process of endowment was resumed after the widespread secularization of the ninth century enabled the subsequent benefactions to remain largely undisturbed (though not, after the thirteenth century, to continue everywhere unchecked) until the period of the Protestant Reformation in northern Europe, and elsewhere until that of the French Revolution and beyond. Since that re-endowment was also the key to the reordering of social relations in the eleventh and twelfth centuries themselves it may properly be seen as epoch-making.

The oscillation of advantage between central and local power which lay behind the alternations of 'reform' and 'reaction' in the endowment of monasteries was also reflected in fluctuations in the balance of power within the neighbourhood itself. That is why at this very time of hectic generosity we also hear of a sustained and determined counter-attack, of the relentless harrying and usurpation of ecclesiastical, and especially monastic lands by lawless and predatory knights. The complaints which reached a crescendo in the movement for the Peace of God – directed precisely against people like the Giroies, who were also the most munificent benefactors – were echoed everywhere in the charters and chronicles of the period. The contradiction is too great to explain simply by saying that some members of noble families objected to the donations made by others. Certainly that was often the case, but it does not explain why the churches should have complained most loudly of ill treatment at a time when they were in fact the recipients of greater largesse than ever – and there is no doubt that land was being transferred to them on a very large scale indeed.

It is even less obvious why the aristocracy should have been disposed to such generosity at a time when its members were competing desperately among themselves for land, and impoverished, or feeling themselves impoverished, by the fragmentation of estates which resulted from partible inheritance, the sharply rising cost of equipping and maintaining a military entourage, and the reappearance of a market in high-status luxury goods such as silks and spices.[34] The 'quitclaims' which are recorded in a growing number of charters from this period certainly seem to show that tension arising from the over-generosity of donors (as perceived by their kinsfolk) was prominent among the conflicts which raged in Francia around the millennium. They record the settlements reached between a monastery and a neighbouring lord who had seized land from it, often with the claim (*calumpnia*) that it had been given improperly, or not given at all, by one or other of his forebears. Even the conclusions of the most learned discussions, which have attributed this excess of generosity to a growth of 'lay piety', or the more specialized form of it which resulted from the passing of land through the operations of shared inheritance into the hands of unmarried women, who were particularly prone to give it to the church, do not so much answer as rephrase the question raised by such seemingly reckless enthusiasm.[35]

The apparent contradiction has been resolved, and the implications of attacks on monastic endowments from the point of view of castellans also anxious to consolidate and legitimate their local standing – people like the Giroies and their followers – by founding a new monastery or supporting an existing one have been brilliantly illuminated, by Barbara Rosenwein's analysis of the charters of Cluny. Just as gifts to monasteries were often not merely altruistic, but intended to shore up the local position of the donor, or to give the protection of the monastery to property whose use and revenues the donors continued to enjoy, Rosenwein has shown that the 'usurpations' recorded in the *calumpniae* were not always prompted by simple hostility to the monks, or really intended to deprive them of the land in question. In 981 or 982, for example, Abbot Maiolous and the monks of Cluny gave a villa at Fontana to a woman named Eva as part of an exchange. Some time between then and his death in 1014 her son Antelmus gave it back to Cluny. On three occasions between 1014 and 1039 three different women, Antelmus' two sisters and his sister-in-law, all claimed the land from Cluny, and then abandoned, or quit, their claims; and each time the claimant was acknowledged as a benefactor to Cluny, and received a payment in return. All three women were buried in the abbey, and their families became important associates of it. Antelmus himself had been involved both in giving land to Cluny and in claiming – and quitclaiming – land from it on a number of other occasions in the 980s and 990s, in association with several groups of other donors. He was eventually buried in the monastery.[36]

The land at Fontana was entirely typical of donations to Cluny in this period in having been 'given' and reclaimed several times over, and by several different people. From the records of many such claims and counterclaims Rosenwein concluded that the 'gifts' of land which they record were not meant to represent the permanent conveyance of absolute rights over immovable property which such acts suggest to the modern mind. Their role was rather that of the cowrie shell in

Malinowski's description of gift exchange, which by passing from hand to hand and creating the obligation of a counter gift each time it was given, wove a network of duty and reciprocal obligation between givers and receivers.[37] That insight immediately explains what had previously seemed inexplicable, why it was precisely in the most difficult and unstable times that people were anxious to associate themselves through donation with the increasingly powerful network of alliance and influence of which the monastery was the centre. They saw their land as a source not so much of income as of the means to secure, consolidate and defend their position in the neighbourhood and in regional society, at whatever level and across whatever distances their standing and resources permitted. The monastery, for its part, acted as a sort of banker (under the control of one or a consortium of the leading families), not only in the economic sense, that it could and did make loans of land or resources in hard times and recover them in better ones, but in the subtler but no less contentious currency of reputation and local standing, which could be finely and accurately expressed in many degrees of association with its religious life (donors, most obviously, were remembered in prayers) and its social calendar.

The same insight suggests another reason for the intensification of conflict between monasteries and their neighbours towards and after the millennium. In all of these transactions the value of the land in question had been largely symbolic. It carried authority and legitimacy, and provided the basis of political and social power, but these things did not depend very directly or significantly on the use, if any, to which the land was put. Once the monks began to think of their land as a permanent economic asset – and it was certainly the monasteries, by and large, which took the lead in the new forms of agricultural exploitation – once they wished substantially to increase their production of cereals, or to plant vines which required a period of several years to repay an initial investment but then became increasingly profitable, they could no longer accept the fluidities of the old outlook. Long-term investment and purposeful management meant that boundaries must be defined and proprietorship established. The cowrie shell, in effect, was withdrawn from the circuit of exchange, to be polished and given pride of place in the display cabinet of one of the participants. Naturally the other members of the circle were outraged, and felt that the terms on which they had given land had been violated – that the monastery was not so much owner of the land (as we would put it), as its custodian on behalf of a kin group or neighbourhood community which was defined by the complex and interlocking network of givers and receivers.

The accusations of avarice so often levelled against the monks by 'usurpers' who took the disputed lands back into their own hands were very often, therefore, not mere rationalizations of lawlessness, but expressions of a real indignation that traditional decencies and understanding were being flouted. Repugnance for the notion that land might be treated as a commodity had been embodied in the opinion of an early exemplar of Cluniac values, Count – and Saint – Gerald of Aurillac, that buying land was a sin to be scrupulously avoided.[38] That Gerald felt it necessary to say so also suggests, however, that already in his lifetime, the second half of the ninth century, the buying and selling of land was becoming more common. David Herlihy showed a generation ago that in southern France and Italy this was indeed the case.[39] By the end of the tenth century the land market around Milan, Marseilles and Barcelona, at least, was active enough to be causing a rapid inflation of prices. Northern Europe provides no evidence for direct comparison, but similar economic forces were certainly at work by the early decades of the eleventh century, at least in relatively advanced regions like Flanders and the Rhineland. Indeed the clear desire of great monasteries like Cluny, or Marmoutiers in the Loire valley to define the boundaries of their possessions more precisely, in conjunction with the indications of the growing rate at which new land was being brought under cultivation and the increasing pace of seignurialisation, is itself evidence that the growth of markets for agricultural produce was a good deal earlier and more rapid than is directly recorded by the documentary sources. In other words, during the tenth century, and especially its second half, the incentives for the monks to try to stabilize their land holdings were increasing just as rapidly as the need for the facilities of association and social consolidation which had been provided through the flexibility of the traditional outlook which Gerald of Aurillac defended.

Hence in the years around the millennium the slow, gradual but cumulatively profound changes which were overtaking European society produced a crisis in the relations between the monasteries and their lay neighbours. The movement towards a market economy and the agrarian changes which accompanied it not only heightened competition for control over land and its workers, but by drawing the monastery itself into the competition undermined its capacity to act as a disinterested mediator and arbiter, just at the time when those services were most acutely in demand. Further, the most intense and dangerous aspect of that competition, the struggle within kin groups for control of the territory which was being divided into patrimonies, enhanced the urgency to command the monastery's economic and spiritual resources (that is, its social power), while increasing the danger that its estates might provide patrimonies for rival dynasties. The complaints of usurpation, the multiplication of *calumpniae*, the movement for the Peace of God, did not, therefore reflect a simple attempt to take the land back, another oscillation in the traditional relationship between the church and lay society. 'Usurpation' rather represented the opening move in a renegotiation of the usurper's relationship with the monastery. It was designed to win a reaffirmation or a reassessment of the usurper's standing in the community of which the monastery was the centre, and to ensure that his interests would not be jeopardized as the monastery consolidated and extended its holdings, thereby strengthening and deepening its relationships with his neighbours and rivals.

The monasteries responded to this crisis in their relations with lay society by offering a dramatic clarification and redefinition of the terms upon which they held their lands, including a thoroughgoing revision of the services which they offered and the ways in which their relationship with the community was formed and expressed. This was worked out in the canons of the councils associated with the Peace of God, and under the leadership of the order of Cluny, and defined the goals of 'reform' throughout the eleventh and twelfth centuries. Its starting point was celibacy, not only of the monks but, crucially, of the clergy as a whole. The immense importance of the idea of chastity (in particular of male chastity) in the religious movements of the eleventh century has long been obvious, but more recently Dominique Iogna Prat has uncovered a critical step in its development precisely in these years around the millennium.[40] Between 999 and 1010 the scriptorium of Cluny and that of its dependent house of St Germanus of Auxerre produced the core documents of one of the largest and most widely circulated hagiographical dossiers of the period, designed to secure the canonisation of Maiolus, abbot of Cluny from 954 until 998. It contained, in addition to a *life*, a sermon which Maiolus had preached, and a poem describing the election of his successor, Odilo, under whose aegis this dossier was compiled. Cluny reached its greatest extension of wealth, power and political prestige in Odilo's abbacy, and we have already met him as one of the leading propagators of the Peace of God. The theme of the sermon is virginity, which is also heavily stressed in the *life*, and it is specifically related to the possession of land by monks, who were dedicated to poverty. The bishoprics of France had been founded by saints and martyrs, whose sacrifice provided the warrant for the authority and the wealth which their successors enjoyed. The founders of monasteries such as Cluny, of much more recent appearance, were men of great wisdom and holiness to be sure, but they had not been called upon to shed their blood in witness of their faith. What equivalent legitimation, therefore, did the monasteries possess for the wealth which they were accumulating so rapidly, and for the independence of episcopal authority which they were so determined to establish? Odilo's Maiolus resolved the dilemma by reviving a theme which had been popular in the early church. Virginity, he maintained, was a sacrifice comparable with that of martyrdom, a grace which enabled the monks of his day to witness their faith as fully and painfully as might, in happier times, have been required of them by the most savage of tyrants or the most blood-thirsty barbarians. For the individual monk it provided an alternative route to salvation. For the monastic community as a whole virginity defined its status in the traditional three-fold ordering of society, and distinguished it sharply from that of the warriors (*bellatores*). Hence, among other things, celibacy rendered the monks and their possessions untouchable by profane hands.

Chastity, together with the personal, as opposed to the institutional poverty of the monks, stood for freedom from worldly interest and connection. In identifying it as the condition upon which monks enjoyed their communal property, therefore, Odilo reaffirmed the fitness of the monastery for precisely the role of arbiter of status and obligation in the community which was being compromised by its changing economic and social interests. At the same time the monks, not only at Cluny but throughout the Latin west, set out to restore harmony and reassure their neighbours by devising new ways of conferring the benefits of respect and solidarity in the community which the gift of land had originally been designed to secure, in the shape of new or more emphatically advertised forms of association between the monastery and its lay patrons. Hence the dramatic elaboration of the liturgy, the increasingly prolonged and impressive commemorations and intercessions for benefactors, the multiplication of prayer associations and confraternities, and the discreet retirement of the bodies of the privileged into the privacy of the monastic cemeteries which constituted the eleventh-century revival of lay piety, and which committed the monasteries to the legitimation and support of the dynastic principle which their patrons were fighting to establish.

By making the monks' claim to property depend on their virginity Odilo also removed at a stroke the greatest threat that it represented to the secular nobility – that it might provide the basis (as secularized church lands had done in the past) for dynastic power to rival their own. His argument was not relevant to monastic property alone. From the very beginning, as we have already seen, it had been held by reformers that the root of the church's troubles was the alienation of its property and revenues into lay hands, which had become almost universal since the middle of the ninth century. Already at the council at Le Puy in 975, which foreshadowed the Peace movement, the restoration of church property and the establishment of a division of the revenues between bishop and chapter was the bishop's immediate objective. But everything has its price, and this surrender or restoration of land was coupled with another change to which it would remain inextricably linked: the members of the cathedral chapter were required thenceforth to lead the common life – that is, to submit themselves to the regime of individual poverty, chastity and obedience.[41] In other words, they guaranteed that the land which was handed over to them would not at any time in the future become the basis for the foundation of a new secular dynasty, and that its fruits would remain available for the support of younger sons in future generations.

By generalizing and conceptualizing the principle that celibacy conferred a right to the enjoyment of property held in common, and was an indispensable condition of doing so, Odilo's dossier on Maiolus provided a definition and sharpening of social boundaries directly equivalent to that which conceived of the land itself as bounded, fixed and immoveable property. It also provided an articulate basis for the provisions of the Peace Councils, which consistently equated the poor, the unarmed and the celibate as those who fell under their protection, which was withdrawn not only from armed warriors but also, with increasing firmness, from corrupt and uncelibate clergy. Thus, the frontier of celibacy was extended during the next half century or so to include not only monks but all clergy, and hence, notoriously, to become one of the central issues of the Gregorian reform. In 1059 Nicholas II, at the second Lateran Council, forbade married priests to participate in the liturgy or administer the sacraments, to live in the presbytery of the clergy or to receive eccelesiastical prebends, and prohibited the laity from attending the masses of simoniacal or married priests. Turning the aspiration into something more or less corresponding to reality would take several more decades of determined struggle, but in principle the distinction between clergy and laity was now entirely clear. In establishing it the terms and conditions upon which property was to be held by the church had been a crucial consideration.

4   Incest, Matrimony and Chivalry

The First European Revolution, like its successors, had victims among the powerful as well as among the poor. The most conspicuous were those who were deprived of a traditional claim to a share of their family's lands, or prevented from exercising it. How they were compelled or persuaded to accept their fate remains utterly mysterious. There was, after all, no authority entitled to pronounce that the claims of younger sons and of daughters on their patrimony were thenceforth to be abrogated or severely curtailed, let alone with the power to enforce it. On the contrary, in a profoundly conservative society every prejudice of tradition and propriety would have reinforced the natural resistance of those whose most fundamental interest was threatened by overturning the customs which governed inheritance. As we have seen, that resistance was often both determined and bitter. To be secure the new regime must be not only established but accepted, and accepted not only as necessary, but as right. It was all very well to devise new family stratagems, and to incorporate them in new rules and customs governing inheritance, but unless everybody concerned, and especially those whose material interests were most obviously affected, could be fully persuaded that it was not only expedient (for some) to adopt new customs and expectations, but right for all, the violence and instability of the eleventh century would not have diminished. The most remarkable thing about the new regime, in short, is that it was quickly based on consent. Within two or three generations the young men and women of Europe's landed aristocracy – not a group previously notable for either docility or altruism – were persuaded to accept a radical and sweeping reconstruction of the norms and values of social life which was greatly to the disadvantage of most of their number. Its first and fundamental demand was that in relinquishing the expectation of inheritance most of them should postpone for many years, and perhaps for ever, the prospect of legitimate sexual activity.

The ideal of Christian marriage as it has been known in the west, together with the body of law and teaching which gave it form, were very largely the work of Carolingian churchmen. Charlemagne incorporated into much of his legislation the principles of the *Collectio-Dionysio Hadriana*, the authoritative collection of relevant texts, which had been given to him by the Pope on his first visit to Rome in 774. Throughout the reigns of his son and grandsons the bishops of their kingdom promulgated and elaborated these teachings and regulations in councils of the church and instructions to their clergy, and laboured by direct intervention to have them observed by the nobility as well as the peasantry.[42] Their success was severely limited, however; the ecclesiastical principles that marriage was monogamous, contracted at the free will of the partners, and indissoluble, conflicted too sharply with the mundane necessities of forging as many alliances and begetting as many sons as possible, while the demand that the partners should not be nearly related too often obstructed the consolidation of great kin groups and the union of their territories.

Those considerations remained powerful in our period, of course, and long afterwards. Philip I was not the last king to make scandal (though he was the first king of the Franks to incur ecclesiastical sanctions for doing so) when he was repeatedly excommunicated for divorcing his own wife Bertha of Frisia, and making off with someone else's, Bertrada,

Countess of Anjou, whom he married at Senlis in 1093; nor was Philip II, when he cast off Ingeborg of Denmark after a single night with her in 1193, and bigamously married Agnes of Méranie three years later, on the basis of a spurious claim that Ingeborg was his fourth cousin.[43] Nevertheless, the intervening century had seen profound changes. Clerical writers continued to refer to Bertrada as a concubine right up to Philip's death, twelve years later, and Suger of St Denis, mentor and biographer of Louis VI (Philip's son by his first marriage, and his successor), disparages his two sons by Bertrada. This did not prevent all the bishops of his kingdom from attending Philip's wedding to Bertrada, except the zealous reformer and canon lawyer Ivo of Chartres, who led the campaign against him, and even Ivo admitted the validity, though not the legality, of the marriage. Nor is there much sign that Philip's magnates – including the Count of Anjou himself – took any serious exception to his conduct, which they understood as necessary to provide cover for the single delicate heir whom Bertha had given him. Agnes of Méranie died in 1201, but although Philip II was the most powerful king in Christendom his efforts to get rid of Ingeborg were unavailing, and he was eventually compelled to take her back in 1213, in time to secure the Pope's blessing for the invasion of England by his son Louis. He could afford to do so because Louis' own wife, fortunately, had just produced an heir.

What had changed in the century which separated these two scandals, in short, was not that kings, or indeed other great lords, had ceased to give their dynastic interests priority over Christian morality, but that they had to pay a very much higher price for doing so, because that morality, as expounded by the Pope and the bishops, now reigned unchallenged. Its ascendancy contributed indispensably to the creation of the dynastic family, and therefore of the consolidation and preservation of the patrimony that supported it, by sharpening the distinction between legitimate and illegitimate offspring, thereby eliminating competition between the children of different unions. Inheritance was the greatest issue at stake in the vigorous, and at times bitter conflict which was waged during our period between what have been called 'two models of marriage'. When the lord was principally the leader of a band of warriors it had been an advantage to have many sons to support him in his prime, while daughters could be given to followers and rivals, sealing treaties and consolidating alliances. A barren wife was a wasted opportunity at best, and a fruitful concubine a useful asset. It availed little to insist pedantically on magnifying differences of status between them – or between their children. The Church might be determined that marriage should be monogamous, exogamous, free and indissoluble, but the magnates insisted on their right and duty to select wives according to the social and diplomatic requirements of their situation, and to replace those who failed in the primary and urgent obligation to provide their lords with male children. If the Church won in the end it was because the benefits of the secure transmission of property came to outweigh the risk – though it remained a very real one – of dying without an adult male heir.

When the transmission of an undivided inheritance became the over-riding consideration, however, the heir must be designated as clearly as possible, and the number and standing of his potential rivals minimised. The stigmatization of bastardy was therefore one of the clearest signs of the transition from the economy of plunder to that of property, as well as the inevitable counterpart of the glorification of the *genus*. There is little to suggest that this was of the slightest significance among the many obstacles that William had to overcome to assert his right to the Norman duchy in the 1040s, but it prevented his grandson, Robert of Gloucester, from being regarded as a serious candidate to succeed Henry I in 1135, even though Robert's ability and integrity were as generally admired as the claims of the legitimate contestants, Stephen of Blois and the Empress Matilda, were distrusted and their characters disliked.[44]

Insistence on legitimacy inevitably elevated the importance of the marriage from which the heir would spring, and of the purity of the vessel in which he would be conceived and nurtured. The elevation of female virtue, both through the promulgation of the cult of the Blessed Virgin and in her secular aspect in the tales of chivalry and the so-called cult of courtly love, is one of the most familiar aspects of twelfth-century civilization. Its novelty, however, is worth stressing. Virginity had always been honoured in Christian tradition, of course, and the groundwork for the high medieval cult of the Virgin had been laid, especially in England, during the previous two or three centuries. Nevertheless, it was male, not female chastity that really commanded the attention of the writers of saints' lives in the eleventh century. It was not until the twelfth that Mary's role as the universal saint of Christendom really began to be reflected in an increasing domination of church dedications, among them those of the entire Cistercian order. There were many reasons for the rise of her cult, including the identification of the papal reform with the suppression of liturgical and disciplinary variations from Roman practice associated with the veneration of local saints, most famously that of Ambrose at Milan,[45] and the movement towards a gentler and more compassionate theology. One of them, however, was certainly the interest of the aristocratic family not only in persuading many daughters into nunneries – more than one-third of all the nunneries established in France and England during the middle ages were founded between 1126 and 1175[46] – but in promoting the status of the loyal and virtuous wife.

It was even more important to define and regulate what marriages might take place. Since early times the church had set its face against the marriage of partners too nearly related, without agreeing consistently or clearly just what that meant. At the beginning of the seventh century Pope Gregory I, writing to Augustine of Canterbury, had been content to exclude marriage between the children of full brothers or sisters – that is, with two common grandparents; in the middle of the eighth Pope Gregory II specified to Boniface, who was dismayed by the contradiction, that there should not be common ancestors in four generations.[47] Perhaps an attempt to reconcile these rulings contributed to the emergence in the ninth century of a consensus that the partners should not be related within the seventh 'degree' of consanguinity. This, according to the prevailing 'Roman' method of calculation, meant counting the number of sexual acts interposed between the prospective partners (so that I am related to my sister in the second degree, my niece in the third, my first cousin in the fourth and so on). Marriage within the seventh degree was formally prohibited, and bishops required to see that those already married should be separated on pain of excommunication, by the Lateran Council of 1059 – a council at which some of the most fundamental acts of the papal reform were promulgated, such as that which placed the election of the pope in the hands of the cardinals. The ostensibly traditional phraseology, however, concealed a massive change of meaning. The Lateran decree was accompanied, or directly followed, by a momentous alteration in the method of calculation. The Roman principle of counting by acts of generation was abandoned in favour of the so-called Germanic reckoning, which defined a generation as all the members of a sibling group and counted accordingly (so that I am related to my sister in the first degree, and to both my niece and my first cousin in the second). This change was given normative force by the treatise of one of the leading reformers, Peter Damiani, *de parentelae gradibus* (c.1060), and incorporated shortly afterwards in legislation of Pope Alexander II, and subsequently in Gratian's *Decretum*.[48]

The purpose of this change, which increased the probability that a given match would fall within the prohibited degrees by a factor of about twenty, and caused such difficulties that it was virtually reversed by the Lateran Council of 1215, has puzzled historians. There is no obvious scriptural or theological reason for it, and it is not elucidated by other contemporary texts. Whatever the rationale, however, one consequence is clear. An important function of incest prohibitions in tribal societies is to increase the authority of the older generation over the younger by making marriage more difficult to achieve.[49] This was a consideration of particular interest to eleventh-century parents, since the church's awkward insistence that a marriage was made by the consent of the partners meant that it was not invalidated by the lack of parental approval. The anthropologist Robin Fox, writing essentially of very much less developed societies, describes as the essential ingredients of systems of kinship and marriage: (1) a power struggle between older and younger males (2) over the control of women for sexual purposes (3) leading by one route or another to the invention of exogamic restrictions (4) through the intermediary process of the development of conscience and guilt.[50] It would be difficult to offer a better short account of the changes which took place in the eleventh- and twelfth-century west.

How practical and formidable a barrier the new rules on consanguinity presented, even after they had been significantly relaxed by the Fourth Lateran Council in 1215, is shown by the complaint of the peasants of Rosny-sur-Bois to Pope Honorius III in 1219, that by upholding the claim of the Abbot of St Denis that they were his serfs the church was making it impossible for them to secure wives from neighbouring, but free, villages, and thus forcing them to marry incestuously among themselves.[51] The promulgation of the new mode of reckoning in its full rigour between 1059 and 1215 meant that since, notoriously, almost no two members of an aristocracy still closely descended from two hundred or so Carolingian comital families did not have a common ancestor in seven generations, it followed that almost no socially acceptable marriage was not incestuous. Our political narratives are full of examples of the exploitation and counter-exploitation of this familiar fact to annul marriages which had become inconvenient, as in the case of Philip II's attempts to get rid of Ingeborg of Denmark. Fewer traces, obviously, have been left by marriages which never took place because they were prevented, as when Henry I of England checkmated the match arranged by Louis VI of France between Louis' candidate for the duchy of Normandy, William Clito, and Sybil, the daughter of Count Fulk of Anjou, whose support was crucial in the conflict between Henry and Louis over control of the Norman succession, by arguing that it would be consanguineous. Even at much humbler levels of society the extension of the prohibited degrees meant that virtually no acceptable marriage could take place without the agreement of everybody concerned, since any objection was very likely to be sustained. To maintain a marriage that was generally considered desirable in effect required a conspiracy of silence, as no less an authority than Pope Eugenius III acknowledged in 1149 when, reconciling Louis VII and Eleanor of Aquitaine after Eleanor's rumoured affair with Raymond of Tripoli during the second crusade, 'he forbade any future mention of their consanguinity', which was common knowledge, and 'commanded under pain of anathema that no word should be spoken against (the marriage)'.[52] Thus the eleventh-century redefinition of incest not only inhibited the common tactic of securing a wife by abduction (as Philip I had done in the case of Bertrada of Anjou, only to face the accusation that their union was incestuous), but ensured that no marriage could take place without the assent of all those who had claims on the lands involved, as patrimony or dowry.

A less direct consequence of increasingly firm control over marriage has been made very famous by Georges Duby.[53] The narratives of the twelfth century are full of references to *juvenes* – literally youths, or young men, but specifying a stage of life rather than a calendar age. A man became *juvenis*, as opposed to *puer* or *adolescens*, when he had completed his training as a knight, and remained one until he had married and become head of a household. If he were a younger son and his father was unable or unwilling to diminish the patrimony to provide for him it might be a long wait. William Marshal, perhaps the most famous knight of the twelfth century, was knighted in 1164, and married in 1189, when he was about forty-five years old. With extensive estates in southwestern England, Wales and Ireland, Isabella de Clare was worth waiting for. Her lands made the Marshal one of the greatest lords in the kingdom, as befitted a man who had been the most celebrated tournament-fighter of his age, and whose exemplary chivalry and shrewdness had made him tutor to Henry II's eldest son and a trusted and intimate adviser of Henry himself.[54] In the vernacular *life* composed (probably) by a member of his household the Marshal exemplifies the theoretical ideal of knighthood which had developed apace since the middle of the eleventh century, though its beginnings go back much further.[55] In real life William the Marshal fulfilled in the most enviable fashion the ambitions of the 'youths' who crowded the retinue of every great lord and supplied the muscle of the innumerable military enterprises which made up the twelfth-century expansion of Europe. Most of them were younger sons. Certainly the eldest, reaching maturity while his father was still in his prime, would be sent off with a group of companions and an older mentor to complete his education (*studia militiae*) and win his spurs. But barring accidents, which were common, he would return in a few years to marry a daughter of some greater lord to whose connection he might be added, and take over the estate. For his younger brothers it was a far more serious matter. They were driven by the ruthless promotion of the dynasty to seek their maintenance at the courts of prospective patrons, and by the restrictions of consanguinity to find fortune in the arms of distant brides, providing in the process the settings and plots for a new genre of vernacular literature. The most famous were the sons of Tancred de Hauteville, of whom there were twelve, as well as several daughters, by his two lawful wives. 'He passed on his whole inheritance to his son Geoffrey and advised the others to

seek their living by their strength and wits outside their native land'[56] –
advice which they took to such good effect that, to mention only the
most spectacularly successful, Robert and Roger led the Norman con-
quests in Apulia and Sicily, and fathered respectively and among many
others, Bohemond of Antioch and Roger II, the Great, of Sicily, the most
powerful and magnificent king of his day. The 'aristocratic diaspora'[57]
produced in this way scattered the scions of northern French families,
and then their counterparts from other former Carolingian lands all over
what in these centuries became Latin Christendom. By the end of the
eleventh century Grandmesnils were active and successful in England,
Wales, Calabria and Syria; early in the twelfth century Bertrand of Laon
became count and Robert Burdet castellan of Tudela, only two of many
Frenchmen and Gascons who did well in Spain; in the twelfth and early
thirteenth centuries Joinvilles from Champagne became great lords in
Ireland, Apulia and the Holy Land; as did even more Germans over great
stretches of eastern Europe, from the Balkans to the Carpathians.

The socialization of 'the youth' was powerfully reinforced by the
military apprenticeship of the knight, which was no mere formality.[58]
Since around the beginning of the eleventh century improvements in
every aspect of training and equipment and increasing sophistication in
tactics and manouevring had rapidly differentiated the knights from the
traditional levy of freemen. The use of the cavalry charge, several ranks
of knights riding abreast with lances held horizontal ('couched') before
them, demanding great dexterity and coordination from both men and
horses, is a sufficient index of the arduous and often dangerous preparation which was now required. It was as formidable a weapon against the
armies of sophisticated enemies at Hastings, in Spain, Sicily or the Holy
Land, as against less powerful, though equally ferocious adversaries on
the shores of the Baltic or in the Polish forests. Such a training served not
only to remove young men from the breeding cycle for many years,
reducing the pressure which they and their sons would place on the
patrimony of their family, but to inculcate a discipline which improved
the likelihood that they would accept their fate, and place their skills at
the service of those who had inflicted it on them.

Not all younger sons became knights of course, nor was there room
for all of the rest in the monasteries which their families founded so
eagerly. The great expansion of education in the twelfth century is the
subject of the next chapter, but we may notice now that the formaliza-
tion of the curriculum which lay at its core was a development which
paralleled that of the training of the knight, and that literacy, like both
chivalry and the monastic life, was understood to demand severance
from the family and abandonment of a claim on the patrimony.[59] Less
well documented than knights or scholars are the many younger sons

who became merchants. Social ambition, as ever, led in the opposite direction, and those who made money by trade hastened, in as few generations as possible, to convert it into the lifestyle and trappings of the landowner. Nevertheless, younger sons of the landed families of the region in question have been found among the earliest consuls of cities all over Europe.[60] In short, as Georges Duby insisted, the younger sons are to be found behind every aspect of the growth of Europe, military, cultural and social, in the twelfth century.

That does, however, leave one important question unanswered, and it cannot be answered here. Our impression of the fecundity of these eleventh-century warriors rests heavily on the endlessly entertaining stories of Ordericus Vitalis, several of which have been quoted above. 'From Ordericus Vitalis,' wrote Duby, 'we learn that, in the houses of the nobility, five, six or seven sons usually reached manhood'.[61] On statistical gounds alone that inference must be doubtful. We must add that Norman society in the early eleventh century, the period of Orderic's work from which almost all these famous examples are drawn, was still organized on the basis of the predatory kin group in which it was advantageous for the leaders to breed as rapidly and prolifically as possible.[62] In this discussion, however, we have been chronicling, very much in the footsteps of Duby himself, a rapid transition not only in Normandy, but everywhere in the former Carolingian lands, precisely to the opposite situation, in which the patrimony was to be protected by every possible means against the threat which was posed by multiple claims upon it. So successful were these strategies that by the twelfth century there are clear indications that the opposite situation frequently obtained, in which a significant proportion of noble lines had difficulty in maintaining themselves, a difficulty exacerbated by the policies of family limitation which we have discussed.[63] The family of Ubaldo of Gubbio had to implore him to give up his vow of chastity to defend the patrimony: he refused.[64] Aswalo I, who was Lord of Seignelay from about 1100 to 1139, arranged his affairs more successfully. He had five sons and six grandsons, but only two great-grandsons in the male line, of whom only one had children. The eldest son died while still a *juvenis*, allowing the second to marry at an early age; he died, leaving an infant son, who eventually had a son of his own through whom the line was continued; of his four sons one succeeded and three died, unmarried, in the Holy Land. Aswalo's third son also married, but only after the death of his elder brother, and had three sons. Of these, one went into the church and two died, unmarried, on crusade: in other words, they had provided insurance for the continuity of the dynasty which was abandoned, in effect, when it turned out not to be needed. The fourth of Aswalo's sons eventually found an heiress, but late in life; again, one of his sons went into the church and the other died on crusade. Aswalo's fifth son went into the church and prospered, as Gui, bishop of Sens from 1176 to 1194.[65] In consequence of these strategems the number of men with claims on the lordship of Seignelay hardly varied throughout the twelfth century. This family therefore provides a model illustration of the techniques for limiting claims on the patrimony which lay at the heart of the twelfth-century transformation. But we cannot have it both ways: it must also be admitted that they raise a question how much, demographically speaking, it is reasonable to expect of the younger sons who remained.

5   Brothers in Christ

At the heart of our revolution was the unspoken agreement between the eldest son and his tonsured brother to confirm the lands and privileges of the monastery in return for recognition of the eldest as sole legitimate heir to the patrimony, and on condition that the monks would remain celibate. The rehabilitation of the remaining siblings who had become knights was one of its earliest results. The *miles*, who in the early eleventh century had been constantly represented as the source and instrument of the evils of the time, the violent and lawless oppressor of the church and the poor, was transmuted during the following three or four generations into their heroic defender, the champion of Christendom against the infidel and the embodiment of courage, selflessness and honour. To this transformation the Church made an essential contribution by bestowing on those who lent their swords to the cause of the papacy during Gregory VII's struggle with the Emperor Henry IV the title of Knights of St Peter (*miles sancti Petri*: a *miles Christi* to Odo of Cluny had meant a monk[66]); by combining in the early years of the twelfth century the notion of knighthood with that of monasticism, in the military orders of the Temple and of St John of Jerusalem (the Hospitallers), 'monks on horse-back' vowed to poverty, chastity and defence of the Holy Land; and by giving its blessing to the military life itself through its participation in the ritual of creating a knight ('dubbing'), which seems to have been widely adopted around the same time.[67] In the early years of the twelfth century knights were represented in triumph on the facades of several Aqui-tainian churches – including one with a falcon on his wrist, riding down a pedestrian (a vice personified? a peasant?) at Parthenay – and on the cathedral at Angoulême, on whose west front are portrayed two scenes from the *Chanson de Roland*.[68]

The real initiative had already been taken by the lay aristocracy themselves, manifestly in abandoning the Roman-sounding titles beloved by the Carolingian nobility – *clarissimus, nobilissimus, illustris-simus* – in favour of *miles*, which was also substituted in the same documents for words like *fidelis* and *vassus* that implied subordination and unfreedom. This substitution, which occurred at different rates in different regions – with great rapidity, between 970 and 1060 or so in Duby's southern Maconnais, much more gradually in Barthélemy's Vendôme[69] – shows very plainly that all the differences within the military order – between the eldest son triumphant in his inheritance and his brother desperate for employment for his lance, between the Emperor himself and a landless fighter – were to be accounted less profound than the chasm which separated those who bore the arms of a knight from those who did not. The structure of society had changed so radically and rapidly that the seemingly fundamental distinction between freedom and unfreedom no longer corresponded to reality. *Miles*, like *vassus*, had formerly implied unfreedom, and many knights, especially but not only in the Empire, remained strictly speaking unfree – except that, necessarily, since it was they who enforced it, they were not subject to the *bannum*, the power to demand payments and services in the name of the king. On the other hand, as we have already seen, the fusing and confusing of the powers of the *ban* with the rights of lordship, and the imposition of both on the rural labour force as a whole, were in these same decades reducing the formal differences between free and unfree among the peasantry to practical insignificance. So the old attributes of freedom, imprecise and often precarious, though to many very precious, were swept aside by a new, harsh and very clear practical distinction, to all intents and purposes universal, between those who were subject to the *ban* and those who were not. Hence the bath which a Philip Augustus or Richard Coeur de Lion took before being dubbed a knight proclaimed to the world not only how strong was the bond which united them to any landless adventurer who could wield a lance, but how deep was the chasm which separated them all from those by whose toil they lived. Like every successful ritual it flourished because it expressed a profound truth. It also concealed a truth, that within the ranks of the privileged another old distinction, that between the eldest legitimate son and his brothers, had been made, with no less brutality, far clearer and far more momentous than ever before.

The role of the monasteries in this reconstitution of the aristocratic order was no less central in death than in life. There was nothing new in the eleventh century about a connection between the remembrance of ancestors and the handing down of a patrimony: that was why in the ninth century Dhuoda had admonished her son to 'pray to your father's relations who left him their possessions as a lawful heritage'.[70] Nevertheless, Archbishop Hincmar of Reims had forbidden not only the acceptance of payment for burial places in churches (*c.*876), but the assertion of hereditary claims to particular spots: everybody must be content to go where the priest directed. In 1025, however, Bishop Gerard of Cambrai was prepared to justify the purchase of favoured burial places in the church or sanctuary because it was a means of maintaining family identity and exclusiveness. 'The holy fathers,' he said, citing as examples various Old Testament figures, including Abraham, 'wished to keep themselves apart from strangers not only in life but in death.'[71] Whatever the quality of his theology he was in tune with his time. As the nobles were drawing apart from the poor in life with the elaboration of the ban, so they did in death. In Provence it was precisely after the crisis of the 1020s, which brought about the collapse of comital power and set the castellans on the road to domination of the countryside by simple force, that they ceased to live and to be buried in the episcopal churches and retreated to the monastic cemeteries which they had patronized; in Normandy the impetus of monastic patronage passed from the princes to the aristocracy in the decades after 1040, just when the formation of patrilinear dynasties was gathering pace, and the great abbeys became 'as much symbols of family power and prestige as any castle or bourg'; in the Maconnais it was a sign both of tightening ecclesiastical control over everyday life and of increasing social differentiation that by the end of the eleventh century 'only the nobles could be buried near the great abbeys, far from the village sanctuary'.[72] Only they could evade prohibitions like that of the Council of Beauvais which in 1114 forbade monasteries to accept bodies for burial without the permission of the parish priest, whose monopoly of other services was gradually confirmed.[73]

In commemorating their benefactors in written records, solemn and magnificent liturgies, and splendid tombs and monuments, the newly invigorated monasteries of eleventh-century west Francia provided the authoritative record of the structure and membership of their founding families – which is as good as to say that they created and preserved them. This was a new, and obviously crucial role. It superseded the older practice still visible in the Empire, where the much higher status of women in monastic life was closely related to their role in mourning and remembering the dead. Such a pivotal position in acting as the custodians of the kin and its collective memory was hardly consistent, Patrick Geary points out, with the drastic diminution of women's rights in the family and their claims on its property which was taking place in Francia. He contrasts the way in which Thietmar of Merseburg – a member of the high German nobility as well as a great historian – shows the Empress Adelaide active and independent in making arrangements for several monasteries to commemorate her son Otto II after his death in 983, whereas she is represented in the same business by a west

Frankish abbot – and who should it be but Odilo of Cluny? – as acting through him, and subordinating herself to his religious authority.[74]

In this way the alliance which religious benefaction represented between the eldest son and those of his siblings who enjoyed the benefits of the family patronage was sealed by the role of the monasteries as family shrines. In a parallel movement of the twelfth century, families of the lesser aristocracy, or those who made their way towards social position by way of royal service, acquired their burial places through the less expensive patronage of the new monasticism and of canons regular. Later in the twelfth and thirteenth centuries as knights began to escape from the retinues of their lords and settle in the countryside they too sought to secure the position of their families for posterity in the same ways, often through the parish churches. One of the earliest sets of English lay estate records, those of the Hotots in Northamptonshire, offers an example of how it was done. During the reign of King Stephen (1139–54) William of Clapton took over one-third of the churchyard to extend his manor house, disturbing many graves and destroying a fine grove of ash. His action was well enough resented for the daughter of one of the diggers he employed to be able to point out long afterwards just where the ancient boundaries of the cemetery had run. When William brought his bride home some years later he arrived to find the house and all the fineries which had been prepared for his wedding in flames – obviously an act of divine vengeance for his sacrilege, says the local chronicler, discreetly omitting to specify the particular agency the Divinity had employed. In 1182 William gave the rights over this parish to the priory of St Neots. Since there is no reason to think that they were his to give, and the incumbent at the time was his younger brother Reginald, it looks very much as though the benefaction was designed to legitimize, and also to consolidate, William's usurpation. Reginald replaced the old wooden church with a fine new stone one, handsomely built in the latest style (which we now call early English) and with a splendid tomb for its founder, his brother. The chance of knowing that Reginald had been bald since infancy and that his successor as priest of Clapton was a master John Calvus, betrays that not only the church but the parsonage had been annexed to the family as a hereditary possession.[75]

The family necropolis which had been reserved to the greatest nobles in the tenth century had by the end of the twelfth become the prerogative of all the privileged, as every parish church was turned into a mausoleum by the graves of its patrons and their relations. And for every one of them, from the Plantagenets at Fontevrault to the squires of Clapton, that mausoleum provided in stone and marble exactly the same service as the family histories and genealogies whose construction, whether from real or bogus materials, they pursued so eagerly in the twelfth century, constituting a solid and sanctified proclamation of their identity, origins and grandeur which was periodically renewed and reinvigorated in the natural course of events. As Duby once remarked, though marriage was the organizing principle of the new dynastic structure it was burial which provided its great landmarks.[76]

6   Apostacy and Betrayal

It was not for this that the crowds had flocked to the relics in the fields, or that they responded so readily to those who called for support against the simoniacs. Despite the rhetoric of the Peace of God and of later calls for popular underwriting of reform, including those issued so resoundingly by Pope Gregory VII, the material interests and developing political consciousness of the little community were plainly irreconcilable with those of the church, as well as of the secular aristocracy. Of course the leaders of the reform, in any of its aspects, neither designed nor desired such a conflict. They needed to enlist the people on the side of their ideals, but there is no reason to doubt that their aspirations were rooted in an authentic vision of the unity of the Christian community, or sincerely believed to be in the best interests of the people themselves. The identification of spiritual humility with poverty, and hence of the truly religious with the poor, was the first and most universal precept of the religious revival of the eleventh and twelfth centuries, proclaimed by simple and drab clothing, the avoidance of meat and the adoption of chastity which not only imitated the apostles, but advertised the renunciation of worldly power by spurning the equally universal privileges and prerogatives of the powerful. The hagiographers seized upon every opportunity to emphasize how in adopting the religious life the sons of *potentes* abandoned the prerogatives of their rank. The son of a certain Count Guido was worthy to be honoured as a saint because he spurned the inheritance of his carnal parents, and his late tenth-century contemporary Wulstan of Bamburgh, a relative of kings, not only gave up his inheritance but lived for thirty years as a farm labourer. For Giovanni Gualberti a generation or so later the renunciation of landed privilege and worldly wealth (*terrenas honores atque falsasque divitias*) was a condition of conversion. In 1074 Simon de Crépy not only renounced his inheritance but by moving the body of his recently deceased father Count Ralph of Valois, from a town that he had acquired by usurpation to one which was his by inheritance 'for the greater safety of his soul', publicly acknowledged the wrongs that Ralph had committed.[77] Occasionally the distancing of the evangelical movement not only from the means by which the seigneurie was brought into existence but from the seigneurie itself was quite explicit, and marked the clearest possible repudiation of the old monasticism by the new. The founder of the Cistercian order, St Robert of Molesme, said that in accepting tithes 'we feed upon the blood of men and share in their sins' and his followers, 'finding no evidence in the Rule or Life of St. Benedict that he, their teacher, had possessed churches and altars, offerings or burial dues, ovens or mills, villages or peasants...renounced all these privileges ...and declined to arrogate wrongly to themselves another's rights'.[78]

The difficulty which many found in living according to their ideals is no less notorious, and was no less evident from the outset. Disillusionment was nourished, however, not so much by the backslidings of individuals, which were easy enough to identify and bewail, as by the inherent contradiction between the interests of the leaders of the reform, or rather of the institutions which they headed, and those of the poor and the dispossessed whom they rallied in their cause. Once again, the tensions quickly became visible in Aquitaine. The character of the Peace of God as an alliance between church and people had been resoundingly proclaimed by the Council of Charroux in 989, and was fostered at the great rallies of the 990s, making full use of the liturgical skills which the monks had honed so well. It was reiterated by Duke William V when he presided over another great gathering at Poitiers, perhaps as late as 1010. But the fervour for social unity which was displayed on both sides did not last for long. In 1028 the Duke summoned another council at Charroux 'to extinguish the heresy which the Manichees were spreading among the people. All the princes of Aquitaine were there: he ordered them to keep the Peace and venerate the Catholic church.' Ademar of Chabannes, a notable liturgist as well as a prolific historian, who years earlier had added tropes and sequences to the mass at St Martial of Limoges to emphasize both the idea of peace and the involvement of the people as active participants in the liturgy, applauded him for it.[79]

The accusation of heresy had previously been used sparingly, and in the context of conflicts among the privileged. William himself, for example, had threatened in 1015 that those who resisted his institution of the common life at St Sernin of Toulouse by asserting their hereditary claims to canonries would be tainted with the Arian heresy, classically the source of division in the Church.[80] The proclamation of 1028 turned the accusation outward, against the lower orders. Its sequel, if there was one, is not recorded, and it would be more than another century before the claim that heresy was rife among 'the people' became a routinely institutionalized instrument of repression, but this is the first clear example shown by our selective and fragmentary sources. Ademar had anticipated it in the chronicle whose first draft he finished two or three years earlier, with the famous assertion that in the year 1018 'Manichees appeared in Aquitaine, leading the people astray. They denied baptism, the cross, and all sound doctrine. They did not eat meat, as though they were monks, and pretended to be celibate, but among themselves they enjoyed every indulgence. They were messengers of Antichrist, and caused many to wander from the faith.'[81] The year after the second Council of Charroux, in August 1029, Ademar himself suffered a devastating public humiliation when a Lombard monk named Benedict of Chiusa confronted him with the accusation that the campaign to establish the apostolicity of St Martial to which Ademar had devoted his life and writings was nothing but a fraud to increase the revenues of the monastery. What is particularly significant from the present point of view, as well as particularly painful for Ademar, is that Benedict was vociferously supported by a crowd of local onlookers.[82] In short, the alliance between prelates and people over which Duke William had presided and which Ademar had chronicled so enthusiastically only a few years earlier had turned sour.

In general terms it is not difficult to see why. The summons of the Peace Councils called for unity in opposition to a common enemy, the *milites*, and their main provisions were directed against the abuses of the seigneurie. But they did not outlaw it altogether, and could not have done so. Their purpose was not to oppose the extension and intensification of lordship over land, but to regulate and therefore to legitimate it. The calls to Peace, like the lives of the saints, are full of lamentations about the wickedness with which the goods of the poor were seized, their animals stolen, their persons held to ransom. The rhetoric, however, masked something a good deal more subtle than mere anarchy. The words which described the prohibited practices – *praedae, rapinae, redemptiones* and so on – referred not to simple brigandage, but to the powers conferred by the Carolingian monarchs on their counts, vicomtes, provosts and other officers, including ecclesiastical officers, to collect royal revenues and services, raise and provision armies and see to the construction of public works.[83] In other words, they were precisely the royal powers and rights whose diffusion from count to castellans in the last decades of the tenth century and the early ones of the eleventh had heralded the final collapse of the Carolingian state and the consolidation of the seigneurie. In one of the most celebrated acts of the early Peace the Council of Charroux excommunicated 'anyone who takes as *praeda* sheep, oxen, asses, cows, nanny-goats, billy-goats, or pigs from *agricolae* or *pauperes, nisi per propriam culpam*'.[84] The ambiguities of the language chosen are untranslatable. *Agricola*, in classical Latin a farmer, is rather conspicuously not one of the many words used in our period to refer to those who worked the soil, all of which implied (or were capable of implying) degrees of servitude: its use, perhaps, implies without trumpeting it that the protection of the Council was intended for the free. *Pauperes*, of course, were not *potentes* – but they might very well be monks. *Nisi per propriam culpam* – unless on account of their own wrongdoing. Who was to say what action constituted a *culpa*, and whose it had been? This meant that rights of justice were to be reserved to those who already possessed them, and that the Council did not condemn the common practice of distraining people or their goods for rents they were alleged to owe.[85] Similarly, at a council held at St Paulien, near Le Puy, probably in 993, anathema was pronounced upon those who committed a vast repertory of abuses, including seizing hostages and building castles – the very practice from which all these evils have commonly been held to flow – unless he does it on his own lands – *aut de suo alodo vel de suo beneficio vel de sua commanda* – his own property, or his benefice, or his *comenda*.[86] The *comenda* was a contract or agreement permitting the lord to control lands that were not his own – by origin, those of a church under his protection, but by extension, of another alodialist (property owner) who had 'commended' himself. In either case, the *comenda* was a powerful instrument for the imposition of lordship and the extension of *consuetudines*: as a document from Marmoutier put it about this time, 'what these customs are it is unnecessary to relate by listing them, for at their head stands the *comenda* of which we have spoken, and it is from this that all the others have proliferated'.[87] The Peace Councils, in short, did not resist the consolidation of the seigneurie in the hands of the lords. They endorsed it, on the condition that each should respect the boundaries of the others. Certainly this did mean offering protection, at least in principle, to the small alodial holders who were prominent among both the victims of seignurial aggrandisement and the supporters of the Peace. That is not an insignificant exception, but it remains the case that in reality the Councils were a very long way from spreading their mantle over the mass of the *pauperes*, in the Carolingian sense of those who lacked power.

The reason is not far to seek. The next clause from St Paulien says that nobody shall dare to take various levies from 'ecclesiastical, episcopal, canonical or monastic land' – unless it has been acquired from the bishop or the brethren as a voluntary gift. The protection of anathema, in other words, is not extended to those who work the land, from whose surplus the exaction in question must come, but to the church which claimed its lordship. In the following year Abbot Odilo of Cluny appeared at the council at Anse in Burgundy, to secure from the assembled prelates protection for a long list of properties which had been given to his abbey, against *invasores aut raptores* – which is to say, against indignant or unconsenting relations of the donors. We have already seen that Cluny at this time was consolidating its hold over many properties by interpreting the terms of donations much more inflexibly than had previously been customary or intended by the donors, in respect both of boundaries and of exclusive long-term control over the land in question. The properties listed by the Council of Anse constituted the strategic core of Cluny's future domain, which was enormously expanded during Odilo's long abbacy to provide the foundation of perhaps the greatest monastic estate of the ancien régime in France.[88]

Against this background it is not difficult to understand why the accusation of heresy should have been transferred from those within the ranks of the privileged who resisted the 'reforms' promoted by the princes and great abbots to spokesmen of the less privileged who began to query whether the game of Peace was worth their candle. Ademar of Chabannes offers other pointers to the mounting tale of bitterness, disillusion and recrimination. In 1021 Bishop Gerard of Limoges was forced by popular anger to consecrate the duly elected Abbot of St Martial, the successor to his uncle, Abbot Josfredus, who had died in 1019: Gerard had been stalling in order to keep the abbatial revenues in the family. In 1018 more than fifty people were trampled to death in the basilica of St Martial as they crowded towards the tomb of the saint. In his first draft Ademar placed this story directly before the report of the appearance of the 'Manichees', but when he revised the text in 1027–8 he inserted a comment on the rebuilding of the basilica between the two reports, and amended the sentence about the 'Manichees' as though to remove – or disguise? – the previous implication that their appearance was a result of the tragedy.[89]

The trampling in the basilica of St Martial points to a source of tension more specific than the general disharmony between the aims of the Peace movement and the hopes which it aroused in many of its supporters. There has been a long and romantic tradition of identifying the construction and use of the great churches with 'popular religion', based largely on the connection between so many of the earliest and most striking architectural innovations with the pilgrimage routes, and on the vivid and often moving depictions of ordinary people in Romanesque and Gothic sculpture. Assertions like Abbot Suger's that the great extension of St Denis which he began in 1135 to produce what is widely hailed as the first Gothic building was necessary because the narrowness of the old church 'forced the women to run towards the altar over the heads of the men as though upon a pavement'[90] have encouraged acceptance of overcrowding of the typically tiny churches of the early middle ages as a sufficient explanation of the constant building and rebuilding of the eleventh, twelfth and thirteenth centuries. A handful of stories from similar sources in which poor people (or in the case of Laon, oxen) spontaneously offer help with construction have been taken as proof of popular enthusiasm and support. All of these say more about the responses which the builders hoped to excite or sustain than how their efforts were in fact received. Similarly, the civic pride and social aspiration immortalized in many fine windows and monuments paid for by merchants and craft gilds – especially from the later part of the twelfth century, when the urban elites were closing their ranks and consolidating their privileges – are not to be taken as somehow representative of the sentiments of the population at large. On the contrary, they reflect the ambitions and advertise the success of an emerging patriciate consciously distancing itself socially and culturally from the masses. The hostility of the early Cistercians to elaborate building and decorations, of a piece with their refusal to accept tithes and cultivated land, was based on their cost and its implications for the poor, as well as on the spiritual considerations trumpeted in Bernard of Clairvaux's blistering denunciation of Cluniac magnificence. Even in circles where enthusiasm for fine building might be expected it was not universal: Peter the Chanter the Parisian master (and canon of Notre Dame) complained (*c.*1180) that 'monastic and cathedral churches are being built by deception and avarice, by cunning and lies, and by the deceptions of the preachers'.[91]

It would be in no way surprising if the dreadful accident in the basilica at St Martial in 1018 had triggered a backlash against the building work itself, or won support for its critics (the 'Manichees'?). Heresy appeared, or was alleged, only a few years later at Cambrai and at Arras, where major building was in progress, and perhaps in the 1050s at Nevers; at Le Mans when Henry of Lausanne led his insurrection there in 1116 and at St Gilles du Gard, where Henry's contemporary, and perhaps for a time associate, Peter of Bruys, was burned alive in 1139/40. The list could be considerably extended; indeed, it might fairly be objected that church building was so universal and so sustained a feature of town life in the twelfth century that it must inevitably coincide with any other activity one cared to propose, and certainly that a great deal of building was done in places which, so far as we know, were never polluted by a heretical breath. Nevertheless, the relationship is worth considering. Itinerant craftsmen (classically, weavers) have been prime suspects of the dissemination of heterodox ideas ever since the twelfth century, and as Heinrich Fichtenau (noting these coincidences) points out, building sites swarmed with such people.[92] More generally, the very qualities which made church building the great engine of the economic revival, as we have argued above, could also bring hardship and unrest: if it created concentrations of capital and demand and nourished ever more sophisticated craft skills it also accounted for innumerable demands for higher rents and taxes, and for corvée labour. The serfs who were conscripted to build the basilica at Vézelay rose three times in protest against it before it was done.[93]

Still, man does not rebel for bread alone. Peter of Bruys, who preached in Provence and the Rhone valley in the 1120s and '30s, maintained that 'there should be no churches or temples in any kind of building, and those that already exist should be pulled down', because God would hear the prayers of the faithful 'whether in a tavern or a church, in a street or in a temple, before an altar or in a stable, and he listens to those who deserve it'.[94] Henry of Lausanne also held that churches should be constructed of neither stone nor wood, implying that the church did not require a physical location because it subsisted in the community of the faithful. Even the challenge which such a teaching implied to the whole structure of ecclesiastical authority, confirmed by Henry's denial that the Gospels gave priests the power of binding and loosing, was outstripped by another concomitant which each man spelt out in his own way, to the horror of his Catholic opponents. That 'God laughs at ecclesiastical chants, because he loves only the holy will and is not to be summoned by high-pitched voices or caressed by well-turned tunes',[95] as Peter of Bruys is said to have argued, is more than an attack on a style of worship, though to the Abbot of Cluny who reports it that would have been bad enough. But we have seen how, and why, the *opus dei* was directed above all else to the cult of the dead, whose efficacy Henry had directly denied: 'no good can be done for the dead, for they are all either damned or saved as soon as they die'.[96] In those words he dismissed the entire basis of the construction and legitimization of the dynastic family, of the endowment of the church, and of its commanding place in the post-revolutionary world.

Peter of Bruys denied the efficacy not only of prayers for the dead but of infant baptism and of the eucharist. Henry of Lausanne also rejected infant baptism, the authority of the clergy and the controls over marriage which were being so painstakingly imposed in his time. These were the commonest and most fundamental objections recorded or alleged against Catholic teaching in the eleventh and twelfth centuries. Some or all of them are included, with or without additional accusations, in every appearance or assertion of popular heresy throughout the period. We are fortunate to have in Henry of Lausanne a preacher both articulate enough and well enough documented to show clearly that it was not by accident that they were directed precisely against the changes and innovations which have been identified in this chapter as the foundations of the new social order which was created by the First European Revolution. Henry is sometimes, pedantically but misleadingly, called Henry the Monk. There is no evidence or suggestion of a monastic education or upbringing, but he had been educated – since childhood according to the monk William, otherwise unknown, whose *contra Henricum*, effectively rediscovered and now being edited by Monique Zerner, is our most important source of information about him.[97] Henry had written a book or pamphlet to which William refers throughout the debate described in *contra Henricum* and which is also mentioned by Peter the Venerable in his treatise *against the followers of Peter of Bruys*, composed *c*.1139/40.

Even through the highly selective though not apparently dishonest eyes of his opponent Henry's arguments and references are not those of an illiterate. We have already met him on his first appearance at Le Mans, in 1116,[98] which he entered not as an enemy of the church but as an itinerant evangelist who sought and received the permission of the bishop to preach in the city during Lent. During the insurrection which he provoked, however, the nature of the views which he would circulate and defend against William in the 1130s became startlingly clear, even, or especially, as they were recorded by the scandalized and still, in retrospect, terrified canon of Le Mans who wrote the official biography of Bishop Hildebert. Its climax is a description of 'the sacrilegious meeting which Henry summoned at the church of St Germanus and St Vincent', where he preached that 'no-one should accept any gold or silver or wedding presents with his wife, or receive any dowry with her: the naked should marry the naked, the sick marry the sick and the poor marry the poor, without bothering whether they married chastely or incestuously'.[99] He put his teaching into practical effect by calling upon the prostitutes of the town publicly to confess their sins – a traditional practice which he would implicitly defend in debate with William by condemning the private confession to priests which the church now demanded – and marked their forgiveness and reintegration into the community by encouraging young men to marry them, making a public collection to replace the clothing that had been burned as part of the ritual. Another shocking story from about this time, told about Tanchelm of Antwerp, is that he used to pronounce his own nuptials to a wooden statue of St Mary in each of whose hands he placed a purse, saying 'Let the men put their offerings in this purse and the women in the other. I will see now which sex shows the greater generosity towards me and my wife.'[100] This also suggests a satirical attack on the marriage market, as well as on the cult of the Virgin. Henry's reported words, like his later contention to William that a marriage could be dissolved only by reason of fornication, clearly and explicitly repudiated the use of marriage as a mechanism of family aggrandizement, and the concept of incest as a means of controlling it.

The first and last chapters of Henry's pamphlet attracted the longest and most painstaking of William's rebuttals. It opened, perhaps unsurprisingly, with the contention that 'bishops and priests should not have money or honours' (that is, lands which yielded feudal rents and services), and concluded with apparently the most passionately debated of Henry's contentions that 'the children of Christians, Jews or Saracens will not be damned if they die unbaptised before they reach the age of reason' (that is, seven years old), quoting 'Suffer the little children to come unto me, for of such is the kingdom of God' and 'the occasion when Jesus called a child and set him in the midst of them and said "Unless you be converted and become as little children you shall not enter into the kingdom of heaven". By his authority therefore you should admit that those children, if they died without baptism, were to be saved. And at that time children were not baptised.'[101] In so arguing, as William pointed out, Henry denied not only the doctrine of original sin, and hence 'the necessity of benefiting from the death of Christ' – that is, in effect, from the sacraments and services of the Church – but also the principle that a child too young to have its own faith could nevertheless be baptized 'in the faith of those who baptize them, in the faith of their parents, in the faith of the whole church'.

Read in the light of his debate with William, which is perhaps most probably to be dated shortly before his first formal conviction for heresy, at the Council of Pisa in 1135, Henry's conduct in Le Mans and the confrontation with Bishop Hildebert which preceded his expulsion from the city offers a *tableau vivant* of the struggle between two worlds which this chapter has recounted. Hildebert of Lavardin, reformer, scholar, accomplished Latinist and elegant poet, was a perfect product of the early stages of the educational revival which is the subject of the next chapter, and a perfect representative of the metropolitan culture being constructed by that revival, as well as by the far-flung aristocratic marriages and the emerging code of chivalry which were its secular counterpart, and by the universalization and centralization of the practice and government of the church. His journey to Rome for the Easter synod, leaving Le Mans at Henry's mercy, was the product, vehicle and symbol of that larger world. As a reformer and a champion of universal authority Hildebert was also, of necessity, at odds with what were, by the account of his own biographer, the singularly unreformed canons of his cathedral. In welcoming Henry as an ascetic and preacher in the mould of his friend, protegé, and ferocious scourge of private property and marriage among the clergy, Robert of Arbrissel, he cannot have failed to anticipate that Henry's message in the season of penitence would be calculated to shake up the chapter and create pressure for the introduction of the common life, as such men had been doing over much of northwestern Europe for the last half century and more, and even in this backward corner of it for a generation. If Hildebert got more than he bargained for, it was not so much in the public unrest that Henry created – reformers had lived with that often enough since the reign of the Patarenes in Milan – as in the throughgoing and uncompromising nature of Henry's teaching, directed not only against the abuses of the old world which he and Hildebert were united in condemning, but the very foundations of the new one which Hildebert was committed to putting in its place. As Bernard of Clairvaux complained in the letter which he addressed to the people of the Languedoc before setting out to preach against Henry in that region in 1145, 'At the voice of one heretic you close your ears to all the prophets and apostles who with one faith and spirit have brought together the Church out of all nations to one faith in Christ.'[102] Henry, for his part, continued to reject abstract structures of authority in favour of those which were firmly rooted in the community itself, to affirm the values of the little community in which small groups of men and women stood together as equals, dependent on each other, suspicious of outsiders, and hostile to every external claim on their obedience, loyalty or wealth.

The tale of trust and betrayal between the leaders of the Peace of God and the people of Aquitaine, between Hildebert and Henry, was repeated many times during the first European revolution, as during its successors. It arose from a contradiction in the process of 'reform' which remained unresolved, and indeed incapable of resolution. Both spiritual respectability and intellectual coherence demanded ecclesiastical conformity to a long spiritual tradition of 'apostolic' poverty, strongly rooted in late Carolingian neoplatonist theology and given programmatic form and European-wide publicity by the Gregorian papacy and its agents. Further, the entrenched control of local elites over the lands and offices to which the church laid claim could often be overthrown only by tapping popular indignation arising from grievances which, though very widespread, appeared to each community as very much its own – demands for tithes and services, the unfitness of priests for their offices, and so on. Yet, however dramatic, even violent the crisis of that struggle might be, it inevitably led not to the new Jerusalem, the millennial dawn of freedom and justice which the rallies and the sermons implicitly or explicitly evoked, but to an alliance between the church and the local magnates still more intimate than before, an exploitation more efficient and a society more hierarchical by far than their predecessors had ever been. In interpreting the fragmentary and impassioned texts which are the sources for popular heresy in the eleventh and twelfth centuries it is often difficult to be sure whether the accusations show the reality of popular protest or the suspicions and anxieties of the accusers. From the present point of view it does not make a great deal of difference. It is possible that the 'Manichees' whom Ademar believed to be at work among the people were real, and had begun to articulate the opposition of the poor to the seigneurie and the imperial church; it is certain that by asserting such a presence the powerful had begun to prepare their defences.

4

The Ruling Culture

1 The Highest Learning

'To her master, or rather her father, husband, or rather brother; his handmaid or rather his daughter, wife, or rather sister; to Abelard, Heloise.'[1] As his former pupil who had become his lover, then his wife, then his sister in religion when both of them took monastic vows after he had been castrated by her vengeful kinsmen, and as the prioress of the convent of the Paraclete whose spiritual direction Abelard, himself by now an abbot, had for a time assumed, Heloise was entitled to remind him as she opened their famous correspondence that their relationship was more than usually complicated. It was a theme to which both returned constantly in the passionate debate which ensued. What were the duties and obligations which each owed to the other, and to others such as Abelard's students or Heloise's nuns, in the various capacities in which they stood, or might have stood, to each other? It was a question not only of behaviour and demeanour, but of sentiment and conviction. How should a nun remember her former passion, and what obedience did she now owe to her husband, or to her spiritual superior? How, as a husband now separated by circumstance and the monastic vow, should Abelard think of and write to his wife? Could marriage and the prospect of children have been reconciled with his vocation as a philosopher? Would the role of mistress have been a more fitting one for Heloise – she insisted that she would have preferred it – than that of wife, and could it have permitted their life together to be continued in harmony with Abelard's career as a teacher?

These letters are perhaps the most intensely personal documents in the whole of twelfth-century literature, but in this preoccupation with role and identity, with what is fitting behaviour and feeling for people in given circumstances and position in the world, they are entirely typical of the age.[2] In particular they are typical in conducting their debate almost entirely in religious terms: what is pleasing to God, and therefore how Heloise is to be saved, is the constant issue for Abelard, while Heloise's willingness to question the justice, and indeed the wisdom, of God's treatment of them, and to renounce the prospect of salvation rather than her feelings for Abelard ('I can expect no reward from God, for it is certain that I have done nothing for the love of him'[3]) is the most powerful possible statement of the depth of her love, and her despair.

Though she accused herself bitterly of hypocrisy because while she led her nuns in worship her mind dwelt on the memory of making love to Abelard, Heloise was no hypocrite, any more than Abelard, haunted by the fear that for love of him she courted damnation, was heartless or false in insisting that she must set aside those memories to devote herself single-mindedly to her religious duties. They found themselves on a path that led they knew not where, confronting in their personal lives, as the whole of their world did in its daily experience, new dilemmas and agonizing choices. They needed a language of precision and subtlety in which to frame them, a technique to define their approaches and test their solutions, and a stock of ideas, examples and arguments rich enough to explore the many aspects and dimensions of their long and multi-faceted relationship with all its shattering reverberations, and flexible enough to explore and express every shade of the passions, certainties, doubts and desires which had shaped and reshaped both their lives. They found the language in Latin, the analytical technique in the legacy of Greece (not directly, for the most part, but preserved in the translations and example of Latin authors), and the materials, examples and arguments in the Bible, the writings of the Fathers of the Church, and (Heloise especially) the literature of pagan Rome. But they also needed – and here Abelard's need is perhaps the more obvious – to place their lives and misfortunes in a larger scheme of things, not simply to make sense of the catastrophes which had befallen them, but to secure that degree of comprehension of one's fate which is possible only in a consistent and rationally accessible universe – and only at the price of acknowledging that freedom entails responsibility, that to steer a course is to choose a destination. That required the faith not only in the love of God, but in his justice, consistency and accessibility to human reason, which Abelard had devoted his adult life to demonstrating.

The questions which Abelard and Heloise debated were uniquely theirs, but in seeking right belief and conduct through the dialectic of which Abelard was the age's most celebrated exponent they showed themselves creatures of their time. No activity was more characteristic of this age than the composition of rules. In the past the world itself – *regula* – had almost always referred to one rule in particular, that of St Benedict, by which, since the Synod of Aachen in 816, all monks and nuns had been expected to live. Indeed, monks and nuns themselves had then been almost the only people who were thought of as needing a rule to live by: peasants had few choices to make, and nobles were not expected to be constrained. Now the world had become a great deal more complicated. The monastic revival had brought into being new orders – including Camaldolesi, Carthusians, Cistercians, Fontevristes, to mention only a few – and individual houses, many of which were given new rules (including the one that Abelard composed for Heloise's nuns at the Paraclete) to express their founders' visions of the religious life or accommodate their particular circumstances. Ecclesiastical reform and urban growth created a host of communities of canons regular – that is, clerics who lived according to a rule, generally a variant either of the Rule of Aachen, based on the decrees of the Synod of 816 and revised in the eleventh century to prohibit private property, or the one attributed to St Augustine, of which several variants were in use. The transformation of the secular world was generating new occupations and groups, new problems and new dilemmas, which meant rules for markets and rules for merchants,[4] rules for trade guilds and rules for knights; even, when Andrew, the chaplain of Marie of Champagne, was disposed to make hilarious fun of the whole process, rules for lovers, that laid down how a lord should approach a lady and a clerk a shepherdess, and whether there could be love between husband and wife. (There couldn't, of course: their affection was constrained, and love could only be free[5]).

At a higher level, the greatest intellectual achievements of the century rested upon a rigorous application of the principles of dialectic to the enormous, scattered, inchoate and often contradictory statements and pronouncements of the Fathers and the Councils of the Church upon every conceivable question of faith and doctrine. The middle decades of the twelfth century produced the Ordinary Gloss, which served as the foundation of all subsequent commentary on the Bible, and the *Sentences* of Peter Lombard, which provided the universities of Europe with their basic text in theology until the seventeenth century. Still more remarkably, a mighty application not only of scholastic method but of the principles and precepts of Roman law to the enormous and inchoate mass of materials accumulated over the centuries as bishops and teachers grappled with the theoretical foundations, practical implications and organisational necessities of their faith, produced in 'Gratian's' *Concordance of Discordant Canons*, a body of law which governed the daily lives of all Europeans for the rest of the middle ages, and remained definitive for Catholics until the beginning of the twentieth century.[6] We think of these works as great academic edifices, called forth by the fundamental issues of authority and belief – the truth of the Christian revelation and whether it could be reconciled with the observations of nature and the lessons of reason; the coherence and consistency of its scriptures and those who had commented on them; how, by whom and on what conditions its precepts and teachings were to be transmitted to the ordinary believer; the authority of its ministers and how it should be exercised and sustained; how that authority and the laws upon which it was founded related to the rights and prerogatives of secular rulers; and so on. So they were, but they also impinged directly and repeatedly on the difficulties and dilemmas of personal and public life, as we have seen so plainly in considering the transformation of family relationships and claims to property by which everyone mentioned in this book was profoundly affected. It was no accident that the schoolmasters of the twelfth century were adept at illustrating their most abstract reflections with mundane examples, or that one of the largest surviving bodies of their debates and reflections addresses such questions as whether the canons of Notre Dame would be profiting from immoral earnings if they accepted the offer of the guild of prostitutes to present a window to the new cathedral.[7]

The people who confronted these issues built the imposing and massively coherent pile which was the scholastic thought, the ecclesiastical law, the religious teaching and practice, the social theory and social relations of medieval Europe, from the debris of a world transformed by the upheavals of the preceding century. Most of them, as younger sons of the minor nobility or illegitimate sons of clerics, came from the ranks of its most conspicuous victims, the disinherited. All of them, by definition, were typical of the new world which was emerging from the ruins. They were, in the famous phrase, 'new men' (*novi homines*) in the most profound sense, that irrespective of their background or origins they were men of a new sort, leading a new kind of life, performing new, uncertain and ill-defined functions, indispensable in countless ways to the construction of the new world, but also – and often for that very reason – widely resented and chronically insecure.

To men so placed formation was everything. It gave them not only their hope for employment and material success, but their status, their place in the world and their loyalties and affections. It is no accident that the twelfth century is the first since antiquity to provide us regularly with stories from the schoolroom. 'I was pelted almost every day with a hail of blows and harsh words while he was forcing me to learn what he could not teach. In this fruitless struggle I passed nearly six years with him, but got no reward worth the time it took.'[8] So Guibert of Nogent learned his Latin. He would not complain to his mother about the beatings which his master administered so regularly, but one day she took off his shirt and 'seeing my little arms blackened and the skin of my back all puffed up with the cuts of the twigs she said, "You shall never become a clerk, nor any more suffer so much to get an education". At that, looking at her with what reproach I could, I replied, "If I had to die on the spot I would not give up studying my lessons and becoming a clerk." '[9] Guibert saw his master's brutality as a cover for incompetence, but even if he had studied with Bernard of Chartres, 'the greatest fount of literary learning of his day' (some half century later), he would have found, according to John of Salisbury, that 'In view of the fact that exercise both strengthens and sharpens our mind, Bernard would bend every effort to bring his students to imitate what they were hearing. In some cases he would rely on exhortation, in others he would resort to punishments, such as flogging...'[10] Peter Abelard was luckier, for 'the more rapid and easy my progress in my studies the more eagerly I applied myself, until I was so carried away by my love of learning that I renounced the glory of a soldier's life, made over my inheritance and rights of the eldest son to my brothers, and withdrew from the court of Mars in order to kneel at the feet of Minerva.... I began to travel about in several provinces, disputing like a true peripatetic philosopher....'[11]

Abelard's classroom memories were not of the beatings he received as a boy learning grammar, but of the resounding logical defeats which at a later stage, as a student of dialectic, he himself inflicted on his masters. His power to draw students to his own lectures figures prominently in two reminiscences to which we owe much of our knowledge of developments in Paris in the crucial decades of the 1120s and '30s. Otto of Freising was a son of the Margrave of Austria and grandson of the Emperor Henry IV; John of Salisbury had his early teaching from a parish priest who dabbled in magic, and kept himself as a student in Paris by acting as tutor to the children of nobles – boys like Guibert – because 'I lacked the help of friends and relations, and God thus aided me and relieved my poverty'.[12] Otto became Bishop of Freising in 1138, by gift of his half-brother, the newly crowned Emperor Conrad IV, and was the adviser and biographer of yet another Emperor, his nephew Frederick Babarossa. John served long and hard in the households of two Archbishops of Canterbury, Theobald and Thomas Becket, sharing the exile and dangers of the latter as one of his most loyal supporters, before earning as a fitting reward the bishopric of Chartres, in 1176. Their political and ecclesiastical loyalties contrasted as sharply as their backgrounds and careers – John was a passionate protagonist of the papacy in all the great issues which divided the Europe of their day, of which the long conflict between Frederick Barbarossa and successive

Popes was the greatest – but they remembered their celebrated teacher and the controversies in which he engaged in very much the same terms and very much the same polished and elegant Latin. It is as good a reminder as any of how rapidly the schools were creating a common high culture and a single educated class.

Few generations of Europe's intellectuals have been so fascinated by their own education, and few so enthusiastic in their display of its trophies – the quotations from the classics, the allusions to and echoes of classical and patristic writings, with which their own prose overflows. We cannot be sure whether Guibert, describing his beatings, intended to remind his readers of the Roman grammarian Quintilian, whose precepts were followed by Bernard of Chartres, but he certainly meant to echo the similar complaint of Augustine of Hippo's *Confessions* about his own schooldays, and he may also have had in mind, by way of contrast, the milder recommendations of Pope Gregory I. In likening himself to a peripatetic philosopher Abelard implied, with what his enemies would have considered characteristic arrogance, that he was a disciple of Aristotle, and anticipated the compliment that John of Salisbury would pay him in his turn, calling him 'the peripatetic from le Pallet, who won such distinction over all his contemporaries that it was thought that he alone really understood Aristotle'.[13]

The few sentences which we have quoted from their writings illustrate a great deal not only about the culture which these three shared, especially in their love of the Greek and Roman classics, but about developments between the three crucial generations which they represent. Guibert was born, most probably, in 1064,[14] Abelard in 1079, and John of Salisbury, who went to Paris as a young student (*adolescens modicum*) in 1136, about 1120. Guibert, like Abelard, saw learning as a vocation which he had chosen, in conscious preference to knighthood. He was not the eldest son, but he says that in the conversation quoted above his mother promised that if he wished to become a knight she would provide arms and equipment so that he could enter some noble household for training – he did not lack appropriate connections. The offer underlines her distress at the beatings, for she was a pious woman, and when she almost died while giving birth to Guibert his distraught father had sworn that if all went well the child would be dedicated to religion. The vow had referred specifically to the clerical and not the monastic vocation (probably reflecting his father's expectation of the patronage that might be available rather than any assessment of the relative merits of the two ways of life), and one of Guibert's complaints against his master is that he 'seemed to require of me the conduct of a monk rather than a clerk'. When he decided a few years later to become a monk both mother and master resisted it strongly; it was not what had been envisaged either in his father's promise, or in his upbringing.[15]

As befitted those of uncertain place in the social order, scholars must needs be wanderers. When Abelard set out from le Pallet it was still necessary to go from one school to another, learning at each what its master could teach from the books that he happened to know. When he reached Paris, probably in 1098, it was dominated by a single master, William of Champeaux, and when Abelard wanted to set up as a teacher himself he had to go to Melun. His own success and the students it brought flocking to him was one of the reasons why the situation was transformed in the next generation, though under the spell of his brilliant memoirs we probably exaggerate his role. When John of Salisbury left England in 1136 he went straight to Paris, and stayed there for twelve years. It now eclipsed all other centres not only for the eminence but for the number of its masters. John tells us how he was able to work with specialists in all of the liberal arts, both *trivium* (grammar, rhetoric and dialectic, in the first two of which John already had some grounding, for he went immediately to the lectures of Abelard, in dialectic) and *quadrivium* (arithmetic, astronomy, geometry and music), before he proceeded to the higher study of theology. The institutional arrangements which created the University of Paris, however, were not yet in place. It was not until 1174, for example, that the Chancellor of Paris was exempted by Pope Alexander III from the recent prohibition of taking a fee for the licence to teach without which nobody could teach in the diocese, and not until the Third Lateran Council in 1179 that he was forbidden to refuse that license to anyone who had been admitted by the masters as one of themselves, which confirms that by this time they were formally organized as a guild. Nevertheless, the curriculum of study whose successful completion would provide the basis for admission as a master for the rest of the middle ages was clearly in place by convention and practice in John of Salisbury's time. Abelard's fluctuating successes and failures up to the 1120s, by contrast, depended far more on the influence at the royal court of his patron Stephen of Garlande than on the disposition of his fellow masters.[16] Even so, his dramatic accounts of the manoeuvres of his rivals to prevent him from establishing himself, both in Paris and in Laon, like John's sunnier description of how he went by agreement from one master to another, show that the masters were beginning to act as a collectivity, for better and worse. Certainly it is easy to agree that the failure of Bernard of Clairvaux in 1148 to secure agreement to the condemnation as a heretic of another of John of Salisbury's masters, Gilbert de la Porée, at the Council of Reims, as he had that of Abelard at Sens in 1140, was in large part a result of their having learned to do so.[17]

The pre-eminence of Paris did not remain unchallenged for long. By the late 1150s Otto of Freising thought Bologna a better bet for an ambitious young man.[18] Bologna had emerged, even more suddenly than the Paris of Otto's youth, as a stronghold of teachers both of civil law – that is, the law code of Justinan – and of canon law. With their students they were rapidly providing Europe with the capacity to create a single body of law, promulgated and enforced through a uniform set of courts and procedures, for the first time since antiquity. This was made possible by a single book, the *Concordia discordantium canonum*, or *Decretum* of 'Gratian'. The *Decretum*, as we now know thanks to Anders Winroth,[19] was the work not of one author but of two. It was first compiled in the 1130s, apparently as a text for use in the classroom, and its essential feature was the lucidity and consistency with which its author used the dialectical method to subject to an orderly and systematic analysis more than two thousand opinions gathered from a vast and miscellaneous collection of papal letters and decrees, decisions and judgements of councils and synods, and the Fathers of the Church, and of earlier canon lawyers like Burchard of Worms, Anselm of Lucca and Ivo of Chartres, to reconcile their contradictions and obscurities and bring out (as he saw it) their underlying harmony and coherence. 'Gratian 1', as Winroth calls him, made use of the principles of the Roman civil law which had been preserved in fragmentary form as it was adopted and adapted down the centuries in the legal systems of the peoples and towns of northern Italy, but he seems not to have been directly acquainted with the *Corpus iuris civilis* itself, the definitive compilation of Roman law created for Justinian in the 530s. 'Gratian 1' completed his work by about 1140. By the early 1150s it had been revised and greatly expanded, probably by one of his students, making much greater use of Roman law. Unlike his master, 'Gratian 2' knew Justinian's *Codex* at first hand, presumably because it was studied and used (though not systematically taught) by some of the large and active community of lawyers in Bologna. It was this direct knowledge which made possible the effective fusion of Roman civil and canon law into the *Corpus iuris canonici*, and made Bologna in the 1150s and '60s the place from which excited and ambitious young men carried the weaponry of legal knowledge and technique to the courts of Latin Europe, placing a formidable new technology of power at the disposal of its rulers both secular and ecclesiastical, and laying the foundation of a single legal culture and practice, irrespective of the formal fragmentation of sovereignty, for the first time since the disappearance of the Roman Empire.

It seems to have been teaching in law which in the 1170s and '80s began to attract advanced students to Oxford, a city which in the twelfth century had many teachers but no School, but it was theology which, from the chancellorship of Robert Grosseteste in the 1220s, made Oxford the second great university of northern Europe.[20] The legal status and formal structures of all three universities were established within a few years of one another, when statutes were promulgated by papal legates for Oxford in 1214 and Paris in 1215, and by Pope Honorius III himself for Bologna in 1219. The need to do so arose very largely in all three cases from the increasing frequency and serious- ness of disputes between the masters and students on the one hand and the authorities of the cities in which they found themselves on the other, and in the case of Paris also between the masters and the bishop. One or other of them provided the model for most of the thirty or so universities that were founded in Europe during the following hundred years.

If there were no other indication that the overwhelmingly powerful reason for the growth of higher education was demand for the skills of government the enthusiasm of kings and their ministers for the new universities would be enough. The University of Paris owed its first statutes to Philip Augustus. Its first residential college was founded by Robert de Sorbon, a chaplain of Louis IX, c.1257, and Oxford's first college by a Chancellor of Henry III, Walter de Merton, in 1264. Soon every monarch considered a university indispensable to the maintenance of royal authority and the well-being of the realm. The University of Naples was founded by Frederick II in 1224 as a base for his propaganda war against the papacy, and that of Toulouse by Pope Gregory IX in 1229 to combat the Albigensian heresy. The Spanish Reconquest was punctuated by a series of foundations beginning with that of Salamanca by Alfonso IX of Leon (c.1220–30, with a charter from Alfonso X in 1255), and including Lisbon and Coimbra in the new kingdom of Portugal (1290). Prague, founded by Charles IV in 1347, was the first in the Holy Roman Empire and of many foundations which throughout the fourteenth and fifteenth centuries marked the growth of the new king- doms of central and northern Europe and the interests of their kings in fostering congenial regional elites.[21] It is not surprising that few of these attained the cosmopolitanism and none the exuberance of Paris and Bologna in their salad days, but, for better or worse, they equipped the intelligentsia of the new Europe, including all its higher clergy and many of its public officials, with a common language, formation and outlook.

2   The Giants' Shoulders

Together with chivalry, its secular counterpart, scholasticism (as the system of education whose beginnings are described above and the modes of thought and expression associated with it have come to be known) was the most articulate and highly developed expression of the European high culture which was formed during the twelfth century and completed in the thirteenth. The essential and most characteristic achievement of this culture was the weaving of many local variants into a universal model. Until Abelard was in his prime each master taught what he could on the basis of what he knew and the books which happened to be available to him; when the student had learned it he moved on to a new place and a new master. By the early thirteenth century the university – *studium generale* – was defined by the ability of its masters to teach between them the whole of the liberal arts. It followed that the curricula in arts of the emerging universities were in all essentials identical. Where they differed was in their emphasis and approach to the advanced study of theology, civil or canon law (all three of which were themselves examples of this same process of welding disparate and fragmentary antecedents into coherent and unified systems of thought) or medicine. The change is directly analogous to that which took place in church-building. A panoply of local forms exuberant in their variety though united by an obvious family resemblance which justifies us in calling them all Romanesque was replaced, north of the Alps, by the uniformity of the Gothic style which spread from the Isle de France after the middle of the twelfth century. Its subsequent variations, spectacular as they are, are related far more closely to chronology than to geography. Similar changes occurred in the dedications of new churches, as the cult of the Blessed Virgin rapidly superseded those of innumerable local saints, and in their liturgies, as the dissemination of the musical notation invented by the Cluniac monk Guido d'Arezzo in the 1030s, the direct ancestor of modern notation, made it possible for the first time for music to be precisely reproduced from a written score. Even in pilgrimage, to mention one last example, we can see the same process. Better communications, more frequent travel and increasing social differentiation encouraged especially the more prosperous to make pilgrimage further afield, and local shrines increasingly found themselves integrated into a clearly-defined hierarchy in which (for instance) a Northumbrian might expect to win progressively greater merit and prestige by visiting Finchale (on the Wear, near Durham), and then Canterbury.[22] The emergence of the great shrines, attracting pilgrims from all over Europe, helped to weave the threads of community ever more closely: in the twelfth century all pilgrimage roads in transalpine Europe ultimately led to Compostela – and hence, for the greater part of the journey, away from Rome.

These are some aspects of the formation during the twelfth century, and especially during its second half, of a new high culture more integrated by far than its predecessors not only in the formation and outlook of its elites, but, through the greatly enhanced authority and prestige of the Roman papacy, between its northern and Mediterranean elements. More frequent and regular movement, between churches as well as between markets, and the release of manpower to permit less mundane and more specialized tasks and consumption, had created a more closely woven and more resilient infrastructure for the production and exchange of knowledge and ideas as well as of goods and services. Up to the time of Abelard probably no classical or patristic work was taught, or indeed read, in western Europe which had not been read and taught, at least occasionally, since the age of Bede. There were even a few people – Gerbert of Aurillac (Pope Sylvester II, d.1002), who taught the *quadrivium* as well as the *trivium* when he was master at Reims, was the most famous – who had read so widely as to have mastered virtually the whole body of extant learning. Gerbert, however, was not typical. On the contrary, his knowledge and ingenuity were so far beyond the ordinary as to fuel the rumours of sorcery which, perhaps inevitably, accompanied the rise of an obscurely-born Auvergnat to the heights of the imperial court and the Roman papacy. What was changing, and changing with increasing rapidity by the turn of the eleventh and twelfth centuries, was that access to virtually all that Gerbert had known could be aspired to, and substantially attained, by almost any young man with the ability and energy to pursue it, and a modicum of patronage to sustain him on the way.

Attempts to weigh the elements of novelty or originality in the intellectual movements of the eleventh and twelfth centuries against those of continuity with the ninth and tenth decline all too rapidly into mere semantics. Though few of its individual elements were new, the enormous growth between the age of Gerbert and that of Abelard of the common stock of knowledge, the capacity to use it, and the uses to which it could be put, transformed the range and sophistication of European thought and learning. Between the middle of the twelfth and the middle of the thirteenth centuries they were transformed again by the recovery of the philosophical and scientific inheritance of ancient Greece, which had been preserved and enriched in the Muslim world, through a flood of translations from Spain, Sicily and Constantinople. The struggle to absorb this vast body of new material and ideas, and to reconcile it with the patristic legacy and Catholic authority of Latin Christendom, culminating in the *summa* of Thomas Aquinas (1265–73), was the great work of the later twelfth-and early thirteenth-century schools. The essential point, observable in many other fields, is again most obviously illustrated in that of building. The structural elements of Gothic architecture, the pointed arch, the rib vault, the flying buttress, or their immediate forerunners, can easily be pointed out in many

'Romanesque' churches – all of them are present in Durham cathedral (built between 1093 and *c*.1130) – but the combination, once consciously achieved and systematically exploited, was revolutionary, and opened the way for buildings of a size, splendour and technical and aesthetic complexity hitherto undreamed of. The continuity of the parts did not add up to continuity of the whole, and did not detract from its originality.

The creation of the new high or learned culture not only depended on the reconstruction of the social and economic order but provided the mechanisms for transmitting and disseminating the skills – ordered thought, literacy, numeracy, legal agility – which were essential to the securing and distribution of the profits, and the exercise of the power which the new order could generate. It therefore became urgently necessary to identify the custodians of learning, and the means by which the skills and authority it conferred were to be granted, acknowledged and transmitted from each generation to the next. Who were to be the dwarfs on the giants' shoulders? This is what was at stake in the struggle of the *magistri* to secure their autonomy. Much of it was expressed through and symbolized in the tension between faith and reason which was the *leitmotif* of the rise of the schools, especially in the earlier part of our period. The confrontations which attracted the greatest attention and reverberated for longest were not between the masters themselves, but between a brilliant and charismatic teacher, the current cock of the scholarly walk, as it were, on the one hand, and a senior and weighty churchman on the other.

The first and in many ways the greatest of these controversies raged for more than thirty years around the questions raised by Berengar of Tours about the meaning and interpretation of the doctrine that during the mass the bread and wine become the body and blood of Christ, in the light of what Berengar claimed to be the observable fact that they were still bread and wine when the mass had been concluded.[23] Its significance for the present argument is not only in the substance (as it were) of the controversy but in its extraordinary political reverberations, and in the fact that while Berengar attracted a long succession of powerful opponents, each in turn conducted the argument increasingly on Berengar's terms, and with Berengar's methods.[24] Berengar was born of a noble family in the early years of the eleventh century, and became a canon of Tours in 1031 and archdeacon of Angers about ten years later. He was a pupil of Fulbert of Chartres, the most famous teacher of his generation, but also a highly political figure (he had been involved, for example, in the intrigues which preceded the burnings at Orléans in 1022), whose correspondence shows him at the centre of a widely spread network of friends and pupils. Berengar himself attracted numerous and loyal pupils – his enemies said that he supported them financially in order to disseminate his heretical teachings – and was prominent at the court of Count Geoffrey 'Martel' of Anjou. The first condemnation of his teaching was the result of a combination of Geoffrey's enemies. The case against Berengar was argued by Lanfranc of Pavia (the future archbishop of Canterbury), also a renowned teacher and dialectician, by origin a Lombard lawyer, but now abbot of Bec, and a close adviser of William of Normandy; the condemnation was pronounced in 1050, at Rome and Vercelli, by Pope Leo IX, who had recently placed Geoffrey and his domain under interdict; and it was embraced by Henry I of France as a war against heresy, justifying his planned invasion of Anjou. That project was abandoned in 1052 when a peace was made, but not before a synod in Paris had threatened Berengar's supporters with the alternatives of recantation or death. Berengar continued to defend his position passionately and publicly, while several times disowning positions attributed to him by his accusers, until he was prevailed on to affirm the presence of the body on the altar 'in substance' (*substantialiter*), and not merely metaphorically, at the Lenten synod of 1079, in terms spelt out by Gregory VII, who seems to have behaved in the matter with both caution and sympathy.[25] Thereafter Berengar remained silent until his death in 1088, though the arguments for and against his teaching, real or alleged, continued to rage.

A similar pattern may be seen in Peter Abelard's trials for heresy, which by his own account were the revenge arranged by his vanquished opponents for his triumphs in the classroom. Abelard is less forthcoming about their political context, but his connection with Stephen of Garlande makes it certain that there was one. His first trial, at Soissons in 1121, was the result of his being accused by two pupils of Anselm of Laon, Alberic and Lotulph, of teaching that the three persons of the Trinity were, in effect, three gods, not one. The trial was presided over by a papal legate, and attended by a galaxy of secular as well as ecclesiastical dignitaries. Abelard brought along a copy of his book on the Trinity, so that he could prove the falsity of the charges, but his opponents were too cautious of his power in disputation to allow that, and he was condemned unheard, made to burn his book and sentenced to stop teaching and withdraw to a monastery. It took him perhaps as much as fifteen years – the date of his return to the Paris schools in the 1130s is not known – to recover his old pre-eminence. He was soon under attack again, this time by Bernard of Clairvaux, egged on by William of St Thierry and others, and was arraigned before another Council, this time at Sens, in 1140. Once more his trial provided the occasion for a great public spectacle, presided over by another papal legate, and attended by the King, Louis VII, himself. The assembled magnates of church and kingdom were cheated of their entertainment, for when Abelard entered the chamber he stopped the trial by announcing an appeal to Rome, and set out to argue his case there. He was preceded by a storm of letters from Bernard which secured a condemnation from Innocent II (who owed his continuing occupancy of the throne of St Peter during a period of acute schism very largely to Bernard's tireless support over the previous ten years), and took refuge in Cluny where he remained under the protection of Peter the Venerable until he died two years later.

There was, of course, far more at stake in these long and bitter conflicts than can be considered here,[26] and they are themselves only the most notorious of many clashes between masters and the higher clergy. These were not merely (as we say) academic disputes. Of course, the philosophical difficulties inherent in reconciling classical logic with faithful acceptance of the Trinity, the Incarnation and the transubstantiation of the body and blood of Christ in the eucharist were very great, and in themselves of profound significance for believers: critical chapters in the histories of both philosophy and Christianity are not to be dismissed as mere tokens or pretexts. Indeed, if the questions they raised had not appeared both intractable and fundamental they could hardly have supplied the material for what concerns us here, the shaping over a century and more of new solidarities and allegiances between teachers and their students on the one hand, and the emerging structures of both ecclesiastical and secular authority on the other. The political manoeuvres for which Berengar's difficulties so obviously provided a focal point are probably concealed beyond recovery in the case of Abelard, but Abelard's tribulations and trials were not independent of each other. His first great enemy, William of Champeaux, went on to become bishop of Châlons and a patron of the Cistercian order of which Bernard of Clairvaux was the effective leader, and his great public contests were carried on against the members of a network of overlapping and interconnected opponents which remained active even after his death. At the Council of Reims in 1148 Bernard accused Abelard's successor (and probably his pupil) as the most charismatic teacher of the Paris schools, Gilbert de la Porée, of heresy, and failed to secure a conviction largely because the assembled prelates recognized and disliked a repetition of the tactics which had been successful at Sens.

The common factors in all three cases, and others less famous and less documented, reveal a series of contests to establish who among the *oratores* were to have the decisive responsibilities of interpreting and transmitting the textual legacy of the ruling culture, and identifying and training its future guardians – how, in other words, the elite was to be reproduced. In each case (though important details remain uncertain) the confrontations were set up by the enemies of the schoolmen, and there was intensive lobbying to secure a condemnation. In each case the use and scope of dialectic, the weapon of the schools, was at the heart of the issue. That is not to say that the position of the schoolmen themselves was the only or even necessarily the most important thing at stake, but whatever else was at issue in any particular case, 'reason' stood for the claims of the clerks to intellectual and pedagogic autonomy and to the extension of the territory in which it might be exercised, while those who sought to contain them fought under the banner of 'faith'. Bernard's failure to secure the condemnation of Gilbert de la Porée was the last of these great gladiatorial contests between the champions of the clerks and their monastic or episcopal rivals, and the first occasion on which we can see clearly that the clerks were mounting a collective defence of the interests which they would continue to advance so effectively.

3   New Monarchy, New Men

The history of Paris in the twelfth century is that of a three-way relationship between the city, the Capetian kings and the masters and students, in which each gained immeasurably from, and contributed immeasurably to, the growth of the other two. From the beginning the development of the university was intimately bound up with that of the monarchy. It was not until 1200 that Philip II granted the masters and scholars immunity from secular jurisdiction, or until 1231 that the independence of the university itself was formally acknowledged by the queen regent, Blanche of Castile, but the presence of the court had long been one of the magnets that drew both students and masters to Paris, and its politics had been closely if still obscurely intertwined with those of academic appointments and reputations at least since the beginning of the twelfth century. The independence which Blanche of Castile confirmed had been secured, in the first instance, by a series of papal interventions since the 1170s, designed to sustain and protect the masters against the power first of the Bishop (through his chancellor) and then of the crown. Neither monarchy nor papacy acted to secure the interests of learning for its own sake, but because each was determined to prevent it from being controlled by the other. The papacy was the greater benefactor precisely because it was a great deal farther away. Then as now, appreciation by the powerful of the practical value of learning and the learned was no guarantee of academic freedom. It was the rivalries of the court, not enthusiasm for his pedagogy, that brought Abelard the support of Stephen of Garlande in his campaign to instal himself in the city in opposition to the well-connected archdeacon William of Champeaux, and later protected him when he had upset the abbot of the royal abbey of St Denis. Political division created the opportunity for growth and diversity. Without it the school would have remained under the control of a single master. The transfer of patronage from the individual master to the corporation of masters in the later part of the century is in itself a significant index of institutional development.

Wise kings had always surrounded themselves with scholars; there was nothing new in that. On the other hand, it is not at first sight obvious why the Capetians should have been such early and important patrons of higher education. Especially by comparison with their neighbours and rivals in the Anglo-Norman kingdom they were rather slow to develop the use of writing and calculation in government and to build a bureaucratic organization; it was not until the 1150s that a *magister* Mainerius appeared in the royal household, and not until Normandy fell to Philip Augustus in 1204 that he developed a systematic financial administration on the Angevin model.[27] Nonetheless, it is in the Capetian entourage that we can see reflected from the middle decades of the eleventh century the changes in the nature and basis of political power which eventually gave rise both to the needs which educated men could satisfy and to the insecurities which drove them to respond with ever-increasing energy and ingenuity. In doing so they made the royal courts of northwestern Europe the pioneers of the intensification of government and the penetration of society by governmental power which was to be the distinguishing mark of the new regime – or, as it would come to be called, the old regime – in Europe.

The court was the visible incarnation of the body politic, the kingdom given form. On the great occasions when the crown was worn the notables of the kingdom came to declare their loyalty – or stayed away ostentatiously to withold it, if they wished to give notice of discontent verging on rebellion. In the Empire this was still in the twelfth century its most important function,[28] but in the new monarchies the representation of power, while still essential, was becoming less and less the equivalent of power itself. Since nearness to the king (*königsnahe*) remained the most potent source and sign of power for those within his reach the composition of the royal court naturally reflected the geography and sociology of power. Hence as it became increasingly obvious in the middle quarters of the eleventh century that the area in which the Capetian monarchs held sway had shrunk to their own demesne, the bishops and counts from all over west Francia who had formerly composed the court gave way to castellans and knights from the Ile de France, and especially those of the king's household (the *familia regis*) itself. These men were far from being grandees: the taint of serfdom was not unknown among them, and they were directly dependent on the king for maintenance, often by means of an annual *stipendium* or money fief. The courts of the great feudatories underwent a similar transformation; the Dukes of Normandy and the Counts of Anjou had stipendiary knights in their *familiae* by around the middle of the eleventh century. Likewise unfree knights (*ministeriales*) seem to have replaced free vassals in the entourage of bishops and abbots in Flanders and Lorraine even in the later part of the tenth century.[29]

From the point of view of the future of royal government this was by no means a negative development. These petty knights provided their lords with a close-knit and highly trained elite force whose loyalty could be depended on – and with it, a continuing need to assure the flow of cash which secured it. As the following generations confirmed, they were precisely the people who did not despise the inglorious pursuit of mundane claims and local rights on which the political structures of the twelfth century and beyond were built. If Louis VI needed frequently to call upon the military skills of his entourage in the traditional fashion as he steadily reasserted control over his demesne, neverthless the continuation of his determined insistence on his judicial rights and claims to income is attested by the charters of Louis VII and Philip Augustus. For much of his reign his most powerful courtiers were the Garlande brothers, who had become prominent as brave and hardy fighters but who also took over the administrative duties of his court. These duties in turn placed an increasing premium on the newer talents of men who could cast accounts and write charters, formulate legal claims and devise the procedures to pursue them.

The difference in circumstances between the French and Anglo-Norman kingdoms, and in the respective relationships between the royal court and the production of the historical sources, conceals an essential identity in the goals of their kings. Their avarice was legendary. William I, said the Anglo-Saxon chronicler, 'was not ashamed that there was not a single hide, not one virgate of land – it is shameful to record, but it did not seem shameful to him to do – not even one ox nor one cow nor one pig which escaped notice in his survey'.[30] Guibert of Nogent was no less withering in his contempt for the way Louis VI allowed himself to be bribed and counter-bribed by the canons and citizens as they argued whether Laon should have a commune.[31] But William was a conqueror whose chronicles were written largely by the conquered. Louis was a conqueror too, but our picture of him now is dominated – Guibert's observations being altogether exceptional – by his close friend and adviser Suger of St Denis, the scriptorium of whose abbey had already for more than a generation been devoted to the project of representing the Capetians as the legitimate heirs of Carolingian authority and legend. Suger's *Life of Louis VI* provides a stirring account of the rebellions suppressed and the castles besieged as the lords of the Ile de

France were subjugated one by one to the royal command. We are left to assume, what the subsequent prosperity of the French crown makes obvious, that once political control had been established Louis found the means to tap the wealth of his compact kingdom, which sat astride the immense granary of the Ile de France, with the tariffs from the Seine, the Loire and the fairs of Champagne flowing into its coffers. In England it is just the reverse: the conquest was swift and brutal, and the conquered were not silent, but the legacy of the Conqueror's establishment and recording of royal rights and opportunities is one of the most extraordinary documents to survive from the whole European middle ages, and one which tells us a great deal about the present and future of eleventh-century kingship.

In the early eleventh century England was perhaps the most commercialized and urbanized part of northern Europe, and possessed a royal administration sufficiently advanced, when driven by the brutal vigour of the conquering Normans, to produce in a very short time an astonishingly complete and detailed survey of the wealth of the king and his subjects. The Domesday survey was ordered by William I at his Christmas court in 1085, and nearly enough complete when he died less than two years later for the returns from the last half dozen counties to be hastily sewn together to complete the great Book before the work was stopped. Most of the administrative techniques and personnel employed were those of the Old English state (though the director of the operation, Samson, later bishop of Worcester, was a Norman), but it is impossible to imagine the subjects of Edward the Confessor meekly submitting to such an examination.[32] For anything remotely comparable in administrative sophistication we should have to look to Apulia and Sicily. There also Norman kings took over wealthy territories, from Byzantine and Muslim predecessors, with ancient and well developed legal and fiscal traditions, and skilled officials to operate them. They did not secure by any means so complete a domination of their own followers as William and his successors achieved in England, but they left a tradition of magnificence and uncompromising autocracy which for the rest of our period dazzled the imagination of the whole of Europe, and helped to keep a good part of it at war.

It was not so much that William I and Louis VI were greedier than their predecessors as that the world was changing. When William Rufus summoned the fyrd to Hastings for service in France in 1094, his right-hand man Ranulf Flambard rode along the ranks collecting the ten shillings each man had brought for his keep, and sent them home again. Mercenaries were more efficient and more reliable. Money created new perceptions and new possibilities, but the novelty caused resentment. Just as in the church the exchange which had seemed perfectly natural of a favour for a benefice became positively indecent when the favour was a fistful of cash, men who would not have stinted whatever their lands could yield to their lord in traditional hospitality and service felt quite differently when he sent his clerks round with a notebook to count it.

Men who could see the new opportunities and knew how to exploit them were invaluable to their masters. As William of Malmesbury explains: 'If at any time a royal edict was issued, that England should pay a certain tribute, it was doubled by this plunderer of the rich, this exterminator of the poor, this confiscator of other men's inheritances [Flambard]. He was an invincible pleader, as unrestrained in his words as in his actions, and equally furious against the meek or the turbulent.'[33] There we have exactly the value of a royal minister to his master, and the strength and limitation of Ranulf Flambard. His energy, his ingenuity, his ruthlessness and his cleverness in exploiting law, memory and custom increased the king's revenues impartially at the expense of all his subjects, rich and poor – and his greed and unscrupulousness further increased the burden on the king's subjects as he enriched himself. Moreover, Flambard was a self-made man and like his master William Rufus flamboyant, reckless, and contemptuous of clerical opinion – qualities which certainly damaged William's posthumous reputation, and may even have contributed to his death, if it was not accidental. Their successors were men of a different style. Rufus lost his temper with Anselm of Canterbury when the Archbishop denounced the effeminate fashions and lewd behaviour by which the king was surrounded, and called upon him to control the libertinism of his court. It was said of Henry I that on his accession he restored the lights to the corridors of the palace by night – but he also left, admittedly from a reign of thirty-five years, more bastards than any other monarch in English history.

Ranulf Flambard was indeed low born, the son of a poor priest in Bayeux, though 'raised to eminence by his wit and subtlety',[34] but the jibes which were levelled at him and his kind reflect not so much their social origins as the tension which always exists where there is competition between those who expect to command office and status by right of birth or custom and those who are given the opportunity to attain them through energy and talent. Those tensions are most fully displayed in the ambiguous reputation of King Henry I. He did not by any means embody the qualities that were generally admired in twelfth-century kings – the chivalric virtues of his bastard son Robert of Gloucester, his grandson Richard Coeur de Lion, or Frederick Barbarossa. He had not the military reputation of his father the Conqueror, though he won his crucial battles. He rivalled neither the magnificent ostentation of the

Sicilian kings nor the ostentatious modesty of the Capetians, which would be brought to its pitch of perfection by the image-makers of St Louis in the next century, but was fully captured in this one by the widely quoted and disingenuous remark of Louis VII that while other kingdoms produced enormous wealth 'we in France have nothing but bread and wine and gaiety'.[35] Henry was cunning, cruel and shifty. To this day the castrations and blindings which he habitually inflicted on his defeated enemies arouse disgust. The rapidity with which he secured his throne by taking possession of the royal treasure at Winchester when one of his elder brothers, William Rufus, was accidentally shot in the New Forest near by, in the nick of time before the return from crusade of the other brother, Robert Curthose, continues to excite suspicion.[36] But for all the shadiness of his succession to a kingdom neither united nor secure Henry ruled for thirty-five years, and died in bed, rich. And there is no disagreement that he ruled well. 'He surpassed all his predecessors in the tranquillity of his rule, in his wealth, and in the great sums he laid out all over Christendom', says Walter Map. 'He arranged with great precision, and publicly gave notice of, the days of his travelling and of his stay, with the number of days and the names of the vills, so that everyone might know without the chance of a mistake the course of his living, month by month. Nothing was done without preparation, or without previous arrangement, or in a hurry: everything was managed as befitted a king, and with proper control. Hence there was eager sailing from the parts beyond the sea to his court, of merchants with wares and luxuries for sale, and likewise from all parts of England, so that nowhere save about the king, wherever he went, there were plentiful markets. His greatest glory he reckoned to be in the keeping of peace and in the wealth of his subjects. He would have no man to feel the want of justice or of peace.'[37]

This is Henry I as Beauclerk, the king who welcomed clerks to his court, and knew how to put their talents to use. He understood them; he was a younger son himself, and whatever his part in the death of William Rufus had schemed and manoeuvred his way to the throne from a very small resource base, and with many enemies as well as two direct rivals. He knew, above all, how to secure loyalty by judicious reward and preferment, and it is in his kingdom that we can see the most extensive and systematic exploitation of ecclesiastical patronage, which with a certain historical irony had been greatly increased by the success of the Gregorian reform. The outcome of the great struggle over lay invest-itures, resolved in a series of compromises early in the twelfth century, had been that kings gave up the formal right to invest bishops, but retained considerable and often decisive influence in their selection. Until the end of the century, when the papacy began to flex its muscles again (and as the development of its own administrative machinery began to swell the demand for benefices for the pope's *curiales*) the compromises worked reasonably smoothly, whether because, as in the Norman kingdoms in England and Sicily, royal power was too great to be needlessly confronted or because, as in France, it was sufficiently emollient to be worth conciliating. Either way, bishoprics were generally available to royal favourites, and with their connivance a handsome selection of other offices rewarded those who served the king well. Thus the bishopric of Ely, one of the richest in England, was occupied during the twelfth century by a succession of royal treasurers, and that of London, founded by Henry I and first occupied by his chancellor Robert de Sigillo, together with the canonries of St Paul's, provided support for an extensive (and *de facto* hereditary) network of Anglo-Norman and Angevin administrators.[38]

The bishoprics were able to provide this support because the attack on simony, as we have seen, had been mainly directed against aristocratic patronage, especially over cathedral and collegiate churches and the offices and revenues associated with them. In the regions with which we have been most concerned it was largely successful. That success, in combination with the decline of child oblation, which was offensive to the religious sensibilities of reformers, greatly increased the power of the bishop to give preferment to men with the qualities and abilities that suited him, which increasingly meant those with educational attainments. The household of Archbishop Theobald of Canterbury to which John of Salisbury returned from Paris in the late 1140s contained six or eight clerks. In contrast, Theobald's predecessor Ralph d'Escures, like St Anselm before him, probably had in his household nobody trained in the schools; his successor Thomas Becket was famous for the twenty scholars (*eruditi*) he maintained, his need admittedly swollen by the propaganda war against King Henry II which consumed the later part of his episcopacy.[39] Similar considerations worked at every level in the church, encouraging lay and ecclesiastical patrons to send young men like John of Salisbury to the schools, whence they returned with the knowledge of money, letters and law to protect the interests and augment the revenues of their lords. By the end of the century every household of any size or pretension contained its quota of *magistri*.

The much greater social, political and cultural continuity which prevailed in the German Reich until the late eleventh century, and in many respects beyond, produced a rather different pattern of development. The principal forces which undermined the Carolingian regime in the west were absent in East Francia. There an open frontier and military success permitted the Ottonian and Salian monarchy to preside over an aristocracy which continued to look to warfare as its primary source of wealth and prestige. Its members were able to secure the positions of a good proportion of their surplus sons and daughters, by means of child oblation, in handsomely supported monasteries and cathedrals and in collegiate churches. There they lived, on the whole, without scandal (or at least without intemperate reformers to draw attention to it), in the aristocratic style permitted by the Rule of Aachen and expected by their peers, usually living in their own houses and keeping their own table, wearing linen rather than the wool that was thought fitting for monks. In short, the German church experienced neither the wholesale secularization of the ninth and tenth centuries nor the vigorous but sternly conditional re-endowment from the late tenth century onwards whose terms and consequences were at the heart of our revolution in western Francia. Consequently, it did not experience either the most deplored consequences of the secularization and impoverishment which was the lot particularly of the cathedral churches of the tenth-century west, or the most extreme of the reactions which followed. Hence the imperial church could remain largely 'unreformed' in the twelfth century not only because the emperor and princes kept the pope and his legates at bay, but because much that was being done in the west was not necessary here: the *reichskirche*, though certainly unsatisfactory in the eyes of a Humbert or a Hildebrand because of the firmness with which its appointments were controlled by the emperor and the lay aristocracy, was an imposing, well organized and well disciplined body, largely satisfactory to the society in which it found itself. One consequence was that canonries remained, for the most part, under the control of the canons themselves, and hence of the family networks at whose centre they lay, instead of coming under that of the bishop. The continuation of child oblation, in combination with the high calibre and reputation of the cathedral schools, led by those of Hildesheim, Magdeburg, Bamberg and Würzburg, and their firm and generally effective constraints on absenteeism, meant that it remained rare for Germans to leave for the schools of France or Italy until late in the twelfth century. For the same reasons, the magnates and the bishops, unlike their counterparts in England or many parts of France, had relatively little in the way of patronage to bestow on highly educated outsiders, to build up administrative and legal expertise in their households. It is a good example of how revolution may be averted, for better or worse, by a modest degree of reform.[40]

In the secular sphere too it might be said that the greater success of the political institutions of East Francia in the tenth and most of the eleventh centuries saved them from the transformation of the twelfth. The imperial court retained its traditional function as the visible presence of the Reich, the occasion upon which its leaders, secular and spiritual, gathered together around the emperor to embody the 'kaleidoscopic commonwealth' over which he presided.[41] The courts of the princes in their turn had the same character, except that being drawn from less far-flung and more cohesive territories they had perhaps a greater potential to develop their authority beyond the essentially symbolic – but if so, they did little to realize it during our period. Though silver from German mines was essential to the commercial revolution in the rest of Europe, the German lands themselves remained at a much lower level of monetization and market development than those to the west and south, so that renders in kind continued in most places to represent a large proportion of the agricultural surplus.[42] Without the ability to turn their revenues into cash lords continued to rely on the services performed in return for land by their *ministeriales*, the unfree knightly class which may have originated in the late tenth century, and which developed rapidly from the late eleventh. Consequently both the incentives and the opportunities to recruit experts in the bureaucratic arts were very much less in the east than in the west, though by no means entirely lacking.

4   Courts and Courtiers

Twelfth-century graduates gravitated to courts as surely as their modern successors do to corporations and government offices – and as surely as their brothers who had become knights. 'I may say that in the court I exist and of the court I speak, and what the court is, God knows, I know not', said Walter Map,[43] and indeed it is not easy to define the shifting crowd of friends and relations, followers, servants and hangers-on in which any great man lived and moved, performed his public duties and enjoyed his private pleasures. Walter, whose *Courtier's trifles (de nugis curialum*, also the sub-title of the more systematic and generally much more highly regarded *Polycraticus* of his older contemporary John of Salisbury) is one of the shrewdest as well as one of the earliest examples of a new genre of literature about courts and their activities, was himself very typical of the 'new men' of the twelfth century who are the central figures of the argument of this book. He was born in the early 1130s, of a family in the Welsh marches not prominent, but substantial enough to have been 'faithful and useful to [King Henry II] both before his accession and after it'.[44] He was a student in Paris in the 1150s, joined the household of his Bishop, Gilbert Foliot, who was translated from the see of Hereford to that of London in 1163, and moved to the royal household in the early 1170s; he was a canon of Lincoln by the early '80s, became archdeacon of Oxford in 1196 or 1197, and died in 1209 or 1210.

On the face of it the structure of every great court from those of the Pope and the Emperor down was much as it had been in Charlemagne's day, a body of subjects and servants roughly divided between those who served him in his chapel and in his chamber. Even as modest a household as that of Guibert's mother contained both knights and clerks, and they did not form nearly such sharply contrasting groups as we might expect. In 1215 the Fourth Lateran Council found it necessary to go into some detail to insist that the distinction between clergy and laity should be visible in daily life, prohibiting clerks from wearing brightly coloured or daringly cut clothes, frequenting taverns and gaming houses, and so on. Many, probably most of each group of courtiers came from the same backgrounds, as the younger sons of knightly families which would, or could, offer them no prospect of inheritance and sent them out to make their own way. Both groups underwent a lengthy training to equip themselves to do so, during which both, in principle, were expected to remain chaste. For both the only living was in the household of their lord, and the only prospect of long-term security to obtain through his favour, after many years of devoted and unquestioning service, a bride with her dowry – for that phrase was commonly used to describe a church with its revenues. The services they performed also became less sharply differentiated (though in themselves more specialized) as the century passed: thus, of the fourteen men who appear regularly as justices of Richard I of England, in the last decade of the century, seven were laymen and seven in orders.[45] The knights continued to provide the king's personal bodyguard and the elite of his fighting forces, but as internal order was steadily imposed, though at greatly varying rates, on the kingdoms and principalities of Europe, the maintenance of order itself became less exclusively a military function, and more often meant the collection, or overseeing the collection, of revenues, securing the acknowledgement of royal or seignurial rights and presiding over the settlement of disputes – to the point, Nigel Longchamp was complaining by 1192, where many were knights who had no skill in arms. Complaints that too many clerks lacked learning were commonplace, of course, and doubtless as true then as they have been ever since. Clerks in principle were not only *litterati* (literate, that is in Latin, the language of government as well as of learning), but the only *litterati*. Nonetheless, it is clear enough that in England a reading knowledge sufficient for practical purposes could be expected by the end of the twelfth century in anyone who did the king's business, and was common enough among the gentry and even some of the peasantry by the end of the thirteenth. We still lack a full study of the role of women – or rather, of ladies – in maintaining and disseminating literacy in their households, by instructing their young children and through piety and the patronage of clerics, but certainly it was not insignificant.[46]

The extraordinary creativity of twelfth-century court culture is in itself testimony to the novelty of the situation of those who made it, and the pressures under which they found themselves. It is not easy to think of King Arthur and his court, 'the matter of Britain', the stories of Chrétien de Troyes, of Gottfried von Strassburg and Wolfram von Essenbach, the Ring of the Nibelungen and the invention of romantic love, as by-products of a change in the style and techniques of government. Obviously, many of the elements of courtly life were not new in them-selves. The ritual and the jealousy, the intimacy between the king and his circle, the backbiting of the envious and the manoeuvring of the ambitious, are visible enough in Einhard's account of how Charlemagne and the scholars he gathered around him gave one another nicknames from the Bible and the Latin classics, or in the gossip that proclaimed Louis the Pious helplessly enthralled by the allure of his beautiful second wife, Judith of Bavaria, and caused one of her ladies to be drowned as a witch. To move safely in such surroundings it was necessary to possess extremely refined personal talents – to give wise counsel without incur-ring the responsibility for error or ill fortune, to be seen to care only for the security and prosperity of one's lord without ever missing an opport-unity to better oneself, to seem always open and frank while never revealing by a flicker or glance the resentment that might betray an affair or an alliance, or give ammunition to an enemy. The cultivation of such skills, and of the manner and demeanour which proclaimed the nobility, the wisdom, the trustworthiness of their bearer, lay at the centre of the education offered in the great cathedral schools of the tenth and eleventh centuries, most impressively in those which had the closest connections with the Ottonian and Salian courts, and trained the Prince-bishops whose control of the resources of the church in the interests of the crown made them the key figures in the so-called Ottonian system in Germany.[47] Both the Carolingian and the Ottonian courts gave rise, through their patronage of learning, to movements of 'renaissance' which made contributions of permanent importance to the development of European culture. It has, indeed, sometimes been argued that the alleged superiority of the 'renaissance' of the twelfth century to these predecessors was precisely that it was not a court movement but more broadly based in society at large – an argument which underestimates both the power and originality of the innovations which stemmed from the courts themselves, and the extent to which developments outside the courts, such as the emergence of the universities, were driven by their needs and enthusiasms.

'The king only praises those whom he wishes utterly to destroy.' Thus Bishop Robert of Lincoln, who after twenty successful years at court knew what he was talking about, answered his friends when they tried to console him for the withdrawal of Henry I's favour by recalling the king's kind words of former times. Bloet, before whom many had trembled, had been found in tears by Henry of Huntingdon: he was losing his lawsuits, his followers being fined by upstart royal justices, bits of his lands being claimed as royal demesne. The wind had turned cold, and he died a broken man.[48] The rivalries and jealousies which had fuelled faction and intrigue at the court of a Louis the Pious or Otto III were multiplied many times when the courtiers were not great lords in their own right, regarding themselves as the king's equals and natural companions, or imperial brothers or cousins presiding over dignified and opulent ecclesiastical principalities, but men 'from the dust' who had ruin to fear at the merest hint of their lord's displeasure and nothing to hope for but the rewards of his favour. Yet if the courtiers were divided by their distrust of each other they were united in the face of the hostility of almost everybody else, as well as by their common outlook and experience – a unity which a shrewd king, like Henry II of England, went out of his way to foster. And if the daily quest for favourable notice gave a keen edge to the wits and a sharp eye to the observation, the uncertainty of their origins and the novelty of their role in the world gave his servants in even greater measure the preoccupation with the niceties of status and the craving for identity which we have already seen as so characteristic of their time and class.

That craving was expressed through and answered by the 'matter of Britain' which swept the courts of northwestern Europe in the second half of the century, to provide the set, the cast and the plots of one of the most popular genres of fiction, based on one of the most successful literary hoaxes, of all time. It need hardly be said that there is a vast and controversial literature on Geoffrey of Monmouth's *Historia Brittonum* (*c*.1136) and its sources, and that the work contains a good many references to people, places and events which can, with more or less ingenuity, be related to real ones. Nevertheless, the sober reader will find it difficult to improve on the judgement of the twelfth-century chronicler William of Newburgh that 'everything this man wrote about Arthur and his successors was made up, partly by himself and partly by others'. Geoffrey's claim that his book was translated from a Welsh or Breton manuscript given to him by his friend Walter, archdeacon of Oxford, has had almost as many literary descendants as the tales of Arthur and his court at Camelot which it contains.[49] Despite William of Newburgh's scepticism Geoffrey's account of the fourteen centuries or so between the founding of the British kingdom by Brutus, the great grandson of Aeneas, and the Saxon conquest in the fifth and sixth centuries CE was incorporated into a tenacious vernacular tradition around the end of the twelfth century by Wace and Layamon, and has resurfaced regularly in contexts of varying degrees of romanticism and eccentricity. Much more to our point, however, are the stories of Arthur and his knights, which in the hands of the greatest poets of their age, Chrétien de Troyes (apparently writing in the 1170s and '80s), Gottfried von Strassburg and Wolfram von Essenbach, and their many successors, were told and retold to become possibly the most familiar and enduring in the whole of European literature.

What is at first sight surprising is that this popularity, almost total within a generation of the completion of Geoffrey of Monmouth's book, was not achieved for want of an alternative. The *Chansons de Geste*, of which the *Song of Roland* is the earliest and best known, had already achieved wide and rapid circulation in northwestern Europe, in the early decades of the twelfth century. Nobody could complain that the stories were short of incident or excitement, and it might have seemed that the victories over the Saracens of Charlemagne and his companions, Roland, Guillaume d'Orange and the rest, from whom the nobility of the twelfth century claimed descent, would have made far more attractive material for telling and retelling, in the age of the crusades, than the doings of a remote British king. Why should it have been so suddenly and effortlessly superseded by a body of legend which seems to have been circulating in Wales and Britanny at least since the beginning of the twelfth century, and probably a great deal longer, without previously exciting the slightest interest outside its own Celtic milieu? And why did this happen just at the time when the Anglo-Normans were beginning to develop the stereotypes of their fellow inhabitants of the British Isles – the Irish, the Scots, but first, foremost and most virulently the Welsh – as lazy, dirty, ignorant and backward, which over the following centuries would reinforce and justify their conquest and domination?[50]

Geoffrey himself, if his dedications are any guide (which is doubtful) seems to have had some sense of the breadth of his material's potential appeal, for it was presented to two magnates, with both dedications appearing in many of the manuscripts, including the earliest surviving. One was Robert, Earl of Gloucester, who would shortly lead the faction of the Empress Matilda in the nineteen-year struggle for the succession to Henry I (who is also mentioned, and living, in this dedication though he died the same year); the other Waleran, Count of Meulan who with his twin brother Robert of Leicester would be one of the stoutest pillars of Stephen's cause. Geoffrey's motive in writing may have included some impulse to glorify his native culture – for it does seem likely that he was Welsh – by showing that it was older and closer to classical roots not only than that of the Anglo-Normans but even their Old English predecessors. But enthusiasm for Welsh culture certainly would not explain why his tale should have been so avidly seized upon by the

Anglo-Normans themselves, still less by Franks and Germans, or why it should have been so eagerly embraced by Eleanor of Aquitaine and her daughters, and by Philip of Flanders, successively patrons of Chrétien.

The answer may be in part that the *Historia Brittonum*, and still more the literature which was based on it, did not so much include the Celtic past as appropriate it. History bestows identity; a new history either creates a new identity or proclaims an old one which has been struggling for expression. To consider whose history it is which provides the setting for the Arthurian legends, and even more whose it is not, is to see how exactly this literature mirrored the need of the makers and beneficiaries of our First European Revolution – a need which becomes obvious as soon as we recall that neither Roman nor biblical history provides a history for the knights. In the *Chansons de geste* the bishops – think of Archbishop Turpin in the *Song of Roland* – were warriors who carried mitres instead of swords, to avoid shedding blood; in the romances the knights are Christian heroes, whose prosperity and fame rests on their piety and morality, and whose ultimate task is the quest for the Holy Grail. Women, notoriously, are marginal figures in the *Chansons*, mentioned only in passing. In the romances they are, of course, quite central. It is the lady around whom the household has been formed upon her marriage, and with her lord she presides over it, directing and forming the behaviour not only of her maidens, but, in their social being, of the knights. Her role as arbiter of the game of love is famous. However we interpret that delicate and elusive dance, its central purpose in reconciling the untamed vigour of the youthful warrior to the restraints imposed by the necessity (or the ideal) of monogamy are plain. That restraint itself lies at the centre of a wider code of manners and behaviour, designed to inculcate the courtly disciplines, and of these also the lady is arbiter. 'My lady,' says Calogrenant, in *Yvain*, after receiving the rough edge of the seneschal's tongue, 'I'm not greatly upset by the quarrel; it's nothing to me, and I don't care. Though Kay has wronged me it will do me no harm.' 'Don't pay any heed to this attack by my lord Kay the seneschal; he so frequently speaks ill of people that we cannot punish him for it.'[51] In the world of the *Chansons* failure to respond to Kay's insult instantly and violently would have disgraced Calogrenant as a coward, but Guinevere affirms the restraint which lies at the heart of the values of the court, and by her authority a crucial aspect of behaviour is ruled; courage and violence are still expected of a knight, but only at the right time and in the right way – which Guinevere defines. Kay remains silent.

The romances show how inseparable were the elements of our revolution. They yoke together Christian morality and the social institutions

which it underpinned, by not only including but placing at the centre of
the stage those at the cost of whose exclusion the dynastic structure had
been created – women and younger sons. That much, however, could
equally well have been done with the materials of the *Chansons de geste*.
It was not beyond the creative powers of a Chrétien or a Gottfried to
endow the court of Charlemagne with women of spirit and beauty. Even
allowing for the increasingly close identification of the Charlemagne
legend with Capetian propaganda in the middle decades of the century,
which would certainly have reduced its appeal to non-French writers
and audiences, we may suspect that the real attraction of the matter of
Britain lay not as much in what it included as in what it excluded. By
placing Wales, Cornwall and Brittany at the centre of the knights'
perambulations – the places from which they always depart, and to
which they always return – the Arthurian stories incorporate these
regions into the feudal world (anticipating and reflecting in this the
expansionist policies of the new monarchies), while excluding the non-
feudal, as the real Wales, Cornwall and Brittany still very largely were.
The geography of this world of chivalry is somewhat hazy, but at its
centre lies the northwestern Europe of which we write – the British Isles,
France, the Low Countries and Germany. It does not include Byzantium:
when, in *Cligés* Alexander, the son of the Byzantine Emperor, wishes to
travel to Arthur's court to become a knight he tells his father, 'I wish to
leave your empire, and present my service to the king who rules Britain'.[52] And, emphatically, it does not include peasants, presented as surly
and misshapen dwarfs who on the rare occasions when they are mentioned at all, are scarcely human in their presence and attributes. In
short, the world of Chrétien of Troyes and Gottfried von Strassburg is
Latin Christendom, the Europe that was created by our revolution. The
people for whom Geoffrey of Monmouth provided a history were the
makers of that revolution, and those who were made by it.

5   A Governing Passion

Factus de materia levis elementi/folio cum similis, de quo ludunt venti.
(*I'm constructed out of some light and weightless matter/like a leaf, an idle toy for the*
winds to flutter.)[53]

The figure of 'the wandering scholar' is so vividly implanted in our
imaginations by Abelard's and John of Salisbury's descriptions of their
student days, and by so many of the glorious lyrics of their contemporaries that the mention of twelfth-century Latin poetry immediately
draws our minds to young men, students, vagrants and minstrels. That

is highly misleading. The ability to turn witty or moving verses on any subject was (as indeed it for long remained) the clearest possible evidence of the mastery of the language which was the fundamental qualification for membership of the new elite, and the body of such verses that survives includes many by senior and established figures. The unidentified Archpoet whose *Confession* (quoted above) is the best known of them all, was certainly highly sophisticated, as well as highly educated. He almost certainly held some senior position in the retinue of Rainhald von Dassel, Archbishop of Cologne, Chancellor to Frederick Barbarossa, and in his day one of the richest and most powerful men in Europe. The Archpoet parodied everything that was holy, including himself and his patron. He was more likely begging a canonry from Rainhald von Dassel than the crust he specified, more probably wore an ermine robe than the thin cloak in which he described himself huddled against the wind, but in doing so he underlined the universal condition of even the greatest members of this new learned administrative class: they were rootless and wandering men, not only in their student days or in ill fortune, but for life; in their greatest prosperity they lived, like Robert Bloet, in terror of their lord's anger. Rainhald himself was in the same boat. Court life was much less pleasant in reality than the ready generosity and considerate manners of the lords and ladies of Chrétien de Troyes conveys, and much less open and free. As the opening words of the *Confession* – *Estuans intrinsecus, ira vehementer* (Seething over inwardly, with bitter anger) – recall, the first and most constant imperative for the courtier was to hide his emotions. Whether penniless or princely the lot of the clerks (and in this they resembled their brothers the knights) was at bottom the same – treacherous, precarious, open to constant humiliation. If some of them, like Abelard, had renounced their patrimony by choice, many others had been driven from it in the name of dynastic policy. Others were the sons of clerks and therefore illegitimate. Consequently, while they might and very often did succeed their father or 'uncle' in his prebend or even his bishopric, they could never do so by right, but only by the grace of the patron to whose service they devoted their energies, talents and ambitions. All might hope for a career like that of John of Salisbury, who began in poverty and finished his life in wealth and dignity as Bishop of Chartres, but none of them, however talented, however well-connected, could count on it. John was luckier in the end than his master Thomas Becket, who rose even higher from humble origins and was perhaps more typical of the high fliers in serving both ecclesiastical and secular lords; but constant movement, with and between the courts of their lords, and from one lord to another, and the constant uncertainty which stemmed from dependence, was the destiny of both.

If unquestioning and unstinting devotion to his lord's interests was the clerk's constant ideal the reality of service was not always heroic or chivalrous, as Nigel d'Aubigny, believing himself to be dying, recalled when he wrote to his master, King Henry I of England in 1118:

> I beg you my dearest Lord in whom after God lies my whole trust, to have pity on me in my great need. . . . I have been yours while I could, and I have loved you most truly and served you most faithfully. In your service and in my own affairs I have committed many great sins and I have done few if any good deeds. . . .[54]

In yoking together the king's service and his own affairs Nigel goes to the heart of his situation, and of the reputation of his kind for limitless avarice and arrogance. 'For having won for themselves the favours of secular power they assert that all things are opened to them as of right, because (as they say), the prince is not subject to the law, and what pleases the prince has the force of law' says John of Salisbury,[55] and the writings of the twelfth century abound in scathing and bitter accounts of the bribery, corruption, intimidation and blackmail that infested every court and attended every exercise of power. Tanchelm of Antwerp and Arnold of Brescia became radical and eloquent preachers of heresy in disgust at what they saw at the papal court, but neither was more sweeping or more contemptuous in his condemnation than St Bernard of Clairvaux. Autti of Huntingdon, the father of Christina of Markyate, could not understand why Bishop Alexander of Lincoln ruled that her vow of chastity should take precedence over the marriage vows subsequently forced from her to secure an advantageous alliance for her family until his friends told him. 'If you had given him money, you would certainly have won your case.' Autti went back to court, bribed the bishop's servants, and had the judgment reversed.[56]

Walter Map tells several stories to show how Godwine, the son of a cowherd (as Walter alleges) rose to become the father of a king of England (Harold) through the surpassing skill with which he deployed the courtier's arts. One of them is that, having taken a fancy to the property of the convent of nuns at Berkeley, Godwine, accompanied by his handsome nephew and an ample supply of 'rings, girdles and fawn-stones starry with gems', sought its hospitality. Pretending that the nephew was ill, he left him in the care of the nuns, with instructions to seduce as many of them as possible. When in due course the young man reported that 'the swelling wombs of the abbess and many of the nuns were past concealment' Godwine told the news to the king, and sent men to investigate. 'The nuns were cast out, and Godwine asked for and received Berkeley from his lord [King Cnut], who might better be called his fool.'[57] The story may be based on a true one; at any rate it did not lack plausibility.

The burden of countless such tales is, of course, perfectly accurate. Historically speaking, corruption is unremarkable and those with access to previously unexampled power and wealth have not been notable for spurning temptation. More interesting about twelfth-century Europe is the vigour and versatility with which the abuse of power and its appropriation for self-advancement and self-enrichment were ridiculed and excoriated. We do not understand satirists like Walter Map or the Archpoet by taking them at face value. Their anger at abuse is proportionate to the value which they place on the use. Walter is unsparing in his contempt for the hypocrisies of power, the duplicity and cruelty that lay behind the construction of royal government, merciless in the stories that he tells of those who inflated the prince's authority to exalt their own positions. But his epitaph on Henry I shows what he believed that power could achieve. 'His greatest glory he reckoned to be in the keeping of peace and in the wealth of his subjects. He would have no man to feel the want of justice or of peace.'[58] It is not a cynical or an ignoble observation.

Walter also knew that justice and peace were not easily achieved. 'How is our king to rule thousands of thousands, when we poor lords can hardly control the few men that we have?' he asked.[59] The harshest critics were found at the most advanced courts not simply because they offered most opportunity for advancement, though that was certainly the case, but also because they were the places where the highest hopes were entertained and the keenest sense developed of what might be done. Government, throughout the twelfth and thirteenth centuries, was at the leading edge both of science and technology, the solution of its problems a source of satisfaction and excitement as well as reward to its practitioners. The king's greatest servants were not, in the twelfth century, themselves the most highly educated men – the greatest administrative innovator of all, Archbishop Hubert Walter (d.1206), chief justiciar to Richard I of England and Chancellor to John, was mocked for his lack of scholarly polish – but they were ready to look to the schools for solutions to their problems. To Henry I's court, in the second decade of the century, came Adelard of Bath, who had attended the school at Laon, which had links with Muslim Spain, and there learned the use of the abacus, which he introduced to Henry's treasury, thus giving the Exchequer its name. From this time the royal sheriffs appeared before the Treasurer each year to have the balance of the revenues which they had collected and the expenses which they had incurred on the king's behalf cast on the chequered cloth (*scaccarium*: chessboard) behind which he sat, though it is only from 1131 that one of the Pipe Rolls upon which the calculations were recorded survives. The *Dialogue of the Exchequer* (1178), by Henry II's treasurer Richard Fitznigel, a member of one of the greatest clerical-administrative dynasties of the period, adds a new genre to the literature of government. It is concerned neither with moral exhortation or reflection, either directly like the 'mirrors for princes' of which *Polycraticus* is the best known, or indirectly like the satires, nor primarily with history, though it contains a great deal of history, but with explaining carefully and exactly how the king's business is carried on – how his revenues are assessed and collected, what procedures are used and what are the practical reasons for them, and so on. Richard's preface, which attributes sweeping powers and rights to the king, is sometimes cited as evidence of a growing tendency towards royal absolutism, but it evokes less the realms of high speculation than the impatience of the practical man to get obviously necessary business done without becoming bogged down in discussion of the justification for doing it. Its concluding words will strike a familar note to anybody acquainted with the habits and mentalities of the British – and perhaps not only the British – civil service: 'The Exchequer has its own rules. They are not arbitrary, but rest on the decisions of great men, and if they are observed scrupulously individuals will get their rights and your Majesty will receive in full the revenue due to the Treasury.'[60]

The *Dialogue of the Exchequer* was followed within a few years by the *Treatise on the Laws and Customs of England*, a similarly inspired account of the workings of Henry II's judicial system and the sweeping changes which he undertook, by another of his senior officials, though probably not the justiciar Ranulf Glanvill with whose name it has customarily been associated. The author of 'Glanvill' was probably not trained in the schools and was not systematically familiar with Roman law, though he knew some of its precepts. For just this reason, his treatise illustrates very clearly how deeply imbued by the methods of the schools was the reasoning which the courtiers (often joined in discussion of these matters by the king himself) brought to the problems of government. 'Pleas are either criminal or civil',[61] 'Glanvill' begins in Aristotelian fashion, as any lecturer in the schools might have begun by reducing his topic to order with a series of logical distinctions. Again and again the great legal reforms of the age, irrespective of whatever political inspiration they may have had, can be seen as dialectical solutions to logical problems. How to counter the abuse of clerical privilege which allowed a clerk who had committed manifestly secular crimes like rape or theft to leave the ecclesiastical courts untouched except by degradation (the loss of clerical status), which seemed an insufficient penalty and certainly, in one or two loudly trumpeted cases, failed to prevent him from reoffending? Bring him before a royal justice to be charged; send him under escort to an ecclesiastical court, where he is tried and degraded; and back again to the royal court where, no longer a clerk, he can be punished as a layman. Archbishop Becket, contentiously and with momentous consequences, objected that this amounted to two punishments for one crime, which canon law forbade, but whether he was right or wrong the answer which Henry and his clerks had come up with was strictly logical, straight from the schools: a thing cannot be both *a* and *not a*; the clerk is not tried in the royal court; the man who is sentenced there is not a clerk.

Again – no small problem in the England of lordly clienteles and local tyrannies which Henry II inherited after the nineteen long winters of anarchy when Stephen was king and his grandfather's order was only a golden memory – what remedy can be found for a poor man who is ejected from his land by a rich one alleging a bogus claim to it, and who cannot afford the lengthy and expensive legal process of proving his title while the usurper collects the income and runs down the capital? Let the sheriff put a dozen decent men of the neighbourhood on oath and ask not which of the parties has the rightful claim, but who is the aggressor. Did M, or his father, occupy this land as he says, and did N eject him? If so, let the sheriff restore M to the land, and N prove his case in the king's court if he can.[62] Right was too serious an issue for legal short cuts, and often complicated and difficult to resolve, but possession was straightforward and clear-cut – and henceforth, proverbially, in England nine points of the law.

Just as the expansion of higher education in the twelfth century was driven above all by the needs and ambitions of government, so too government was permeated by the outlook and techniques of the schools. The growth of competing and overlapping systems of law – canon law and civil law, royal law and town law, 'customary' law and feudal law, – together with the multiplication of jurisdictions and the multiplicity of titular authority, which we will look at more closely in the final chapter, creates an impression of a twelfth-century Europe in which power was highly fragmented. In the sense that it was dispersed through many individuals, of whom even the greatest were seldom beyond challenge, and that it was rarely the case, among free men, that all the authority concerning a particular matter was in one pair of hands, this was so. But the common formation, outlook and predicament of the *curiales*, the clerks and knights who actually exercised power, makes it also highly misleading. Whoever they served, all shared education, values and experience, and moved easily between masters, and for the most part indifferently between secular and ecclesiastical. One court was much the same as another, and the very intensity of the rivalries between their lords ensured that an argument found persuasive or a technique that proved effective in one would very soon be carried to another. A famous example is that of Master Thomas Brown, for whom, as Richard Fitznigel tells us, a special seat was created at the English exchequer bench so that no opportunity should be missed to profit from his knowledge of the fabulously wealthy and administratively sophisticated Sicilian court at which he had served.[63] Another, the subject of much unnecessary theorising about his temperament and motives, is Thomas Becket, who differed from scores of others mainly in the level at which he made his final transfer.

6   Doubt, Hesitation and Pain

Their shared culture and common destiny, as well as their usefulness to princes, enabled the *magistri* of the twelfth century to establish themselves as the custodians and interpreters of the texts by whose authority, transmitted through them, Christendom was to be ordered – the Latin classics and the Holy Scriptures. If their position was aptly symbolised by the dwarfs perched on the shoulders of the giants whom they often depicted in glass and stone in their great churches, the giants themselves might be taken to stand not only for the wisdom of the ancients, but also for the power, spiritual and secular, wielded by those whom the clerics served. There remained, however, the small detail (easily overlooked now, since they and their successors have embedded the contrary myth so successfully at the heart of western culture) that the *magistri* were not in fact the sole heirs of either the Greeks and Romans or the Prophets and Apostles – or even, as it were, the eldest sons. Establishing their claim to the succession therefore drew their energies with increasing vigour to the denigration of alternative sources of intellectual authority and cultural prestige, both Christian and non-Christian.

The former included the Greek, the English and the Celtic churches. Between the Latin Church and the most obvious alternative, the Greek, rivalry and mistrust reached a quite new level of intensity in our period. The long-standing Roman claim to primacy of authority over the entire Christian church became a demand for obedience. Backed by a denunciation of the laxity of the patriarchate of Constantinople 'sitting at home in delicate security, in pleasure and lasciviousness, in the dissipation of a long leisure, refusing to take part in the fight [against heresy] waged on her behalf by the pious Mother [Rome],'[64] it resulted in the excommunication of the Patriarch by papal legates in 1054. Hostility was further intensified by the accumulating distrust between East and West generated by the crusades, which culminated in the imposition of

Latin prelates and Latin customs throughout the Greek world after the fall of Constantinople to a Frankish army in 1204 and the setting up of Latin states in its territory. The final break between the churches in 1274 followed abortive negotiations which foundered, like several earlier attempts, largely on the westerners' intransigent insistence on their own superiority.

The churches in Brittany, Wales and Ireland had been regarded by Bede as a rival source of cultural authority supported by spiritual prestige, but their missionaries had converted much of the early Germanic world, and their scholars were received with honour at the courts of Charlemagne and Alfred the Great. They began once more to be regarded with suspicion in the eleventh century, and then reviled as founts of heresy and barbarism, preparatory to their conquest and absorption into the Latin Christendom of the twelfth.[65] Guibert of Nogent cited the example of Piro, who was said to have drowned himself by falling into a well while drunk, to show how the cult of saints in Brittany represented every thing that he deplored about popular enthusiasm unsupported by properly – that is, clerically – authenticated literary evidence.[66] For Abelard 'the country (Brittany) was wild and the language unknown to me, the natives were brutal and barbarous, the monks (of his abbey of St. Gildas de Rhuys) were beyond control, and led a dissolute life which was well known to all.'[66] The same rhetoric, magnifying the allegedly unreformed condition of the Old English church, provided an important pretext for the Norman conquest of 1066, and a useful means of legitimizing it, and then supported the extension of Norman and Angevin power into Wales and Ireland. Those who did not live under the obedience and according to the customs of the 'reformed' Roman church were represented as lazy, backward and immoral, the people steeped in vice and their clergy in corruption. The chroniclers of Anglo-Norman England too denounced their Welsh neighbours as primitive and debauched,[67] and Gerald of Wales in turn described the Irish in the same terms after Henry II sent him to Ireland in 1185 with a military expedition led by Prince John. The *History and Topography of Ireland*, read in public performance to Gerald's fellow clerks at Oxford in 1188, is in its own way a classic of the stereotyping process:

'While man usually progresses from the woods to the fields, and from the fields to settlements of communities and citizens, this people despises work on the land, has little use for the money-making of towns, spurns the rights and privileges of citizenship... Little is cultivated and even less sown... not through the fault of the soil but because there are no farmers to cultivate even the best land.... For given only to leisure and devoted only to laziness they think that the greatest pleasure is not to work, and the greatest wealth is to enjoy liberty. . . . They do not yet pay tithes or first fruits or contract marriages. They do not avoid incest. They do not attend God's church with due reverence.'[68]

In short, they had not experienced the First European Revolution.

Further afield, the Arabs had a far better claim than Latin Christians – and indeed than the Greeks – to be regarded as the inheritors and pre-servers of the classical legacy, though it was a title for which, at the time of which we write, enthusiasm was waning rapidly in their increasingly Islamic world. In little more than a dozen years after the death of Muhammed, in 632, the greatest schools and libraries of the ancient world had fallen into Arab hands. In the golden age that followed, unhindered by the effective hostility of theologians either Christian or, as yet, Muslim, and after 750 encouraged by the magnificent patronage of the early Abbasid Caliphs, they mastered the thought and literature of the ancients – and especially the mathematical, scientific and medical dis-coveries of the Greeks – and developed it to quite new levels of compre-hensiveness and sophistication. After the Christian reconquests of Spain and Sicily Arab libraries were the main source of the flood of translations which allowed the west to recover its knowledge of the ancient Greeks, and hence to provide the foundation for the development of mathematical and scientific thought until the age of Descartes, Leibniz and Newton. Already in the tenth century Gerbert of Aurillac owed his knowledge of mathematics, which would not be matched in the west for centuries, to his education in northern Spain and his contacts with Arab-speaking Christ-ians through whom he secured translations of books on astronomy and mathematics. Adelard of Bath (*c*.1080–*c*.1152) brought back from Sale-rno and Syracuse the knowledge which enabled him to produce the first complete translation of Euclid's *Elements* into Latin, and in all probabil-ity to introduce the abacus to the English Exchequer. Adelard had also been at Laon, which had contacts with Spain, as did the masters assoc-iated with the 'school of Chartres' (though no longer with Chartres itself[69]), who without impugning the mysteries of creation embarked on the search for a rational and coherent account of the workings of nature. The frank acknowledgement of a vastly more advanced civilization which was implied in Adelard's claim that 'I have learnt one thing from my Arab masters, with reason as a guide, but you [his interlocutor] follow another; you follow a halter, being enthralled by the picture of authority'[70] was not unique in his generation. It may even have been shared by Abelard and Heloise, for why else did they call their son Astrolabe?

Such openness, doubtless never much felt beyond these limited and specialised circles, was quickly eclipsed as Muhammed was reviled as the spawn of the devil, and Islam as a seat of iniquity and a fount of heresy. For Peter the Venerable, who in the 1140s arranged for the translation of the *Koran* and other texts into Latin, Islam was 'the foremost error of errors, dregs of all the heresies into which all the remnants of the diabolical doctrines have flown together.'[71] Another who urged greater openness to the splendours of Arabic science was Petrus Alfonsi, a converted Spanish Jew who became a courtier of Henry I of England, and one of his doctors. He implored the masters of northern France to take the teaching of astronomy more seriously, and translated the astronomical tables of al Khwarazmi, not very well, and other scientific treatises from Arabic. But these works earned him little notice. What made Petrus Alfonsi one of the most widely read authors of the entire middle ages was his *Dialogues against the Jews* (*c.*1110), in which he denounced the Jews as the killers of Christ, and Muslims as sensualists, idolaters and thieves: seventy-nine medieval manuscripts of this book survive, compared, for example, with three of Abelard's now far better known *Dialogues between a Christian, a Philosopher and a Jew.*[72]

This was the most agonised, and as it turned out the cruellest, of Latin Christendom's relationships with other literate cultures. It was not always obvious that it need be so. Stephen Harding, the Englishman who became Abbot of Cîteaux in 1108, left in his introduction (*monitum*) to the magnificent Bible which he had made for his infant community, dated 1109, a celebrated account of how its text was established. He explains that 'having collected together a number of books, including some from different churches, in order to follow the most accurate, we found one that was often at variance with almost all the others.'[73] The problem of the corruption of texts was not in itself a new one. The Carolingian renaissance had grown from the determination of Charlemagne's advisers, steeped in the precepts of Bede, to secure accurate texts of the Bible, and to ensure that thenceforth they would be accurately copied. But it was an issue which had a very special resonance for Stephen Harding and his flock, typical products of an age in which rising literacy gave a new power to the authority of the written word. The rationale of the new monastic movement, and the justification for groups like the Cistercians who had broken away from established communities, lay very largely in the conviction that traditional monasticism had fallen away from strict obedience to the Rule of St. Benedict, and most of their dietary, disciplinary and liturgical innovations were based on what they understood to be a literal observance of it. In the same spirit Stephen Harding himself had gone out of his way to see that both the words and music of the hymns sung at Cîteaux were authentically those of St. Ambrose. Stephen's great Bible was the most important, as well as the most imposing and beautiful, of the superb series of manuscripts produced in the scriptorium at Cîteaux in his time. Although at first he and his companions preferred the eccentric manuscript because it seemed more complete than the others, they continued to be troubled by the anomaly. 'Astonished therefore at the discrepancies in our books,' he continues, 'we approached certain Jews who were learned in their scriptures and inquired most carefully of them in French about all those places that contained the particular passages and lines we found in the book we transcribed, and had since inserted in our own volume, but did not find in the many other Latin copies. The Jews, unrolling a number of their scrolls in front of us and explaining to us in French what was written in Hebrew and Aramaic in the places we questioned them about, found no trace of the passages and lines that were causing us so much trouble. Placing our trust therefore in the veracity of the Hebrew and Aramaic versions and in the many Latin books which, omitting these passages, are in full agreement with the former, we completely erased all these unnecessary additions, as is indeed apparent in many places, especially in the books of Kings where most of the errors were found. To all future readers of this book we make the strongest appeal not to put back these passages and superfluous lines.'

Stephen Harding's memoir is remarkable in presenting an encounter between Christian monks and Jewish scholars as a cordial and relaxed occasion. It is uncertain for how long and under what conditions there had been Jewish communities in northern Europe. There were Jews in the diocese of Lyons in the ninth century, and in southern Burgundy early in the tenth, and the fact that both groups included landowners (in spite of the theoretical prohibition on Jewish land-owning laid down by Roman law) has encouraged the view that their forebears had been there since Roman times. Nevertheless, it seems unlikely that they were a substantial or influential presence so far north as early as the tenth century. The likelihood is that the Ashkenazi community of the high middle ages, centred in the Rhineland certainly by the eleventh century and spreading quite rapidly from there, originated in recent immigration from the Mediterranean regions, attracted by the growing economic activity in northern Europe at that time, and often by the direct initiative of princes seeking to develop their territories.[74] 'When I wanted to make Speyer a great town I thought I would add immensely to its lustre if I would bring Jews to dwell in it' said Bishop Rudiger in 1084 as he established a protected quarter in the city,[75] doubtless hoping to attract settlers from the already well-established communities in Mainz, Worms and Cologne.

Whenever they came, and wherever they went, Jews brought with them levels of literacy and a depth of learning that far surpassed anything that their Christian neighbours could show, as well as a tradition of looking to their teachers for direction and decision in social and practical matters. This in itself generated flexible and powerful legal skills, and a considerable literature of both ethical and practical wisdom. Among the greatest of their teachers and commentators was Rabbi Gershom of Mainz (*c*.960–1028), one of many attracted in those years to a city already famous among Jews for its schools and for the presence of members of at least five leading rabbinic families, including the Kalonymides, a number of whom had reached Mainz from Rome, by way of Lucca, by 950 or earlier. Another, related to the family of Gershom by marriage, was Rashi (Rabbi Solomon ben Isaac), who studied under one of Gershom's disciples in Worms and also worked at Mainz before setting up his own school at Troyes, his birthplace, which under his son-in-law and grandsons became the major centre of Jewish learning in northern Europe.[76]

The early Cistercians were not alone in recognizing either the value of Jewish learning, or the value which they placed upon it. A pupil of Abelard's remarked that 'a Jew, however poor, if he had ten sons would put them all to letters, not for gain as Christians do, but for the understanding of God's law, and not only his sons but his daughters.'[77] A number of late eleventh- and early twelfth-century Christian scholars became interested in Judaism and Jewish learning, and especially in the contrast between the increasingly central place of the incarnation of Christ in their own theology, and of the eucharist in their faith and worship, and Jewish attitudes (as they understood them) to ritual observance. One of them was Gilbert Crispin, Abbot of Westminster, whose knowledge of Jewish opinion on the incarnation, gathered in discussion with Jews from Mainz whom he had met in London, helped to stimulate the ideas which his master Anselm of Canterbury was already turning over when he visited Gilbert in 1092, as he prepared to write one of the truly revolutionary works of Christian theology, *Cur Deus homo?*[78] Hugh of St. Victor (d. *c*.1140) and his pupil Andrew (d.1175) had contact with Jewish scholars and made extensive use of the works of Rashi and his followers in their biblical commentaries, whose influence was widely disseminated through the widely used *Scholastic History* of Peter Comestor. But the danger which Stephen Harding's innocent zeal for accuracy illustrates so clearly, of conceding authority over the scriptures to the teachers of another faith, was not lost on his successors, and early interest quickly turned to increasingly bitter hostility.[79] Andrew of St. Victor was accused of 'Judaizing' by his brother Victorine Richard, though Richard himself drew on the knowledge of Jewish scholars in his own work. By 1160 the immensely influential canonist Rufinus of Bologna had pronounced the Hebrew Bible corrupt and inferior to the Latin Vulgate, and the General Chapter of the Cistercian Order prohibited the study of Hebrew in 1198.[80]

The crucial question in the demonization of the Jews was whether or not those who crucified Christ knew that he was the son of God. The crucial step in resolving it was taken in the 1090s, when Anselm of Laon, despite Abelard's mockery the most influential teacher of his generation, broke away from the conclusion of St. Augustine, in the fifth century, almost unanimously accepted by subsequent Catholic commentators, that they had not.[81] Anselm's teaching that, on the contrary, they did know, was reiterated a few years later by the converted Spanish Jew Petrus Alfonsi.[82] From this it clearly followed that Jews must be the willing agents of the devil, as Anselm's friend and admirer Guibert of Nogent, writing in 1115, illustrated vividly with the first example of a story in which a Jew summoned his satanic master by making a libation of semen, which became one of the staple elements of medieval anti-Semitism, and later of the European witch craze.[83] In this, far more than in his intellectual work, Guibert was an original. The Jews of both sexes who appear repeatedly in his *Monodiae* as pimps and sorcerers, filthy, debauched and depraved, inaugurate the dreary and sinister stereotype which retained respectability in European discourse until the middle of the twentieth century. His identification of the Jew with sex, money, and excrement, always symbolically interchangeable with each other, was eagerly seized upon and rapidly and ineradicably established.[84] Major themes remained to be added. In the 1140s Peter the Venerable helped to round out the portrait of Jews as enemies of Christ by envisaging the foul indignities to which they might subject holy pictures and vessels entrusted to them in pawn (the chalice, as the container of the body of Christ, naturally figured especially prominently here), and a few years later Thomas of Monmouth manufactured from the unexplained death of a Christian boy just outside Norwich the first complete and grisly account – it would have more than one hundred and fifty medieval successors – of how international Jewry had conspired to avenge its secular history and temporal misery by re-enacting the crucifixion.[85] Such motifs continued to provide material for the creative faculties of theologians, draftsmen and fantasists for centuries to come, but the essentials were firmly in place, and in circulation, by the time the twelfth century was half over.

It remains difficult and indeed artifical to strike a balance between Guibert of Nogent and Stephen Harding – between the mounting vilification of Jews and Judaism during the twelfth century and the clear and solid evidence of material prosperity and cultural brilliance. As Beryl Smalley remarked, 'the works of the north French rabbis show us typically French, prosperous, middle-class people, who keep a rich table, set prudent limits to their families, in spite of the fertility rites of their weddings, lead respectable lives and practise their religion, are not intolerant and seldom saintly'.[86] In general Jews lived on good terms with their Christian neighbours. Residential segregation was by no means universal, though some cities, like Speyer under the charter quoted above, certainly had Jewish quarters. The Jews of Norwich are represented by Thomas of Monmouth as deciding that it would be too dangerous to dispose of William's body in the rented house in which they had murdered him because the next tenants might be Christians,[87] and even in the early thirteenth century Jews were taking new leases among Christians in York, as they began to return to the city which in 1190 had seen its entire Jewish community of one hundred and fifty people killed in the greatest single atrocity against them of the medieval period. As that itself suggests, the outrages which fell ever harder and more frequently on Jewish communities did not necessarily or immediately obliterate them. After the synagogue at Rouen had been burned by crusaders in 1096, and many Jews killed or forced to convert, the survivors were able to purchase from William Rufus the right of the forced converts to recant, to the virulent indignation of the monastic chroniclers, and to rebuild their synagogue in the most elegant and refined contemporary style.[88]

Nevertheless, at the same time the level of daily violence and harassment to which Jews were subject, especially in northern Europe, was rising steeply. Assaults on whole communities such as those associated with the First Crusade did become more common: the Count of Blois hanged thirty-one Jews on the pretext of ritual murder in 1171, though no body had been found, and Philip Augustus executed more than eighty at Bray-sur-Seine in 1191.[89] As both incidents suggest, Jews had more to fear from the political expedients of the mighty upon whose protection they normally depended than from popular animosity, but wherever Guibert and Thomas of Monmouth may have got their fantasies from – and indications have recently been found that stories of ritual murder were current in the Rhineland and the Low Countries in the 1140s, before Thomas went to work[90] – there is every reason to suppose that they circulated as rapidly and were seized on as readily in the twelfth century when malevolence or ill fortune attracted hostility towards the Jews as they have been ever since. Pope Alexander III found it necessary to add to the decrees of the Third Lateran Council in 1179 that Jews were not to be deprived of land, money or goods without judgement, their cemeteries were not to be invaded or violated, and their religious ceremonies not to be interrupted by assaults with sticks and stones. The problem was certainly not a new one. Complaints of such behaviour, often rationalized by accusations of blasphemy or mockery against Christian images or occasions, had been common enough for two hundred years and more, but it appears to have been increasing, and went on doing so despite the continuing insistence of the papacy that the acknowledged rights of Jews within the Christian community, restricted and grudgingly accorded as they were, must be respected.

Both the source of such vulnerability and its consequences, beyond the misery and physical danger which it entailed, were pinpointed with characteristic lucidity – and, we may think, more than a suspicion of sympathy – by the words which Abelard gave to the Jew in his *Dialogue* (*c*.1125): 'We are allowed to possess neither fields nor vineyards nor any landed estates because there is no one who can protect us from open or covert attack. Consequently, the principal gain that is left for us is that we sustain our hateful lives here by lending money at interest to strangers. But this only makes us more hateful to those who are being oppressed by it.'[91] The earlier chapters of this book have described in the former Carolingian Empire, especially of the later tenth and early eleventh centuries, a world in which those with neither substantial resources in land nor the physical protection which such resources alone could sustain were reduced to landlessness and servitude. Wherever they came from, and whatever their history in the post-Roman centuries – and many uncertainties in it remain – Jews in northern Europe unquestionably fell into that category. 'From being Roman citizens', in Dominique Iogna-Prat's words, 'they became "our Jews" (*Judaei nostri*), the possession of the lords on whose land they found themselves – castellans, counts or kings – one more kind of moveable property.'[92] In default of other protection they became utterly dependent on the kings and princes who successively wooed them, when their presence represented enhanced revenues from economic development and connections to international commerce, exploited them mercilessly when their dependence was secured, and got rid of them when their usefulness was at an end. The treaty which Philip II of France concluded with Count Theobald of Champagne (or, as he is described in this document, of Troyes) in 1198, setting out the terms on which he would readmit to the royal demesne the Jews who had been expelled in 1182, makes their situation very clear. 'We shall retain in our lands none of the Jews of our most beloved and faithful neighbour Theobald...none of our Jews will be permitted to lend money to anyone or seize anything in his lands unless with his consent...none of his Jews will be permitted to lend money to anyone or seize anything in our lands unless with our consent.'[93] That the debts owed to a Jew fell on his death to the King or Count, his master, was an increasingly lucrative source both of income and political power. The English crown, with the additional advantage of monopoly, had placed itself in a position to maximize the same benefits in 1194 by setting up the Exchequer for the Jews to administer the debts owed to Aaron of Lincoln, and subsequently to many others. In both kingdoms Jews were now to be exploited ever more ruthlessly until their final expulsion at the end of the thirteenth century. The progressive impoverishment which resulted, of course, further diminished their value to their royal masters, and with it the protection which they had usually been accorded against popular hostility aroused or intensified by the relationship itself.

Fundamental as this relationship was, it would not alone explain the sustained and increasingly successful vilification of the Jews as the agents of the devil working to undermine everything that sustained Christian society, which in the thirteenth century completed the stereotypes that persisted to become a central and indispensable element in European anti-Semitism. The cultural onslaught to which Jews and Judaism were subjected with mounting ferocity from the 1090s was essential to the construction of Latin Christendom, and to the cultural hegemony of the clerks within it. That is not to say, of course, that there was any conscious or deliberate conspiracy among the clerks, or that anybody intended or foresaw the results of the arguments which were placed in circulation in these years and the inferences that were drawn from them. Just as we have argued in earlier chapters that the division of lands and powers between elder and younger sons which entailed, in effect, the acceptance and endorsement of primogeniture in return for the generous endowment of a celibate church, was arrived at not consciously but through a multitude of individual decisions and settlements which tended in the same directions because they arose from the same difficulties and reconciled the same interests, so we suggest here that many arguments arising in different historical, theological, and ecclesiastical contexts and circumstances came to be accepted because they tended towards the construction of a powerful and coherent system of thought and worship which made for consistency and order in a rapidly changing and diversifying world. A particularly searching and illuminating account of one of the central contributions to that process has recently been offered by Dominique Iogna Prat, in his examination of how the monks of Cluny, whom we have encountered so often at critical moments of our revolution, assisted in the increasingly precise delineation of the social order by articulating and representing the fundamental distinctions between the secular and the spiritual, the free and the unfree, order and chaos, especially through their rule of chastity and their cult of the dead. The last of Cluny's great abbots, Peter the Venerable (1092 or 1094–1156), was one of the towering and in many ways most attractive figures of his time. In three powerful works of polemic, all composed in the late 1130s and early 1140s, against the oldest and potentially most dangerous enemies of the faith upon which it was founded, he completed the account of Europe's new social order which his predecessors, especially Odilo, had done so much to construct. Muslims, Jews and heretics all claimed to cherish the same God and follow the same scriptures as Catholic Christians – and claimed the same authority for different revelations and different teachings. Peter the Venerable's treatises against all three groups constituted not only a comprehensive rebuttal, from a Catholic point of view, but a formidably constructed rampart around the Christian community, presenting a bleak and uncompromising hostility to its real and imagined enemies.[94] Peter exemplifies our argument at innumerable points in his career and writings. Not the least important is that in the combination which he presents of high ability, great learning, profound spiritual sensitivity and still sensible charm on the one hand with, on the other, what appear to the modern eye as high authoritarianism, repellent intolerance and inhumanity, and an obvious subservience to the material interests of his order, he stands as an eloquent exemplar of the contradictions of his age and class.[95]

The depiction of Jews as objects of loathing and contempt, filthy and debased in their persons and demeanour, but wielding sinister power through their diabolic associations, served at least three distinct purposes. In the first place, the denigration of Judaism, its characterization as a source of heresy, idolatry and immorality, was one aspect of the general assault on older literate cultures with which the new clerical intelligentsia of Latin Christendom consolidated its own cultural hegemony. In this context, the attack on the Jews had a further advantage for those who conducted it, since it eliminated the most immediate and authoritative challenge to the authority of Christian masters in the exposition of the scriptures. In doing so, it also removed from the arena of competition for place and influence at the courts a potential elite much better qualified for that role by its mastery of the essential skills of literacy, numeracy and legal acumen than the Christian clerks who were so desperate to fill it. In the second place, the degradation and humiliation of Jews fulfilled the purpose that Mary Douglas detected in many systems of social classification which place great emphasis on the dangers of spiritual or sexual contamination arising from the breach of strictly defined social boundaries. Pollution fears, she pointed out, very commonly identify the danger represented by those whose real social power, because of the roles which they fill, is very great, while their status is very low.[96] As the commercialization of European society proceeded ever more hectically through the twelfth century those who could provide local credit and facilitate long-distance exchanges became ever more indispensable. It became correspondingly imperative to maintain social solidarity against them, and to keep them in their places by humiliation, degradation and terror. In this context the association between money and excrement so regularly pressed into the service of anti-semitism was pungently to the point.[97] Pollution fears of this kind are very apt to be directed against the untouchables who assist in the disposal of human wastes; here, money was the pollutant whose passage through the cisterns and conduits of Europe's proliferating markets enabled new wealth to grow and multiply.

Thirdly, and finally, the special intimacy imposed upon Jews and Christians by their shared inheritance and history, and by their long and uneasy coexistence, made the Jews fatally apt for a very special role in the enterprise upon which the clerks were engaged. Its nature was exactly described, in quite another context, by Max Weber, when he remarked that 'the great achievement of the ethical religions was to shatter the fetters of the kinship group [by establishing] a superior community of faith and a common ethical way of life in opposition to the community of blood, even to some extent in opposition to the family'[98] – and in doing so, to tear the world apart and build another in its place. Such work is not achieved by mere calculation. It requires passion and inner conviction, sacrifice far beyond the interests of those who make it, martyrdom. Certainly the clerks made reason – *ratio* – their banner, appropriated it as their warrant and placed it in opposition to the *superstitio* of the rustics as the foundation of their supremacy in the Christian community.[99] But that was only possible on the premise that both the community as a whole and the *literati* within it were united in adherence to a single faith. Unless faith and reason spoke with the same voice neither could provide a principle of unity: that is why the struggle to reconcile them lay at the centre of every great theological debate from Berengar to Aquinas, and why the claims of either could not be allowed to ride roughshod over the other.

It was also why the Jews could not be allowed to be reasonable. Nothing is more obvious, at the level of daily experience, than that Christians in these centuries rationalized and justified their treatment of Jews by projecting on to the Jews the intention of doing as they had been done by. Ever more regularly, especially after the massacres associated with the preparations for the crusade in 1096, Christians stole the property of Jews, murdered their wives and children, descrated their holy places and sacred objects, and forced them to renounce their faith on pain of death. They must therefore not only invent but persuade themselves to believe a mythology which accused the Jews of intending to do those things to them. In Shylock's words:

> O father Abram, what these Christians are,
> Whose own hard dealings teach them to suspect
> The thoughts of others![100]

The projection was necessary to assure the security of faith and intellect, not physical safety. Jews declined to accept the fundamentals of Christian revelation: the incarnation, the resurrection, the presence of the body and blood of Christ in the eucharist. They declined, of course, to accept the justification of these teachings which was arrived at by interpreting the Old Testament (as Christians called it) as a symbolic or allegorical prefiguring of the New. If such objections were conceded to be rational then faith and reason, for Christians, could not be reconciled: if they were valid for Jews they might be valid for anybody. By refusing to convert, therefore, Jews must be shown to deny not only faith, but reason; by denying reason, they excluded themselves from humanity; if they were not human, they could only be the spawn of the devil. The logic if not unavoidable was certainly inexorable, and by the middle of the twelfth century had been very generally accepted.[101]

Yet the obstacles which the fundamentals of Christian faith presented to Jews were by no means unknown to Christians themselves. On the contrary, the struggle with doubt is commonplace in the extensive religious literature of these generations. After all, as was pointed out often enough, there would have been no religious merit in faith in the obvious, and, we may add, no useful bonding or social classification would have followed from it. An Anselm of Canterbury might set himself to prove the existence of God by reason alone, serene in the certainty that it was reason, not God, that was being put to the test – for his famous proof – that since God is that than which nothing greater can be conceived, and since that which exists is greater than that which does not, God must exist – only proves that if there is a God he must be conceived as existing, or that he exists on the assumption that he is. An Abelard might announce that 'through doubting we are led to enquire; through enquiry we perceive the truth', confident that in his sure hand the sharp sword of dialectic would cut away only error and falsehood. But Anselm and Abelard would have been remarkable respectively for their spiritual and intellectual security in any age. Bernard's fear that 'mere human ingenuity is taking on itself to solve everything, and leave nothing to faith', that Abelard's teaching comprised 'not questions about the faith but wounds to the faith, injuries to Christ, insults and dishonours to the Fathers, the scandals of the present generation and the dangers of those to come'[102] was far more widely felt, and won the day. Peter the Venerable gave Abelard refuge at Cluny after Bernard had secured his condemnation as a heretic, at Sens in 1140 – and himself, five years later, quoted as a miracle a dream in which he was visited by the recently deceased Prior of his abbey, and took advantage of the visit to ask, not once but twice, a question which troubled him sorely, 'Is not what we believe about God certain? Is not the faith we hold true without any doubt?'[103]

The deepest mysteries of the Catholic faith as it was being worked out by three generations of its greatest teachers and visionaries – the divinity of Christ, the virgin birth, the miracle of the eucharist, the harmony of faith and reason – were precisely those which the Jews were represented as impugning in the most profound and most damaging accusations against them – that they had knowingly killed the son of God and regularly re-enacted it, that they profaned holy pictures of Christ and his mother, that they polluted the vessels in which bread and wine became his body and blood, in the miraculous sacrifice which Jews denied, and which was placed increasingly at the centre of Catholic faith, worship and passion. For some of the most influential and in later generations most admired of Christian thinkers it was even more difficult, and more painful, to apprehend these mysteries by faith than it was to describe them by reason. It was more than anywhere else in their relations with the Jews, and in their confrontation with Judaism, that the builders of the magnificent edifice of medieval Christianity betrayed the fragility of its emotional and psychological foundations, and the stresses which its construction had imposed upon its makers.

5
Order Restored

1 Pious and Inflexible Severity

Towards the end of 1165, the English chronicler William of Newburgh tells us, 'rather more than thirty' people who had come to England from Flanders were brought before a council of bishops at Oxford, and on being questioned 'attacked holy baptism, communion and matrimony, and wickedly dared to belittle the Catholic unity which is fostered by these divine aids'. They were denounced as heretics, and handed over to the king, at whose orders they were branded and whipped out of the city 'with ringing blows into the intolerable cold, for it was winter. Nobody showed the slightest mercy towards them (the king having strictly forbidden anybody to give them hospitality or any comfort) and they died in misery.'[1]

As William describes it this sect was typical of many which had appeared in northwestern Europe during the past century and a half in its anti-sacramental and antisacerdotal character and in the humble standing of its members, 'simple and illiterate people, quite uncultivated rustics' (except for their leader, Gerard, who 'seemed to have some degree of learning'). It was quite untypical of others we know of in the feebleness of its efforts at evangelism, which netted a single old woman who repudiated the sect the moment it was detected, and in the severity of the response it suffered. In the eleventh century those who were executed as heretics, at Orléans in 1022, Milan in 1028 and Goslar in 1051, had been members of the nobility and higher clergy caught up in political conflicts within the elite. Humble people, by and large, were dealt with calmly and with restraint by the bishops. Those interrogated by Gerard of Cambrai at Arras in 1024/5 confessed in effect to several grave heresies, but he released them after requiring no more than that they should listen to a long sermon and subscribe a confession of faith. Even by the 1140s, though executions, like the burnings at Soissons in 1115, Liège in 1135 and 1145, Cologne in 1143, and Reims in 1148, were becoming more frequent, they were still confined to the leaders of the groups accused, and to those who preached or were thought to preach heresy and sometimes violence against the church, its priests and property.

In this respect the 1160s saw a new and portentous development, reflected in the disquiet which was widely felt in 1163, when a young girl who refused to renounce her sect was burned at Cologne along with four adult men. They had been arrested after their failure to go to church on Sundays aroused the curiosity of their neighbours, while the unfortunates at Oxford 'could not hide for long, for they were tracked down by men anxious to know to what foreign sect they belonged'. In contrast to the great heretical preachers of the last generation, these people did not force themselves upon the attention of the authorities either by inciting violence or by preaching or seeking converts. They fell foul of the new spirit proclaimed by the Council of Reims in 1157, which had denounced 'the most wicked sect of the Manichees, who hide among the poor and under the appearance of religion labour to undermine the faith of the simple, spread by wretched weavers who move from place to place and often change their names, accompanied by "women weighed down with sin"'.[2] Anyone reputed to belong to this heresy was to be denounced and put to the ordeal. If they confessed or were convicted the leaders were to be imprisoned for life and their disciples to be branded on forehead or cheek. Any who refused to renounce the heresy would be excommunicated, and their goods forfeit. Six years later a Council at Tours, presided over by Pope Alexander III himself, addressed itself to 'a damnable heresy' which 'having emerged in the region of Toulouse spreads like a cancer to neighbouring regions and has now infected many people in Gascony and other provinces'. Reports of meetings or of shelter being given to heretics were to be promptly investigated, suspected adherents to be socially ostracized, commercially boycotted and handed over to the secular authorities for punishment.[3]

Whatever the historical accuracy of these assertions the tone is distinctly more melodramatic than that of earlier reports. It reveals what over the subsequent centuries has been the familiar premise of the persecutor. The appearance of 'heretics', irrespective of their number, demeanour or teachings, showed the existence of the malignant and diabolically inspired universal conspiracy of which they were part. If, on the other hand, the heretics did not make themselves visible it was not because they did not exist, but because they were cunningly concealed by numerous and probably influential supporters, which made it all the more urgent to expose and extirpate them, 'the danger being the greater the better they are hidden', as the Council of Tours put it. This is the language adopted by William of Newburgh, according to whom the heretics found at Oxford 'were believed to belong to the sect known as *Populicani*, who undoubtedly originated in Germany from an unknown founder and who have spread the poison of their wickedness through many lands. Indeed so many are said to have been infected by this plague throughout France, Spain, Germany and Italy that they seem, as the prophet says, "to have multiplied beyond number"'.

In this we see the movement on the part of authority from a reactive to an initiatory role which is regarded as a decisive moment in the transition from decentralized ('segmentary' in academic or 'tribal' in popular jargon) to centralized societies that we call state formation. The history of jurisprudence distinguishes between a conception of law and justice which confine themselves to a passive role, responding to conflict between individuals and groups, avenging injuries and resolving disputes which are reported to it, and an active, institution-building authority which seeks out offences on the assumption that they must have been committed, and invents crimes, such as blasphemy, fornication or treason, which are offences not against identifiable individuals but against the system of law itself and the authority and values which it claims to uphold. That distinction is clear in the prosecution, and persecution, of heresy. From the first appearances of popular heresy around the beginning of the eleventh century until the middle of the twelfth, the discovery of a pious conventicle in one place or the denunciation of clerical avarice in another were identified as heretical and reported to the bishop; he could do little but confront the accused and, if he found them guilty, expel them from his diocese or hand them – in many cases, it seems, with genuine reluctance – to the secular power for punishment. Henry II did not wait for the bishops to seek his help. After the heretics had been arrested he 'was unwilling either to release or to punish them without discussion, and ordered an episcopal synod to meet at Oxford...' Although no blood was shed, and no fire was lit, the result was the first mass execution of ordinary people on charges of heresy in the history of modern Europe.

The role of the papacy in these initiatives was a modest one. In 1163, during the preparations for the Council of Tours over which he presided, Pope Alexander III received certain citizens of Arras who had been accused by the Archbishop Henry of Reims and his brother King Louis VII of France of having fallen into the errors of the Manichees and belonging to the sect of the *populicani*.[4] That they were not negligible people is attested equally by their offer of six hundred marks to the Archbishop to drop the case, and their determination to secure justice at the papal court when he refused. The papacy at this time was in schism. Alexander was in France because Italy was firmly under the control of the Emperor, Frederick Barbarossa, following the surrender of Milan to his armies in 1162, and Rome was securely in the hands of the antipope. The Council at Tours was intended to rally Alexander's supporters against Barbarossa, who in turn was pressing Louis VII hard to withdraw his protection and recognition from Alexander. The Pope's evident scepticism of the accusations against the alleged 'Manichees' of Reims, despite the precariousness of his diplomatic situation, completes the impression clearly conveyed by a fragmentary handful of letters about the case that this was essentially a political rather than a religious affair. In preparing for this Council Alexander III was equally in need of the cooperation of another royal son of the church, and one less dutiful than Louis VII. Tours was one of Henry II's favourite cities, and (in marked contrast to his predecessor Stephen, who had forbidden English bishops to attend the Council of Reims in 1148) he sent an imposing delegation of obedient prelates. There is no direct evidence, of course, that he wished to influence the deliberations of the Council, or that his advice would have been swayed by anything but the purest anxiety for the spiritual welfare of his subjects. Nevertheless, it was a convenient coincidence that the Council took place at a period when Henry was much exercised to enhance his control over those very provinces of Aquitaine and Gascony through which, according to the assembled dignitaries, the 'new heresy' was 'spreading like a cancer'.

Soon after the trial at Oxford Henry II, in his Assize of Clarendon (1166), forbade 'anyone in all England to receive in his house or in his land or any area over which he has jurisdiction anyone of that sect who were branded and excommunicated at Oxford . . . And if anyone shall so receive them he shall be at the mercy of the lord king, and the house in which they have dwelt shall be carried outside the village and burned.'[5] This decree is famous as the first secular legislation against heresy in the west since antiquity, and the forerunner of a series of similar acts by other European monarchs in the following decades. But not even the purest religious fervour would provide a wholly satisfactory explanation of why Henry should have thought it necessary to act with such severity against heretics who were already dead and had made no converts. One possibility, no doubt, is that Henry 'knew' from the experience of his continental lands, as described by the Council of Tours, how rapidly heresy might spread, and was determined that it should not do so in England – although, as it happens, no other evidence survives of any case of heresy in Henry's continental lands in the previous twenty years. William of Newburgh's comments on this point might serve very well for any collection of texts designed to illustrate the general conviction of the English that providence has granted them immunity from so many of the evils associated with the continental mainland. Another possibility is that the episode at Oxford provided Henry with a welcome opportunity simultaneously to proclaim his Catholic piety at a dramatic moment in his quarrel with Archbishop Becket, and to make a vigorous demonstration of the range and extent of his power.

Whatever Henry's conscious motives may have been, however, what William calls 'his pious and inflexible severity' at Oxford and in subsequent legislation provides a classic example of a technique very commonly associated with the extension of the power of the state, namely the invention or exaggeration of a danger to the 'common good'. Like Philip II's treatment of 'his' Jews and the legislation of both these monarchs against prostitution in their capital cities, action against heresy, real or alleged, fitted very well into their ambitions for the aggrandizement of their realms and the extension of their power over an ever-greater range of their subjects' activities and concerns. Certainly they found it so when Count Raymond V of Toulouse, himself in need of a weapon against the pressure of the elected consuls of the city of Toulouse to secure their independence from his officers, made his own use of the language of contamination in a famous letter to the chapter-general of Citeaux in 1177, in which he described the ravages wrought upon his lands by the heretics, and the unwillingness of his greatest vassals to raise their swords against it, adding that he had already appealed for help to his lord, the king of France.[6]

In the following year Pope Alexander III dispatched a mission to extirpate heresy from Toulouse, headed by his legate Cardinal Peter of St Chrysogono and Henry, Abbot of Clairvaux, and supported by both Louis VII and Henry II, who had recently made peace. The citizens of Toulouse were not disposed to be helpful in identifying the heretics until 'the bishop and certain of the clergy, the consuls of the city and some other faithful men who had not been touched by any rumour of heresy were made to give us in writing the names of everyone they knew who had been or might in future become members or accomplices of the heresy, and to leave out nobody at all for love or money'.[7] On this basis the legation confronted a wealthy merchant and consul of the city, Pierre Maurand, who was exposed as a leading heretic, subjected to public scourging and confession, deprived of his possessions, required to raze to its foundations one of his towers in the city, and sent on pilgrimage to the Holy Land. The humiliation of Maurand in turn led to the denunciation of many more heretics in and around the city. The victory was pressed home by dividing the legation so that Henry of Clairvaux and Reginald of Bath could pass through the diocese of Albi on their way home, to secure the release of the incarcerated Bishop and accumulate further evidence for the growing dossier on Roger Trencavel, vicomte of Béziers, as a protector of heretics.

The mission of 1178 and its aftermath provide a remarkably complete vignette of the new regime that was taking shape in western Europe. The motives of Raymond V in inviting intervention are uncertain. The region had long been receptive to itinerant preachers, as St Bernard had been reminded in his struggle against the influence of Henry of Lausanne there, in 1145, and it seems likely that by the 1160s there were among them some who had picked up the Cathar (dualist) doctrines which had begun to emerge in the Rhineland and Flanders during the previous twenty years or so.[8] It is possible that Raymond was really worried by their activity, or that he hoped to use them as a pretext to bear down on his greatest rival, Roger Trencavel, vicomte of Béziers, or on the citizens of Toulouse itself, who were increasingly asserting their independence of comital authority.[9] Alternatively, he may have thought that if he could not stave off the excuse for intervention in his lands which the reports of heresy gave to his overlords he had better preserve what independence he could by taking the lead. In any case, his letter unleashed a series of events which destroyed his house, and exposed a region of distinctive social and cultural identity to a sustained and ruthless process of conquest and assimilation. It is impossible to say to what extent anticipation of that prospect accounts for the rare but striking example which the mission displayed of cooperation between the leading and usually dissonant political powers of the day (the Emperor excepted), the papacy and the kings of France and England, rival claimants to the overlordship of Toulouse. It is certainly striking that the clerks of Henry II, so expert at devising and advertising sinister threats to public safety which must be averted by his assumption of new and sweeping powers, had been promoting exaggerated claims about the prevalence of heresy in the Languedoc since the Council of Tours, and ironic that in the long run it was not the Angevin but the Capetian house which reaped the fruits.

The reports of the legates provided the basis for further legislation for the repression of heresy at the Lateran Council of 1179 and led directly to the dispatch of another legation to the Languedoc under Henry of Clairvaux in 1181, setting in train an apparently inexorable succession of crises and confrontations between the Counts of Toulouse, caught between the rapidly growing wealth and vigour of their capital city and the turbulent independence of their correspondingly disgruntled feudatories on the one hand, and on the other a Latin Christendom, headed by an increasingly energetic papacy (especially after the accession of Innocent III in 1198) and a French monarchy increasingly determined to realize its claims to sovereignty, and (especially after the conquest of Normandy from the Angevins in 1204) increasingly capable of doing so.

The growing reputation of Toulouse as a nest of heresy, in whatever proportions responsibility for it is to be divided between reality and propaganda, provided a heaven-sent justification (bearing in mind that God helps those who help themselves) for the invasion and conquest of the Languedoc in the savage wars of the Albigensian crusade (1209–29), the establishment of the Dominican inquisition in Toulouse in 1233, and the incorporation of the county of Toulouse into the kingdom of France in the decades that followed.[10] That is not to say, of course, that these developments were planned, or foreseen, at the time. The army which was unleashed upon the Languedoc by Pope Innocent III was led by a Frenchman, Simon de Montfort, and largely recruited from northern France. But Philip Augustus declined to participate, to allow his son to join the crusade in 1213, or even after his enemies had been scattered and his position as the strongest monarch in western Christendom triumphantly confirmed at Bouvines in the following year, to allow the monarchy to become directly or closely involved. That happened only in 1226, when the southern cause had gone a long way towards recovery, and only after Louis VIII had effectively secured the withdrawal of the papacy from direction of the affair, but when it happened it was decisive. In 1229 the Treaty of Paris required Count Raymond VII of Toulouse to renounce the greater part of his father's lands, and his daughter Jeanne was given into the custody of Louis IX, and in 1236 married to Louis' son Alphonse of Poitiers, who thus inherited the county on Raymond's death in 1249. Since Alphonse and Jeanne were childless it passed directly into the hands of the crown when they died, in 1271. Nor was a ready-made apparatus of repression waiting to be put in place, as Protestant writers ever since the Reformation have been prone to imagine. The Dominicans who were appointed by Pope Gregory in 1233 'to make inquisition of heretical depravity' in Toulouse and Carcassonne (as had one of their brethren in Regensberg two years previously) faced a long struggle and many reverses before the Cathar and Waldensian heresies petered out in the fourteenth century. But in the course of it, as the latest in the long time of brilliant investigators to have been inspired by their terrible history and remarkable archives, James Given, has recently demonstrated, they contributed much to the emerging technology of government by the penetration of communities – as indeed did the villagers of the Languedoc to the techniques of resistance.[11]

2   The Pursuit of Monopoly

In the story of *Tristan and Isolde*, as told by Gottfried von Strassburg, Isolde's husband Mark, increasingly suspicious of her relationship with

Tristan and egged on by jealous courtiers, demands that she should clear herself by the ordeal of the red-hot iron. Isolde agrees, and tells Tristan to wait by the shore at Caerleon disguised as a pilgrim, when she arrives there for the ordeal. On arrival she asks to be carried ashore by the pilgrim, on the ground that at such a time 'she was averse to being carried by a knight'. As they reach shore Tristan stumbles, at Isolde's suggestion, and rolls over with her in his arms. She then, after drawing everybody's attention to the incident, affirms with the hot iron the oath 'that no man in the world had carnal knowledge of me or lay in my arms or beside me but you [Mark], always excepting the poor pilgrim who, with your own eyes, you saw lying in my arms' and, 'in the name of God she laid hold of the iron, carried it and was not burned'.[12]

'Thus it was made manifest and confirmed to all the world,' comments Gottfried (*c*.1220), 'that Christ in his great virtue is as pliant as a windblown sleeve'. That is the sort of thing that clerks had been saying for decades about trial by ordeal, which was effectively abolished when the Lateran Council in 1215 forbade priests to perform the prayers and blessing that were an essential preliminary, deriding it as a barbarous and superstitious practice, which must give way to rational procedure. Posterity has agreed. In the words of one of the greatest of modern medievalists, 'by 1215 the essential steps had been taken in making human justice and government an affair subject to human rules and dependent on the efficacy of human agents'.[13] But in a now famous essay Peter Brown has shown that the ordeal was not just a primitive equivalent of tossing a coin. It was governed by elaborate ritual and careful procedures which created and defined an interlude before 'the judgement of God' was tested – the three days, for example, before the unbandaging of the hand which had grasped the hot iron in one of the most used ordeals. In this time the community could thresh out its view of the affair. The outcome itself – whether the wound had healed cleanly or was beginning to fester, whether the water had 'received' the body cast into it – was not objectively inescapable, but ambiguous and very much open to the interpretation of the onlookers. Hence 'the judgement of God' would enable those who at first had differed to embrace the collective verdict.[14]

This is why ordeals of one sort or another had figured so prominently in the mobilizing of popular sentiment which we have seen as indispensable to the overthrow of the old order.[15] The problem, of course, was that it cut both ways, as Brown illustrated by recalling the occasion when William Rufus was informed by an Anglo-Saxon jury that the hands of men who had chosen the hot iron to defend themselves against the charge of poaching deer from his forest had healed with no sign of putrefaction and burst out, 'Is God a just judge? Damn whoever thinks

it! You shall be judged by my just judgement and not by God's!' Char-
acteristically, his sentiments were just those of our *clerici*, though somewhat more forcefully expressed than they generally found prudent.

This is another and important example of how as the new regime
settled into place it was confronted by the necessity of forcing back into
the bottle the genie of popular power whose release had been necessary
to oust its predecessor. The removal of jurisdiction from the community
to the officials or representatives of central authority is widely recognized as a critical step in the assertion of 'the monopoly of legitimate
violence' which for Max Weber defined the state, or, to put it more
generally, in the centralization of power in increasingly hierarchical
polities. In twelfth-century Europe this was necessary in respect of
spiritual as well as secular matters, since there was in fact, as we have
seen repeatedly, no clear distinction between the two. The abolition of
trial by ordeal, condemned as a supersition because it provided a
mechanism through which royal or ecclesiastical policy might be
thwarted by what a modern lawyer would call a perverse verdict, was
one example of it. The canonization of saints, commonly achieved by
popular acclaim in the tenth and eleventh centuries to the discomfort of
many churchmen, was gradually brought back under ecclesiastical and
specifically papal authority by similar stages. Bishops increasingly
sought papal approval for canonizations – in six cases at the Council
of Tours in 1163 – and the protocol was formalised at the Third Lateran
Council in 1179, and again in 1184 at Verona (when the most sweeping
measures to date against heresy were also approved in the bull *ad
abolendam*); in 1234 the power was reserved entirely to the papacy.[16]
The same development, in which the shift of authority from the bishop
to the papacy tends to conceal their common and more fundamental
determination to remove it from popular hands, is visible in dealing with
heresy. On most occasions when heretics were tried up to the middle of
the twelfth century the examination was conducted in public, and the
accused were required to support their assertions of innocence by oath
or by ordeal, which meant in effect by appeal to public opinion; on the
few occasions when the accused were examined privately, in the presence only of officials, they were not required – or allowed – to vouch for
themselves in that way. The tension between the centralizing justice of
the clerks and the traditional procedures of the community became
painfully evident when, as at Soissons in 1112 or at Cologne in 1143,
the clergy tried to hold people who had been convicted by the traditional
method for further interrogation, or to await direction from higher
authority as to what should be done with them. That was when the
community took matters into its own hands and burned the accused, not
necessarily because they hated heresy or even heretics as such, but in

defence of their own jurisdiction against the encroachment of the outside world.[17] By the 1160s the fact that questions of faith and doctrine were still treated in the Languedoc as matters for public debate was in itself regarded by outsiders as a matter for scandal contributing to the growing sense of a need for a war against heresy, as we may see from the account of Roger of Howden (a former clerk of the English royal chancery) of the meeting held at Lombers in 1165, when the bishops of the region sought in vain to deprive the heretics of their aristocratic patronage. A similar sense of being improperly forced into the public arena is betrayed by the indignation of the legate Peter of St Chrysogono at Toulouse, in 1178, in being forced not only to debate with the representatives of the heretics in public, under safe conduct, but to do so in the vernacular because 'when one of them tried to speak in Latin he could hardly string two words together'.[18]

In 1024 Gerard of Cambrai had made no demur when suspects whom he arraigned at Arras refused to sign a confession of faith until it had been translated because they could not understand the Latin in which it was drafted.[19] The clash of cultures, north and south, Catholic and anticlerical, which is painfully evident in the approach to the Albigensian crusade arose in large part from the fact that towards the end of the twelfth century the south had not progressed, if that is the right word, so far along the road of centralization and modernization which had transformed the north since Gerard of Cambrai's time. Malcolm Barber has noticed the general resemblance of the social and political conditions of the Languedoc at the end of the twelfth century to those in northern France or Normandy at the end of the eleventh, pointing particularly to the lawlessness associated with the presence of a large number of young men possessing military skills and training but no land or expectation of it, and an impoverished and unreformed church whose efforts to secure the endowments necessary to support its activities exposed it to the imputation of corruption and avarice.[20] The Languedoc, like Gerald of Wales' Ireland, had not yet undergone the First European Revolution.

It was no accident, then, that accusations of heresy and the alleged necessity of rooting it out were both the pretext and the occasion of the confrontation which took place so dramatically at Toulouse in 1178. The demeanour and appeal – including the anticlericalism – of Cathar preachers, who were widely present, and widely welcomed, in the region by this time were very similar to those of the hermit-preachers like Robert of Arbrissel, Vitalis of Mortain or Norbert of Xanten who had been so influential in northern France and the Low Countries a hundred years and less before. In the one region as in the other, rapid social change and the tensions and conflicts to which it gave rise conferred great influence on those who could separate themselves from the corruption of the world – power and sex – through their personal austerity, forswearing property and embracing chastity with spectacular fervour, advertising above all that they owed their authority not to an episcopacy enmired in the world, but to popular approbation of their holiness of life.[21] As Bernard of Tiron had said in the 1090s when challenged by the archdeacon of Coutances (accompanied by his wife and children) to say by what right he denounced the clergy of the diocese, 'A preacher of the church ought to be dead to the world…he earns the right to preach by virtue of his mortification'.[22] The phrase that he used, *licentiam praedicandi*, referred explicitly to the bishop's licence, the right to grant which was, in canon law, exclusively his prerogative. It was precisely the refusal of Valdès of Lyons to bow to this claim, in 1181, which caused him and his followers to be denounced as heretics. The issue was absolutely central to the entire reconstruction of the western church, and of western society, in the twelfth century: either the bishop exercised the right to declare who could preach, who could teach and who was a heretic, or those rights would continue to be vested in the community, as they had been in fact though not in principle in the tenth- and eleventh-century west. In secular terms, to return to what remains an essentially anachronistic distinction, the issue was the same. Justice belonged either to the neighbourhood or to the lord; either to the little community of custom, tradition and face-to-face authority, or to the large one of written law, literacy and the clerks.

The events of 1178 in Toulouse make abundantly clear not only the nature of this elemental conflict, but how and with what weapons it was resolved. The formidable unity and cohesiveness which the culture of the clerks had now attained was displayed in the personnel of the visiting party. It reflected the division as well as the distribution of political authority in Latin Christendom: a high theorist might have been as struck by the absence of a representative of the Empire as by the presence of those of the sponsors of the mission, France, the Angevin Empire and the Papacy. But, at least if gifted with hindsight, our theorist might also have reflected that the composition of the party as well as its outcome suggested rather strongly that the division of sovereignty, in principle, between the two swords of secular and spiritual authority and between the many claimants to the secular sword, was in many ways of much less practical significance than the development of a single clerical-administrative class. Peter of Pavia, Cardinal of St Chrysogono, Alexander III's long-standing legate in France, had brought about a reconciliation between Louis VII and Henry II the previous autumn, inspired by the prospect of this joint action in defence of the faith. As Abbot of Clairvaux Henry de Marcy was the successor of St Bernard, who in 1145 had himself led a celebrated but only partially successful preaching mission against heresy in this region. Henry and his order continued to spearhead both the collection and editing of evidence of heretical activity in the region[23] and the campaign against it. The assassination of another Cistercian, the papal legate Peter of Castelnau, in 1208, would provide the final pretext for launching the Albigensian crusade, which was led, as papal legate, by the head of the order, Arnold Amalric of Citeaux. Among the other members of the party, Archbishop Guarin of Bourges was also a Cistercian and John de Belles-mains, bishop of Poitiers since 1162 and formerly treasurer of York, was a product of the brilliant household of Archbishop Theobald of Canterbury: it was said that as a young man he had made a pact of mutual support and advancement with two of his fellow clerks there, Roger Pont l'Evêque, now Archbishop of York, and Thomas Becket. A few years later, it was John, as Archbishop of Lyons, whose withdrawal of the licence to preach forced Valdès and his followers, who had been supported by John's predecessor as Archbishop, Guichard of Pontigny, to choose between silence and excommunication. Reginald Fitzjocelin, Bishop of Bath, the son of Bishop Jocelin de Bohun of Salisbury, sprang from one of the leading Anglo-Norman curial dynasties, and had been in Becket's household in the early 1160s, and active at the royal court ever since. The composition of the legation not only underlines the common culture and outlook of the men who increasingly did the day-to-day work of governing Europe, but the extent to which movement between the courts of Latin Christendom, both secular and ecclesiastical, had become commonplace. Hence the comfort and sure-footedness with which its members worked in harness, not only hitting upon procedures effective for the task of imposing their will upon a well-integrated, vigorous and hostile community (though one not without acute internal tensions and divisions which they were able to exploit), but maintaining political leverage on their host Raymond of Toulouse, himself under considerable countervailing pressure from his restive subjects. They also produced substantial reports from the pens of two of their number, which not only helped to secure the immediate consequences mentioned above, but for the greater part of the following eight centuries sustained their and their masters' reputations for a disinterested regard for public safety.

The device of demanding denunciations by which the legate broke down resistance in Toulouse – putting the leading members of a neighbourhood or community on oath to provide information to the representatives of central government – was the *inquisitio*, a classic procedure of Roman law which had become one of the most flexible and adaptable instruments of twelfth-century government. It had been pioneered with particular precocity in England, providing the basis of William I's Domesday survey and the spearhead of the legal reforms promulgated by Henry II in his Assizes of Clarendon (1166) and Northampton (1176). Its use greatly enhanced that king's reputation as a giver of justice, and helped to undermine the private jurisdiction of his greatest subjects. As former clerks of the royal household, Reginald of Bath and John of Poitiers would have been very familiar with those developments. In a multitude of aspects the inquisition, or inquest – words which, ironically, have developed quite different connotations in our legal and political vocabulary – was a principle central to the entire institutional development of the period, especially through its power, which this episode illustrated so dramatically, to break through the carapace of instinctive solidarity which almost any community, large or small, would instinctively present to the representatives of external authority.

If any single aspect of the twelfth century revolution in government was of decisive importance for the future it was the capacity developed by both secular and ecclesiastical powers to penetrate communities of every kind vigorously and ruthlessly, overriding the restraints of custom, and enlisting, or destroying, men of local standing and influence in the name of order, orthodoxy and reform. We must not, of course, exaggerate either the rapidity or the uniformity of such development: even the Capetian monarchy, as we have seen, though it was learning to wield a formidable degree of power over its subjects in the reign of Philip Augustus, multiplied learned servants and administrative devices far less rapidly and prolifically than its Angevin rivals – if only because a more compact territory and a smaller reliance on mercenary soldiers meant that it had far less need to. If our twelfth-century sources resonate with scornful denunciations of the guile, greed and corruption of the papal court it was largely because, lacking any secure or regular means of assuring an income at a time when demands on it were increasing at every turn, the papacy was largely dependent on the more or less voluntary donations represented by an array of 'customary' payments from various parts of Christendom, on payment for its judicial services, and (when it had access to them) on the profits of tourism to Rome itself. The long history of schism, exile and rebellion in the twelfth century meant that though the popes were always in desperate need of money, and though they steadily and determinedly extended the scope and thoroughness of their jurisdiction and increased the number and variety of those who came to Rome to seek it, it was not until Clement III secured a durable accommodation with the Roman Senate in 1188 that the lasting subordination of the papal patrimony and the systematic reorganization of its revenues could begin.[24]

In secular government the reliance of kings on the traditional council and service of their great vassals is almost everywhere far more obvious than the early signs of incipient bureaucracy. Nevertheless, as Karl

Leyser pointed out, by the third quarter of the century the indications are very widespread of a 'penetrating fiscality' borne by royal agents whose own fortunes depended on their ability to exploit and if necessary abuse the powers of their masters by means of growingly effective local intervention and investigation. Examples are to be found not only where monarchy was relatively strong, as in Sicily or Aragon, but even in the Empire, where though consistent recording is lacking Frederick Barbarossa frequently used the device of inquisition to protect local rights against encroachment, and his peace legislation to get report-backs from his judges.[25] If further reminder were needed that this culture of increasingly vigorous and pervasive interaction between centre and locality for the aggrandizement of lordship was not confined to the territories which nineteenth-century historians hailed as the progenitors of their own nation states it might be provided by Raymond VII of Toulouse. Immediately after the Peace of Paris he set about reasserting his authority and increasing his revenues in his greatly diminished but still substantial domain, demanding the right to appoint the consuls of Toulouse, extending his judicial authority, and founding numerous bastides. 'Ultimately,' as Given remarks, 'all of Raimond's efforts served to enrich the French monarchy... but this should not blind us to the very real success that he enjoyed in laying the groundwork for a strong territorial principality'.[26] Nor should it blind us to the very real success of those who knew how to turn literacy and numeracy into power and money in finding ever more scope for their abilities in the rich variety of political and cultural environments that Europe, still in its infancy, would have to offer.

3 The Community of the Faithful

To establish themselves as the effective ruling elite of Latin Christendom (the division of formal authority among so many titular sovereigns notwithstanding) and ensure that their power would reign supreme, it was necessary for the clerks to complete a dual process of exclusion, removing both warriors and peasants from the political arena. As so often in this argument, it is necessary to emphasize that in using such language we do not imply any conscious strategy or collusion, only that men similarly educated and similarly situated, with similar interests and similar opportunities, naturally tended to make similar recommendations to their masters, and to support and reinforce one another's efforts.

The attack on the little community which is seen at its most brutal and direct in the persecution of heresy was also being vigorously carried forward in the Angevin kingdom from the 1160s and 1170s in Henry

II's drive for 'law and order' for which the anarchy of his predecessor Stephen's reign provided some justification and limitless excuse, and with similar energy in the French kingdom from the accession of Philip Augustus in 1180. The excommunication in 1182 of Valdès and his followers by John de Belles-mains, now archbishop of Lyons, upon their refusal to undertake not to preach without licence was an important local sign – but in the context also much more than a local sign – of growing determination to bear down on unauthorized preaching. It was generalized in 1184 by the decree *ad abolendam*, issued at Verona jointly by Pope Alexander III and Frederick Barbarossa, which condemned, in addition to a lengthy list of named heresies, all who preached without the authority of the bishop of the diocese or the Holy See, or who protected or gave shelter to heretics. Finally, Pope Innocent III summoned at the Lateran in 1215 the largest and most comprehensive Council of the church up to that time, more than 400 bishops and 800 abbots and other senior prelates, as well as representatives of the eastern churches. The decrees of Lateran IV set forth a sweeping programme which drew upon and synthesized the intellectual, administrative and pastoral developments of the tumultuous century and a half since the Gregorian reforms. They provide yet another example, and one of the most successful, of the systematization which was the central characteristic of this age and culture, laying down with lucid precision the foundations and framework for the government of the church and much of European life for the rest of the middle ages and beyond. The dominant note was sounded by the first canon, which laid down a new creed, worded specifically to rebut the heresies which were thought to have multiplied over the previous half century, and to incorporate the sacramental theology which had evolved so rapidly during the same period.

It is easier to make law than to enforce it, and for the rest of the middle ages church history, at every level, might almost be described as a long and often unavailing attempt to put the decrees of Lateran IV into practice. Nevertheless, to whatever extent they represent aspiration rather than reality, from 1215 onwards our sources describe an entirely different world – a world pervaded and increasingly moulded by the well-drilled piety and obedience associated with the traditional vision of 'the age of faith', or of medieval Christianity. All the practices and rituals which we have encountered as mechanisms for the articulation and expression of communal sentiment were firmly suppressed. Priests were forbidden to perform the rituals which preceded the ordeal. Preachers and holy men were ruthlessly subordinated to episcopal authority. Canonization was conferred by ecclesiastical process instead of popular acclaim; miracles (already superstition to Guibert of Nogent when acclaimed by the people rather than ecclesiastical authority[27]) were confined to properly supervised shrines; and shrines themselves were orchestrated and ranked from village upward to mirror and affirm the new order which was regularly proclaimed and renewed by the pilgrimages that had become the universal means of articulating, expressing and reproducing at every level the faith which sustained it.

The cornerstone of all this was the parochial system, and the authority or influence of the parish priest, under the bishop. To him, at least once every year, before Easter, every Christian of either sex who had reached the age of discretion must make confession of all their sins and perform the prescribed penance before receiving the eucharist, on pain of excommunication and denial of Christian burial. The parish, now more than ever the centre of communal life and the place where every significant transition in the social life of every individual was enacted and marked, was, while it was many other things besides, the Church's answer to heresy. But, when viewed from above, the parish and even the parish priest had a murky past, as we saw in Chapter 2, and in many places had already assumed its place all too securely at the centre of the community. If it was the counterpart, as a focus of communal loyalty and support, of the heretical sect, it was often in the following century, under the provisions of Lateran IV, treated in very much the same way. The most energetic bishops and those most in touch with current thinking and (in the sinister phrase of their late twentieth-century counterparts) 'best practice', men like Archbishop Eudes of Rouen or Bishop Robert Grosseteste of Lincoln set out, full of zeal and sincerity, to eradicate ignorance and corruption among their parish priests by regular visitation and inquisition. Sometimes it seems that they were not much more different in spirit than were the inquests they conducted in method from those which inquisitors like Peter Martyr in Lombardy or Jacques Fournier in the Ariège brought to the pursuit of heresy.

Definition implies exclusion, and had done so increasingly thoroughly over the past century. Beyond the rising fear of heretics and Jews, signs of nervousness multiplied among the privileged as they contemplated, more or less consciously, the condition of those whom they had subordinated. A famous example is the nightmare of Henry I of England in which the three orders of society appeared, protesting about high taxation, and led by the peasants armed with scythes and forks: their protest was vindicated by higher authority when the king was caught in a storm at sea which abated only when he promised to remit the geld for seven years.[28] Such anxieties are classically represented by the imagery of pollution or contamination, the breaching of hygienic or sexual boundaries which are perceived as fundamental to the social order. The assertions of sexual promiscuity, massive genital endowment and skill in seduction which are routinely associated with heretics and Jews from the late twelfth century onwards offer an obvious example. From around the same time another anxiety is even more pervasive – the fear of leprosy, which in many societies has been seen to embody untouchability in its most graphic form. Leprosy was regarded as the physical counterpart of heresy, and when first asserted, around the turn of the tenth and eleventh centuries, seems to have been used in much the same way, as a means of suggesting that occupants of high office were unfit for it. By the early twelfth century anxiety about the contagion of leprosy among the population at large was rising fast, and by the 1160s the bishop of Exeter was forbidding lepers to walk the streets of the city. Soon after Lateran IV the full panoply of exclusion was in place. Lepers were not only segregated everywhere as outcasts (the most fortunate in the leprosaria which had proliferated in the last three-quarters of a century), but like heretics and Jews deprived of the right to give evidence in court and to dispose of their property, and in many places required to undergo a formal ritual modelled on that of burial. It is generally thought that these concerns and restrictions were responses to an epidemic of leprosy (Hansen's disease) which had been dormant in western Europe since the seventh century but reappeared in the eleventh and spread very rapidly in the twelfth, reaching a peak around 1250. This may be the case, although it is undermined by the absence of physical evidence from any excavated cemetery of the period less marginal than that at Naestved, in Denmark, in the form of bones which carry the distinctive erosion produced in the advanced stages of the disease. But the perception that leprosy was spreading in the population and especially among the poor, whether founded on a correct medical diagnosis or not, provided a powerful and adaptable metaphor of social exclusion, and of the danger represented by a potentially disaffected population, as the language used of the disease and its symptoms made clear. Leprosy would appear suddenly and unpredictably, after lurking undetected for a long time underground, and once present might move rapidly from place to place; it was disseminated by poisonous air, such as that exhaled by heretical preachers, as well (of course) as by sexual intercourse; it made its victims not only sexually voracious but importunate, dissatisfied with their lot, prone to gossip and to interfere in other people's business. In short, it both arose from and threatened to extend the breach of established social boundaries, and could be controlled only by entrenching and enforcing those boundaries with constant vigilance.[29]

William of Newburgh's description of the heresy destroyed at Oxford in 1165 is laden with the image of leprosy, to which the Council of Tours had also referred. This imagery was not new in the description of heretics and the threat which they represented, but it was used here more systematically, and from this time forward more frequently, than formerly, reflecting a more sinister and less rational analysis of both conditions. As with the Jews, the rhetoric of demonization represents those who are to be persecuted as not only inspired by the devil, but often directly in communication with him. Thus a single account was formed of the victim as enemy of God and society which might be transferred at will to any object, either a class of persons already existing, such as Jews, or a new one created by an act of classification, such as sodomites (another category newly defined in the second half of the twelfth century) or witches. The model was to a considerable extent self-fuelling and self-fulfilling. Those who were cast for persecution were depicted not only as the enemies of God and the family, but as outsiders, bereft of social ties and obligations, often rootless and wandering people, dirty, diseased and desperate – in short, as exemplifying the condition to which ostracism and persecution must eventually reduce them, whatever their initial vigour or prosperity.[30]

The marginalization of the warrior aristocracy was of necessity a much subtler and less complete process than that of the poor. Its members continued throughout the ancien régime to exercise great power – in many places and at many times absolute power – within their own extensive territories, and to command the highest social prestige and all that went with it. Even in the twelfth and thirteenth centuries the distinction between kings and great nobles, and even that between greater and lesser nobles, is a tenuous one from the point of view of the present argument, since by the thirteenth century even relatively modest households in many parts of Europe contained their quota of knights and clerks to bring the same skills and dedication to the enlargement of the incomes and the extension of the power of these lords that their counterparts did to those of princes and prelates. It would be quite wrong to think of the new regime, or the new culture of purposeful administration which sustained it, as being the prerogative of those who may be recognized in retrospect as 'state builders'. On the contrary, that it steadily permeated European society at every level must be the chief sign of its success and the principal reason for its continuing vitality. Nevertheless, the nobles were the chief losers by the long and unrelenting assimilation of power to the institutions of the state. The rhetoric of chivalry and holy war may or may not have distracted the members of the military aristocracy as effectively as it sometimes has their historians from the simple fact of their marginalization during the twelfth and thirteenth centuries. It would obviously be a foolish exaggeration to claim that military power was definitively placed under civilian control at this time. But equally obviously the monopoly of the warrior class was removed from it, and assumed not so much by sovereigns as by their servants, who despite the titular fragmentation of power constituted in effect a single regime, rooted in a single culture, and single-mindedly dedicated to the expansion and perfection of the organs of central power. Michael Clanchy illustrates this with a vivid story from the end of the thirteenth century, when one of the great magnates of the English kingdom, the Earl Warenne, appeared with an ancient and rusty sword before the royal justices who demanded on behalf of Edward I to know by what warrant – *Quo warranto* – he held his land, saying 'Here is my warrant... My ancestors came with William the Bastard and conquered these lands with the sword, and by the sword I will defend them'.[31] It was a defiant but hopeless gesture precisely against the fact that the warrior class to which he and his recent ancestors belonged was being steadily subordinated to the fiscal and juridical power of the state, and their independence and status being undermined by the influence and values of those who operated it. Indeed Warenne's historical perception was itself somewhat faulty, for the *Quo warranto* inquests, though powerfully symbolic in proclaiming the supremacy of the written instrument, were only the latest manifestation of a technique which William the Bastard himself had used in the great Domesday Inquest to assert that the only title to land in England belonged 'to whom King William had granted it', and to secure an exhaustive understanding of the resources upon which he would continue to draw. Nor was the English nobility by any means the only one which felt the chill. Gabrielle Speigel has shown brilliantly how in the early years of the thirteenth century the nobility of Flanders, for a time one of the mightiest and most prosperous powers of northern Europe, but subverted and humbled by its inextricable involvement in a generation of warfare between Angevins and Capetians, and by the ruthless ingenuity of Philip Augustus, sought to recover its ancient sense of dignity and worth by patronizing an entire new genre of historical writing, the vernacular prose romance in which the deeds of Charlemagne and his followers were again immortalized.[32]

In one of his most acclaimed books Georges Duby showed how the new social order was embodied and proclaimed in the celebrations which followed Philip Augustus' definitive victory over the Angevins and the Empire at Bouvines, in 1214. In those celebrations the use of the ancient theme of the division of society between those who fight, those who pray and those who work concealed beneath a rhetoric of tradition and continuity the completion of a new social hierarchy which had taken the place of the essentially Carolingian one which had endured until the early years of the eleventh century, when (as Duby saw it) it suddenly collapsed. During that long interval the image of the three orders, current in the ninth and tenth centuries, had been relatively little used, but in the later part of the twelfth century it began once more to assume great prominence in the public discourse of the courts of northern Europe.[33] There was now, however, a striking difference. In the Europe of Charlemagne, and in the writings of Alfred the Great, commenting on his translation of Boethius' *Consolation of Philosophy*, the *agricultores* had been the peasantry, on whose labour the training and support of warriors and clergy were acknowledged to depend. In 1214, instead of embracing the whole of society the 'three orders' were simply the ranks of the privileged; the peasantry, who constituted some 90 per cent of the population, had been excluded.

As the schematization had been revived by writers like Wace (*Roman de Brut, c.*1170), Benoit of Ste.-Maure (*Estoire des ducs de Normandie*, 1173–5), and John of Marmoutier (life of Geoffrey Plantagenet, 1180), it functioned mainly in the service of the glorification of knighthood, completing the transformation of the knight (*miles*) from the lawless desperado of the Peace of God into the Christian warrior and protector of the weak, and reconciling younger sons with elder, and landless adventurers with kings, to weld the entire warrior class into a single united body.[34] In this version of the three orders the *laboratores* are still peasants, though they are now depicted as made base and ignoble by the degrading nature of their labour. But within a few years another version began to emerge, improbably revealed in the famous treatise *On Love* by Andreas Capellanus. Andreas may once have been in the service of Marie of Champagne, or been connected with the court of her mother Eleanor of Aquitaine, but when he wrote this work, in the later 1180s, he was at the court of Philip II of France: it is dedicated to Walter, the son of Philip's chamberlain. The main part of the treatise, in Latin and in mimicry of the emerging scholastic method, was a series of conversations showing how affairs should be conducted between lovers of varying combinations of social status – a man of the higher nobility with a woman of the lower nobility, and so on. From this game however two groups were excluded: the clergy, who ought not to play at all, but if they must should take their rank from their parents, and peasants, who didn't count, and whose women, if desired by a free man, should simply be taken.[35] Those who could play were *nobiles, nobiliores* and *plebiani*. With the noble or more noble – descended respectively from the vassals of vassals or modest lords and from great lords – we are in old company, but the plebian appears as one who 'throughout the week applies all the strength of his intelligence [that is, not of his body] to various affairs of trade and profit; on the seventh day, resting, he would like to immerse himself in the affairs of love'. He is clumsy in manners and appearance, but he claims that his trade does not dishonour him as manual labour would have done, and that he was a better man than his father, rising by the exercise of his virtuous and useful talents. And in spite of his clumsiness and lack of physical and social grace, Duby pointed out, he was not excluded: the Countess to whom he addressed his plea heard him, and agreed to instruct him in the rules of love.[36]

Thus for better or worse the *bourgeois* or *prud'homme* (*prudens homo*) as he proclaimed himself, was thrusting his way into the numerous descriptions and classifications of the new social order as relentlessly as he ascended to wealth and influence. His metamorphosis was completed in the second version of the *Philippiad* which the royal clerk Guillaume le Breton composed for the celebrations that followed the victory of Philip II over the forces of all his enemies at Bouvines in 1214, and revised ten years later. Guillaume described the royal forces in battle and returning to Paris for a triumphal feast as those of the three orders victorious over darkness. The knights, of course, were in the van and closest to the king, followed by the men of the towns and cities of France (that is, the Isle de France), and then by the clergy. Both in the battle itself and in the celebration which followed it, that is, the ensemble of the *pugnatores* and *oratores* was completed by the *negotiatores*, the *bourgeoisie* which had been so vigorously entrenching its legal and social privilege during the three or four generations in which the traditional threefold image had largely dropped from view. The peasants had been reduced, even more ruthlessly in the second version, to a marginal role as outsiders and spectators.[37] *Negotium* had usurped the place of *labor* as the real world took on ever more the appearance of a great market place. Money was omnipresent and irresistable, widening as ever the gap between rich and poor, between those who lent and those who borrowed, in the countryside as well as in the city. The peasant's service, like the knight's, was now measured in cash which his lord was increasingly desperate to collect. There was almost nothing that could not be turned into money or that it could not be turned into, and the alchemists who could work these transformations had become indispensable to the creation and exercise of power. In short, Guillame le Breton consecrated the domination of the countryside by the city, and described the society of estates which would remain in place until 1789. But he did so with a discretion which befitted the truly powerful. For where in his threefold scheme was there a place for the other class of *novi homines* which had risen so dizzyingly in the century past, and to which he himself belonged – that of the *clerici*?

4 Exporting the Revolution

Like all the great revolutions this was one was quickly exported. The structure of Christian teaching and practice laid down by the Fourth

Lateran Council would last for three hundred years, for a territory which stretched from the Atlantic to the Vistula, the Dneister and the Danube, and from Greenland and the Baltic to Sicily. By 1300 that space was occupied by kingdoms with firmly settled (though not, of course, unchanging) boundaries. In each of them society was organized according to the theory of the three orders, and on the basis of the clear distinction between secular and ecclesiastical land and the opposing principles upon which each was transmitted from generation to generation. Military power and social prestige were displayed by a hereditary aristocracy, its leading families often originally from former Carolingian lands, whose castles controlled the countryside and whose children were raised in the code of chivalry and the Catholic faith. In each there was (or soon would be) at least one university whose graduates staffed royal, noble and ecclesiastical courts, drawing with the same dialectical and legal skill upon the same authoritative interpretations of the same texts to advance the claims, increase the revenues and win the favour of their lords. Everywhere there were chartered cities with their own laws and privileges, with whose assistance they dominated in varying degees and in varying ways the life of the countryside around them. Everywhere markets used currencies and traded according to conventions familiar from one end of the region to the other. Great cathedrals in the same Gothic style were to be found from Trondheim to Naples and from Cracow to Seville; whether Gothic or not, their revenues were enjoyed collectively by their celibate canons, and their bishops ruled over networks of parishes whose inhabitants were baptized, married and buried according to the same laws and by the same rites, who confessed the same sins at the same Easter, and received the same penances, from priests trained according to the same manuals and subject to the same regulations and disciplines. Very great differences remained, of course. It goes without saying that innumerable variations of landscape, ecology, tradition, culture and custom at every level of society and in every aspect of life would continue to exercise profound and frequently decisive influence on the nature and course of European history. Nevertheless, the inhabitants and communities of the entire region now shared essential and fundamental customs and institutions, and shared a culture, as they had not done two hundred years earlier.

Both individual kingdoms and Latin christianity as a whole had already been for several centuries encroaching upon the territories of their less developed neighbours, drawn by the need of kings to reward their followers, and of the church to win converts. Between the sixth and tenth centuries Germanic kingdoms had expanded at the expense of others among themselves, or against less settled and or less belligerently organized neighbours on their internal and external frontiers. But even

Charlemagne had suffered a legendary defeat at the hands of the Spanish Muslims, who were themselves, unlike Charlemagne's descendants, almost untouched by the Viking raids of the ninth century. The greatest military triumphs, those of Alfred over the Danes or Henry the Fowler and Otto I over the Magyars, had been defensive ones. In the eleventh and twelfth centuries, in marked contrast, armies led by knights from northwestern Europe attacked and defeated all comers, including those of the far wealthier and more sophisticated Byzantine and Islamic worlds.

Before those confrontations came about, however, the frontiers of western Christendom had already been dramatically enlarged by the astonishing energy and enterprise of the Vikings of the ninth and tenth centuries, as they ranged over almost every navigable waterway between the Atlantic and the Urals, bringing together worlds which had barely known of one another's existence. They sold their captive Slavs to Arab merchants at Great Bulgar on the Volga, traded with Inuit in Greenland (the North American Indians whom they encountered at l'Anse aux Meadows in Newfoundland – Vinland – may have been less friendly), and sailed great convoys of rafts laden with furs, honey, pitch and wax down the Dniepr and across the Black Sea to sell in Constantinople. They founded Ireland's first towns at Dublin, Waterford, Wexford and Limerick, and Russia's at Starya Ladoga, Novgorod, Smolensk and Kiev. More than 85,000 Arab coins and 70,000 German ones have been found in Scandinavia, and further hordes continue to be unearthed almost wherever they went. These were the profits of the monasteries they plundered and the geld they collected – 150,000 pounds of silver from England alone between 991 and 1014 – but also from the regular trade which they established between the peoples who lived around the North Atlantic, the Irish Sea, the English Channel, the North Sea, the Baltic and the Russian rivers.[38] The routes and regular contacts which the Vikings established and the communities which they created contributed indispensably to the formation of western Christendom, and helped to establish its boundaries, bringing it into direct contiguity with the Byzantine and Islamic civilizations to the east and south. A crucial decision between Latin and Greek was made by the Scandinavian princes of Kiev in 987, when they decided to adopt Christianity rather than Judaism or Islam, and to take it from Constantinople rather than from Rome.

The christianization of Scandinavia, which began with the foundation in 829 of the see of Hamburg, the first bishopric of the Roman Church outside the frontier of the Roman Empire, crystallized with the conversion of kings and the creation of bishoprics at the beginning of the new millennium. The first Danish king to convert was Harold Bluetooth, in 965. He was followed by Olaf Tryggvasson of Norway (995–1000) and

Olaf Sköttkonnung I in Sweden (1008). In Iceland also the Norwegian settlers decided to accept Christianity in 1000. In 968 the Emperor Otto I had Magdeburg raised to the status of an archbishopric 'for all the people of the Slavs beyond the Elbe and the Saale lately converted and to be converted to God'.[39] The Bohemians had a bishop at Prague by 973, and the Poles one at Poznan by 968. In the year 1000 an archbishopric was created at Gniezno for the Polish kingdom, and in 1001 another at Esztergom for Hungary.

Especially since the year 1000 crops up so frequently in the story – many examples could be added to those mentioned above – historians have been accustomed to hail these developments as the beginning of a new age, and thereafter to stress the elements of continuity in the next three centuries, during which the outline of a Latin Europe so boldly and rapidly sketched in the decades around the millennium was filled and coloured to make the great familiar canvas of Medieval Christendom. To leave it at that, however, would be to miss the sea-change in the character of expansion from the former Carolingian heartlands in the eleventh century, and with it in the throughness of the incorporation into Latin Christendom not only of territories conquered after that point, but of those which had already been added in the great sweep of conversions around the periphery of the Carolingian and Ottonian world at the end of the first millennium. The newly formidable military capacity of the Latin west began to show itself in the 1030s, when the Christian rulers of northern Spain, their armies rapidly swollen by recruits from north of the Pyrenees, began to exploit the weakness and disunity of the Muslim principalities, first by border warfare and then by territorial expansion. The fall of Toledo, in 1085, symbolically and practically heralded an accelerating reconquest which by 1270 left only Granada and its hinterland in Muslim hands. In Italy the Normans secured Aversa in 1030 and Melfi in 1041; by the 1050s Robert Guiscard and his followers had established themselves as the effective power in the Byzantine provinces of Apulia and Calabria; in 1062 they captured Messina and in 1072 Palermo, and with it to all intents and purposes Sicily, from the Arabs who had governed the island since 827. In 1098 and 1099 Frankish armies took Edessa, Antioch and Jerusalem. Their precarious maintenance for almost two centuries of a territorial presence in Syria and Palestine depended overwhelmingly on the naval power and commercial interests of the Italian cities, which had first been dramatically manifested when Genoan and Pisan fleets captured Sardinia from Muslim rulers, in 1015–16. The same power and interests were primarily responsible for one of the great barbarities of world history, the conquest and sack of Constantinople in 1204 by an army raised for the Holy Land by northern barons, but transported and manipulated by the Venetians.

The Latin 'Empire' of Constantinople, set up in the wake of the atrocity, installed a Latin patriach and canons from Italy and France in Hagia Sophia, and created metropolitan sees throughout Greece, the Aegean and the Levant. It remains uncertain what many of them amounted to in practice, or what roots they had put down by the time Byzantine rule at Constantinople was restored in 1261, but the diocese of Athens, for example, was reorganized by its new bishop 'according to the customs of the church of Paris'.[40]

The English kingdom which William of Normandy invaded in 1066 was no Byzantine Empire or Abbasid Caliphate, but it was the wealthiest and best governed territory in northern Europe. Its new king, Harold Godwineson, had demonstrated its military power and unity by marching his army the length of the land to defeat an invading host led by the redoubtable king of Norway, Harald Hardrada, at Stamford Bridge. Three weeks later Harold himself was killed at Hastings. Twenty years later his reign was erased from the official record with breathtaking effrontery by two simple questions which William's Domesday Commissioners asked in every hundred court in England: who held this land on the day when King Edward was alive and dead? To whom did King William grant it? Upon the answers, given by sworn juries, legal title would depend thenceforth.

The events of the weeks after the battle of Stamford Bridge and of the years after Hastings provide the clearest illustration of the relationship between the changes of the tenth and eleventh centuries in northwestern Europe and those of the eleventh and twelfth, because England was exceptional both in the extent of its development, economically, culturally and politically, before 1066, and in the rapidity and thoroughness of its conquest and subjugation thereafter. The strength of the kingdom to which Harold succeeded, and the wealth which William's Normans seized, was rooted in the work of Alfred of Wessex and his successors. Alfred had been the only English ruler successfully to defend his kingdom against the Vikings, and had taken advantage of their conquest and occupation of the kingdoms of East Anglia, Northumbria and Mercia to lay his own claim to be protector, and therefore by implication lord, of all the Christians under Danish rule. He laid the military and political foundations of the reconquest which was completed by his son Edward (899–924) and his grandson, Athelstan (924–939). They did their work with such boldness and success that its essentials survived the devastation of the renewed Viking raids at the end of the tenth century (more powerful by far than those of Alfred's own time), England's incorporation into the Danish empire of Cnut the Great, and the long period of acute political instability that followed Cnut's death in 1035. Under Edward the Confessor (1043–66) England's towns were the largest, its trade the most varied and far-flung of any kingdom north of the Alps. Its royal government could deliver the king's writs across the land and assure the stability and prestige of his coinage, taking a tidy profit into the bargain, by changing the coins every third year; its people, organized into townships and hundreds, enjoyed a considerable measure of security and independence in their own affairs; its monasteries maintained a flourishing vernacular culture, and under its efficient if in some cases worldly bishops local churches flourished and multiplied.

There is a strong case for arguing that the achievements of Alfred and his successors brought about just such a revolution in ninth- and tenth-century England as this book propounds for eleventh- and twelfth-century Europe.[41] Alfred's success rested not only on military victory, but on the intensification of trade in the English Channel and the North Sea which provided the basis for the establishment of towns and markets, with the transformation thus implied of productive capacity and social relations in the countryside. His defence against the Vikings was based on a highly organized system of fortified *burhs*, which also became market and administrative centres. The great strength of the monarchy which Alfred left was demonstrated by the sweeping social and cultural changes carried out, its sophisticated financial administration and developing power to tax, and above all its determined imposition of royal order against the traditional procedures of kin and community.

These are certainly grounds for maintaining that Alfredian Wessex met the definition of social revolution offered in the preface to this book – that it 'transformed state organizations, class structures and dominant ideologies' and gave birth to nations 'whose power and autonomy markedly surpassed their own prevolutionary pasts and outstripped other countries in similar circumstances'.[42] If so, however, Alfred's revolution was swept away by its younger and brasher successor. Within twenty years of Hastings the entire thegnage (landowning class) of England was dispersed by defeat, deprivation and exile, to make way for the followers of William of Normandy. The church had been reorganized on Gregorian lines by a Lombard Archbishop of Canterbury, and its Anglo-Saxon bishops and abbots replaced by Normans, Franks and Lotharingians, though a few of them, unlike their secular counterparts, were allowed to die in office. Norman castles, Norman lordship, Norman law, were planted rapidly and ruthlessly in England, to such effect that, as we have seen, the English kingdom became with the French the epicentre of our 'First European Revolution'.

Similarly, it may seem perverse to describe far-reaching and durable transformations such as those which the Vikings brought to the economic infrastructure of an immense tract of western Eurasia and its surrounding waterways merely as preludes to the First European Revolution. The Vikings were not only raiders, traders and colonizers, across vast distances, but founders of cities, on a scale and of a complexity which (not being much described in literary sources) is only now beginning to be appreciated with the extraordinary vividness and precision that scientific archaeology can achieve. Even on this cursory account, the Vikings had a colourable claim to be hailed as revolutionary in their own right, and in the terms of the argument of this book. In the long run, however, the Frankish social order and institutions prevailed in Scandinavia, not the other way round. Cnut the Great (1016–35), who presided over a powerful and wealthy Anglo-Scandinavian empire, went to great lengths to win acceptance from the grandees of Latin Europe, making the pilgrimage to Rome as well as attending the imperial coronation of Conrad II in 1027, and apparently encouraging the greatest of his subjects to follow his example.[43] Danish bishoprics began to be associated with specific territories in his reign, and by 1104 had agreed boundaries and an archbishopric at Lund. Not until then did the many churches which had been founded in the eleventh century themselves begin to acquire settled boundaries, and with them the tithes that a parish system required. Tithes and parishes also implied an agrarian system capable of supporting the castles and mounted knights which made their appearance in the early decades of the twelfth century.[44] Under Waldemar I (1157–82) a centralized royal administrative structure based on a chancery was established, and under his successors Denmark registered its full membership of the new order with the growing participation of its knights in the expansion now vigorously in train around the shores of the Baltic.

In the Slav lands the Christianizing and colonizing endeavours of the late tenth century, impressive as they had been, rested on weak foundations. The creation of the Polish and Hungarian archbishoprics in 1000 and 1001 was part of the attempt of the Emperor Otto III and his advisors to reassert Church and Empire after the disaster of the great uprising of the Wends in 983, when the northeastern frontier of the Empire was overrun, and Hamburg itself sacked and pillaged. The fortunes of the new churches remained uncertain until they were courted, organized and disciplined, according to the high papal principles set out by Gregory VII himself in a series of letters addressed to their rulers almost from the beginning of his pontificate, and by the legates sent by him and his successors.[45] Neither papal policy nor ecclesiastical structures, essential as they were, would have secured the incorporation of these lands into Latin Christendom without a wider and deeper movement of settlement and colonisation. Throughout the twelfth and thirteenth centuries settlers from as far afield as the Low Countries and the Rhineland streamed far beyond the Elbe and Saale, the previous limit of the German-speaking world. Some were brought in by conquerors seeking to populate and consolidate the territory they had won, as in the mark of Brandenburg, or in Prussia and Livonia in the wake of the Teutonic knights; some, in Silesia, Pomerania and Poland, for example, were recruited by frontier lords or Slavonic princes seeking to stabilize their territories and improve their revenues from the taxes, rents and tithes that would flow, even at lower rates than were demanded in the older areas of settlement, from the clearing of forests and the draining of marshes in immense stretches of fertile and under-populated land. Some came as monks and missionaries, some as peasant colonists attracted by the promise of abundant land and relatively mod-est dues and services. All brought with them not only their languages, but the distinctive institutions which were being forged in the lands from which they had come. By the end of the thirteenth century not only could the Roman church be found all the way to the borders of Russia, but also German towns inhabited by German settlers living under German law, in a countryside often responding to the rhythms of German commerce and German custom, though cultivated by Slav peasants.

The victories which continued on every frontier of Latin Europe throughout the eleventh, twelfth and most of the thirteenth centuries built in a variety of ways upon the achievements of the first millennium, and especially its last two centuries, which Peter Brown in an earlier volume of this series, has described so brilliantly as '*The Rise of Western Christendom*'. But they were also the direct result of the social revolu-tion of the eleventh century, and of two of its aspects in particular. The military revolution produced mounted knights equipped and trained to perform intricate manoeuvres with high speed and precision, including the charge with couched lance which at that moment no force in the known world could resist. The dynastic revolution compelled young men to place themselves at its disposal, and defined the terms upon which land and revenue would be divided. Behind the knights followed the monasteries and cathedrals, the towns and the laws, which were equally and inseparably the products of the same revolution. In short, the new expansion of the 'age of the Crusades' (as it is sometimes vulgarly called, after the least consequential if perhaps the most barbar-ous of the military exploits which marked it) was not only engendered by Europe's internal transformation but, as Robert Bartlett has shown with great eloquence and force, exported the structural principles worked out in that transformation to the newly conquered and colon-ized lands, and in doing so laid down the common foundations upon which Europe has been built.

5   The Europe of the New Regime

A civilization is both created and defined by its learned elite. The diagram (figure 1) devised by the late Ernest Gellner to describe what he called 'agro-literate polities' shows why this should be so.[46] It emphasizes a contrast between the communities of primary producers – farmers, fishermen, miners and so on – in the lower part of the diagram, and the ruling elite in the upper. One village is much like another in their internal structures; the differences between their inhabitants in wealth, status and way of life are relatively slight, however important to the people concerned. On the other hand, there may be large cultural differences between one village and another. Even within the same region neighbouring communities may speak different languages, observe different customs, worship different gods or venerate different saints. For the elite – typically described as comprising priests, warriors and merchants, though there may be many further distinctions and gradations within those categories – it is just the opposite. Differences of rank and function are very precisely defined in principle, and are clearly marked in practice by dress, demeanour and manner of life, but all share a common culture, contained in the first instance in the common language (not that all need know it) of its sacred texts, which are guarded and interpreted by the priests and scholars. Further, it was precisely their common culture – the shared language, values and modes of conduct – which enabled the elites of the traditional civilizations of Eurasia – those who had mastered the Chinese or Arabic script, for example – to establish and exercise their domination, communicating effectively and coordinating their activities over great distances, even though their native languages and cultures might have been as various as those of the people whom they ruled. As the cultural community of the rulers sustained their domination, so did the diversity of the ruled, as was recognized in the Chinese saying that a peasant should know of the

ruling class: stratified, horizontally segregated layers,

military

administrative, clerical

commercial

laterally insulated communities of agricultural producers

Figure 1   The general structure of agro-literate polities

existence of the next village because he heard its cocks crow in the morning. That is why the elites of these civilizations insisted on controlling transactions between their producing communities, economically through markets and politically and socially through religion and law enforcement, and why they were quick to suspect unauthorized dealings between their underlings, and to condemn them as heresy or sedition.

Much of what we have seen in the previous chapters might be summarized as showing how during the tenth, eleventh and early twelfth centuries northwestern Europe came to resemble Gellner's diagram very much more precisely than it had done before (see figure 2). The creation of the seigneurie marshalled the peasantry into a far more closely controlled and effectively regulated system of production, stimulated and sustained by an increasingly dense and active network of markets, and the seignorial *ban* marked a frontier between exploiters and exploited infinitely clearer and more universal than the the vivid but imprecise Carolingian distinction between *potentes* and *pauperes* – a distinction which had not excluded many who produced from the ranks of the free, or of those who did not, such as monks, from those of the poor. The re-articulation and re-conceptualization of the social hierarchy not only to eliminate that ambiguity, but to define precisely the ranks of the privileged and their obligations and relationships to one another, was effectively completed by the beginning of the thirteenth century, displayed in the celebrations which followed the battle of Bouvines and codified in the canons of Fourth Lateran Council.

In two critical respects the course and outcome of the eleventh- and twelfth-century revolution distinguished the literate elite of Latin Europe and its interests sharply, and in opposite ways, from those of the older

(*i*) Ninth-century society:

potentes

pauperes

(*ii*) Thirteenth-century society:

oratores

bellatores

laboratores

rustici, illitterati, pagani, heretici etc.

Figure 2   Ninth-century society and thirteenth-century society

and more imposing civilizations of Eurasia. In the first place, the changes in the ways in which learning was transmitted and acknowledged had profound implications for the structure of society, and in particular for the location of religious authority. In the ninth century teaching was firmly controlled by the bishops, but they did not, in principle, restrict access to it. In the eleventh century increasingly strident assertions of the presence of heresy among the people were accompanied from the outset by the assumption that one of its surest signs would be unauthorized attempts to acquire or transmit literacy, and with it the knowledge of the scriptures. This was a change not of principle, but of emphasis and perception, which led rapidly to the presumption that literacy was by definition inconsistent with servitude, or with rusticity. At the same time, while bishops were in this way asserting their authority over teaching more firmly and aggressively in relation to the laity they were losing the ability, in practice though not yet in principle, to exercise it in respect of the clerks. In the eleventh century masters were still appointed by their bishops or abbots, but they attracted students by virtue of their personal reputation, with which the renown of their schools rose and fell. Their twelfth-century successors secured their licence by demonstrating competence in the standardized curriculum to the satisfaction of their teachers, and hoped to find positions in schools whose lustre would bring them students. We have seen in some detail how Abelard's career marked and was marked by the transition from the first principle to the second. Abelard himself won fame and authority by intellectual daring, dazzling and charming the students who flocked to his lectures. His account (beginning in the 1090s) of his journey through the Loire valley, including perhaps Loches, Tours and Orléans, to Paris and Laon, in search of more famous teachers and more advanced methods of reasoning, and of how students followed him in his turn as he was driven from one place to another by the jealousies and intrigues of those whose pre-eminence he threatened, describes conditions which resembled quite closely (in practice) those which obtained in the Islamic world at the same time. His successors, foreshadowed by Alberic and Lotulph who attacked him on Anselm's behalf at Laon and arraigned him for heresy at the Council of Soissons in 1121, made their ways by winning the approval of their seniors through conformity to acknowledged norms of attainment and conduct. By the end of Abelard's life the concentration of both students and masters in Paris placed it on an entirely different plane from any other centre, and made it possible in the next decade or so to institutionalize the curriculum and require formal confirmation of having mastered it as a prerequisite of higher study. Charisma had been replaced by institutional authority, or, in plainer language, intellectual status and access to the power it could confer were passed down from the top, instead of up from the bottom. As in so many aspects of social existence in these centuries, an old order had been superseded by a new one – the authority of the bishop by that of the corporation of masters – after a heady interval of much looser, popularly sanctioned control. The message was heavily reinforced by the imposition on all young men who belonged or aspired to belong to the social elite – in fact, to the free – of increasingly rigorous norms of behaviour as well as of thought and expression, embedded in ever more closely defined codes of dress, demeanour and conduct.

To the extent that pre-Gregorian Latin Christendom was characterized by its devotion to local saints and their cults, by its dependence on the monasteries as the principal *loci* of spiritual authority and cultural prestige, and in tending to perceive the supremacy of Rome in those terms rather than through any regular exercise of institutional power, it differed from the House of Islam much less in practice than in theory. In the absence of overarching ecclesiastical structures Muslim religious life revolved around the mosque, the teachers of the Koran (*ulema*) and those who devoted themselves to meditation and contemplation (*sufis*). Without an institutional church there could be no precise equivalent of the Catholic conception of heresy, and in the early centuries it seems that on the whole, respect for the prophet and observation of the essential obligations of the faithful were sufficient: as al-Ash'ari (d.935–6) put it, 'I do not consider any who pray towards Mecca as infidels'.[47] Where there were no bishops anybody could teach who could find students, provided that what he taught was not considered heretical, or contrary to the Koran. But the Muslim world was changing too, and in these respects the twelfth century reversed the significance of the contrast. The removal from the bishop (in the first instance, the Bishop of Paris) of discretion to withold his *licentia docendi* from anyone who had completed the prescribed course of studies to the satisfaction of his fellow masters, or to grant it to anyone who had not, was the most fundamental of the privileges upon which the thirteenth-century university was founded. Meanwhile, in the Islamic world the transmission of knowledge remained solely on a personal basis, through the relation between teacher and pupil, and provided the currency of an open-ended competition for status, influence and office. This competition was in effect conducted by and between networks of patronage and loyalty created by teachers and their pupils, resembling in their strategies and often in their language and values those of the military elite – rather as Abelard's had occasionally done in his exuberant hey-day.[48] The *madraseh* foundations which multiplied in this period, lacking any organization of masters, curriculum of study or system of licensing, in no sense provided an educational institution analogous to the rise of the universities in

Latin Europe,[49] but the absence of institutionalized authority, rather than nourishing freedom of speculation as it had done in the Golden Age, increasingly left room for anyone who could command a mob to become a censor. As in the west, it was not holding heterodox opinion that called for action, but disseminating it. 'Someone who makes propaganda for his view and leads people astray by his error must be stopped from doing this by whatever means', says Abu Bakr al Razi in the fourteenth century.[50] His words presuppose a judgement of what constituted error, even though there was no bishop to make it. In consequence accusations of heresy readily provided the occasion of conflict between rival schools of teachers or *sufis*, and sometimes the medium through which they competed for popular support. This became increasingly apparent from around our period, with (it is widely supposed) disastrous consequences for the development of non-Koranic, and especially scientific thought. Having attained the highest pinnacle of fame to which intellect and eloquence could bring him, Abelard's older contemporary, Al Ghazzali (d. 1111) renounced his great offices and devoted the remainder of his life to denouncing as superfluous and impious the learning through which he had attained them.[51] In doing so he identified himself as closely with the current of his world and time as Abelard did with his. Abelard's career was ended by the western equivalent of Koranic literalism, as represented by Bernard of Clairvaux, but the memory of his fall saved other scholars from similar persecution. Consequently, his championship of the application of reason even to holy things, and of the right of a teacher to follow his trade without being pitched out of his position, or hauled before a tribunal every time he flouted convention, helped to lay the foundations upon which the great edifices of scholasticism and the university rose in the century following his death.

The claims with which the *clerici* of Latin Europe rationalized and justified the power which they extended so energetically and so ingeniously, to the effect that the business and responsibilities of government were entrusted to them, to be exercised with due concern for justice, the protection of the weak and so on, but nevertheless by the arbitrary will and absolute right of their masters, are of a kind familiar among Eurasian traditional elites. In practice, however, such assertions by no means always implied an effective claim to a monopoly of legitimate violence. Neither the distance which the *ulema* habitually maintained from the display of earthly power nor the sophistication of the juridical and administrative traditions available to those who exercised it could disguise the obvious fact that from the eleventh century onwards most of the Indo-Islamic world was dominated ruthlessly and exclusively by warrior elites. The subtler language of imperial China barely concealed the brutal truth that the splendour of the Son of Heaven rested upon an unspoken compact by which, in return for its acknowledgement, his officials, for all the theoretical comprehensivess of his authority, did not challenge the domination of the countryside – which might be very violent indeed – by the magnate families from which they came, and to which they would return. However dazzling might have been his performance in the examinations through which he had risen to preferment, a magistrate who had to govern perhaps a quarter of a million people with the aid of a couple of clerks and two or three runners was in no position to contest the hegemony of the local bosses.

As we have seen, the aggrandizement of central authority, royal or papal, in twelfth- and thirteenth-century Europe rested upon no such unspoken accommodation with the warriors. On the contrary, the elevation of the warrior class and knightly values through the language of holy war and the cult of chivalry was designed to secure, and at the same time to obscure, the marginalization and subordination of the knights themselves. A single example will make explicit the contrast between western bureaucratic dynamism, the restless and seemingly insatiable appetite for the extension of governmental power, and its most developed Asian counterpart. In his discussion of the Ming dynasty in decline, at the end of the sixteenth century, Ray Huang discusses the career of Hai Jui, a model official, zealous, honest and fearless, determined to expose extravagance and uphold the rights of emperor and peasant alike against the landowners and the grasping and corrupt fellow-officials whom they dominated. He died a failure, lonely, frustrated and embittered. So, of course, have many of his western counterparts down the years. But Huang's point is that Hai's impotence was part not just of the failure or corruption, but of the very nature of the imperial bureaucracy. The countless abuses which Hai details at the level of local government 'testify that the bureaucracy could never adequately dispense justice to millions of peasants... To define and safeguard individual rights the civil officials would have had to involve themselves in such small issues as brothers taking alternate years to use the same fishpond, and the rights of way on flagstone bridges over ditches. Obviously, that would have been impractical. Yet by dismissing such matters as petty and irrelevant the officials would never again find an adequate point of reference to the context of village life.'[52]

It would be difficult to imagine a sharper contrast with the clerks of Angevin England, or the Dominican inquisitors, for whom nothing was too small, and nothing irrelevant. They knew very well that it was in just such petty matters as the use of fishponds and rights of way on bridges that the very essence of power, or as they would have said, lordship, resided. One of the privileges which Robert Pullen, when he became

Chancellor at the papal court in 1144, confirmed for Sherborne Abbey, where his cousin was Prior, was the right to fish in every fishpond in Sherborne for the whole of every feast day of the Blessed Virgin.[53] It was precisely in that from which the mandarins shrank, the regular and continuous penetration of local communities and the ruthless subordination of their leadership and values to those of the high culture, as represented by nascent church and state alike, that the common and formative goals of persecutors and state-builders lay; precisely for that reason that they were in fact one and the same. In Karl Leyser's words, 'A general characteristic of kingship in western and southern Europe in the twelfth century was the growth and intensification of the connections... by which kings transmitted their will to local communities... guidelines and measures passed on from above to competent agents at local level... careers and interest groups formed at the beginnings and ends of these routes of administrative traffic... were the means by which regional societies could acquire statehood. Without such connections and without their local officials and advocates kingship was forced to remain distant and sporadic... irrelevant for the mass of the agricultural population.'[54] These developments in the exercise of secular authority were paralleled, of course, by that of the parochial, and especially of the penitential system, which has no analogue in any other world religion, and which was to all intents and purposes completed by the decree of the Fourth Lateran Council that every Christian should confess to his priest at least once each year. This was one of the religious developments of the period most bitterly denounced by heretics and most vigorously enforced by reformers.

This contrast amounts to rather more than the familiar observation that the Chinese imperial bureaucracy was far too small in size to exercise local power with its own hands: European bureaucracy, after all, has not been accustomed to submit tamely to a shortage of manpower. There does not appear to be any profound mystery about the reason for the lack of dynamism of Chinese imperial government. Beyond the notorious conservatism of the Confucian tradition itself there was a plain social cause in the identification in principle of the imperial bureaucracy and the landed gentry, and the close and sustained relationship between them in practice. The officials did not ordinarily interfere with the local gentry in the maintenance of order, and depended on its support to exercise their authority and carry out their public functions. In return, they were deeply committed to underpinning the status and authority of the gentry. Since each group recruited almost exclusively from the other and there was no clear conceptual or empirical distinction between them it could hardly have been otherwise. Largely from Sung, and certainly from Ming times (that is, from the eleventh and fourteenth centuries respectively) success in the examinations was the necessary route to the privilege associated with landholding rank, to such an extent that by the early nineteenth century the lowest grade of pass had been made available by purchase.[55] Nevertheless, despite its theoretical openness recruitment to the imperial bureaucracy was overwhelmingly from the landowning families. The support of an examination candidate through the long and arduous years of preparation (the normal age of eventual success in the imperial period being about thirty-five) was an investment in which an entire and extended family would join, and from which it would expect to benefit. The result was that by the nineteenth century, on at least one estimate, the gentry families owed perhaps half as much again of their wealth to the profits of office as to the income from their land.[56]

Further, the entire system was designed to place severe constraints on the number of those who might benefit from it. The difficulty of mastering even the script effectively restricted the diffusion of literacy, and the prolonged period of candidature for the examinations, representing a far greater expense than its equivalents in the west, must have been increased (at the same time as the premium on actual talent was reduced) by the growing and minute insistence on conformity in the late imperial period, from the fifteenth century onwards. The rate of success required was not prohibitive, for it seems that one entrant to the imperial service in every three generations or so was generally reckoned sufficient to allow a family to maintain its position.[57] In other words, the system was designed to secure high rewards for a very small number of beneficiaries, avoiding both the need and the incentive for the extension of the tax base which, among its other consequences, would have tended to introduce a dynamic element, in the need to recruit more officials in order to gather more taxes and so on, and also in doing so to draw the imperial administration more closely into the local community and its affairs.[58]

Without a systematic comparison of the relationship between land holding, office holding and family structures in medieval Europe and in imperial China we cannot say whether it is more than a coincidence that some of the developments which were critical in confirming the effective subordination of the imperial administration to the interests of the landed families seem to be traceable to the mid-twelfth century – that is, the half century or so following the over-running of northern China by the Jurchen, in 1126.[59] But certainly in Europe the opposite development, the creation during precisely that period of an administrative class whose members identified their interests with those of their patrons and not their families, laid the foundation for the reshaping of European society and culture in the high middle ages. By contrast, Paul Magdalino points out, many of the same, superficially contradictory tendencies which accompanied it – an expansion of higher education and vigorous enthusiasm for learning on the one hand, increasing authoritarianism leading to persecution on the other, – were present in twelfth-century Byzantium, but did not develop to the same extent as in the Latin west because 'the class which was at the forefront of both remained integrated with the government and society of the imperial city [Constantinople], and did not achieve the status of a separate, international, spiritually dominant social order' that is, of the clerks of Latin Christendom.[60] This was the instrument that prevented the vigour of the nascent states of Latin Europe from running into the sands of tribal or dynastic loyalties and unchallenged local hegemony. Those forces remained potent in every part of Europe and supreme in many for the next seven hundred years at least. Nevertheless, the permanent existence both of a class of young men driven from their families in search of wealth and glory and of a mechanism which enabled patrons to attract and reward their loyalty would continue to stimulate in crucial regions and at critical moments a competition for the favour of central power which was sufficiently general and enduring to assure not only its survival, but its determined and vigorous extension.

The creation of this class of men, and of the conditions which ensured its perpetuation and prosperity, was the crucial achievement of the First European Revolution. Its full significance, however, is visible only in the context of another, much older, longer and broader transformation of which it was part. A map of the Eurasian land mass around the year 1 would show that citied civilization at that time did not yet reach very far beyond the cradles of the earliest civilizations, which had appeared between 2000 and 3000 years earlier. Cities had spread from Mesopotamia and the Nile valley through the Fertile Crescent and around the Mediterranean, from the valley of the Indus to that of the Ganges, and rather tentatively from the valley of the Yellow River to the mouth of the Yangtze. By around 1200 the building blocks of modern world history were in place. What turned out to be lasting citied civilization had extended not only to northern and western Europe, including Russia, as we have seen, but to the entire Yangtze basin, to Japan, south India and both mainland and island Southeast Asia, into central Asia, to the African coast of the Indian Ocean, and the valley of the Niger. During the first millennium of the Common Era, that is to say, and especially in its second half, regions previously incapable of sustaining citied civilization had acquired the economic and social infrastructures and governmental structures that made them able to do so. The point is clearly illustrated by the contrast between the failure of Roman cities and civilization, at the beginning of the first millennium, to take root much beyond the shores of the Mediterranean, and the success and rapid growth in the eleventh and twelfth centuries, from origins on the face of it so much less auspicious, of those which began to break the surface of historical record towards the end of it. Again, a systematic account of how this came about is lacking, but much of this common development must plainly be attributable to common experience. An obvious example is the dissemination of the new (or newly dominant) proselytizing religions of the first millennium, including not only Buddhism, Christianity and Islam, but Brahmanism and Confucianism, which had the capacity to persuade tribal peoples to embrace new forms of social organization and new and more productive agricultural practices, while drawing them into larger and more cosmopolitan networks of economic and cultural exchange. In western Europe this extension of the infrastructures of complex civilization had been under way since before the end of antiquity, and it was not completed much if at all before the end of the twelfth century. In this sense those historians, led by Dominique Barthélemy, who refuse to see a catastrophe or a caesura around the millennium, insisting that slow and gradual changes in society, economy and culture had been under way since the ninth century and before, direct attention to continuities of the greatest importance.

On the other hand, our brief and necessarily superficial comparison of the ways in which Europeans in the twelfth century responded to certain fundamental challenges which their Muslim and Confucian counterparts also faced in broadly similar forms may suggest that it was precisely in the eleventh and twelfth centuries that the complex civilizations of Eurasia began to follow separate paths, and to assume in their social and cultural institutions the increasingly distinctive identities which until then had been more obviously proclaimed in their ruling ideologies. 'It was 800, not 1000, that was in most parts of Carolingian Europe the turning point of local aristocratic dominance', as Chris Wickham has said[61] – but it was 1000 which was the turning point for maintaining it. By transforming the Carolingian elite the First European Revolution saved it from going the way of so many others. The price was the restless dynamism of Europeans – the energy which Burckhardt related also to their inner restlessness, their need to explore themselves and their destiny as well as the world they inhabited. The resulting combination of greed, curiosity and ingenuity drove these first Europeans to exploit their land and their workers ever more intensively, constantly to extend the scope and penetration of their governmental institutions, and in doing so eventually to create the conditions for the development of their capitalism, their industries and their empires. For good and ill it has been a central fact not only of European but of modern world history.

The peculiar fact that it was in Europe that the 'breakthrough' to the industrial economy took place, that it was Europe and the 'neo-Europes' which it strewed around the world that upset the equilibrium between the traditional civilizations and set about reducing the world to a single social and economic regime, has often been attributed to the 'origins' of European civilization both in classical antiquity and in the christian religion. The beginning of 'European supremacy' has been dated variously from the Renaissance of the fourteenth century, the Reformation of the sixteenth, the enlightenment and the colonial expansion of the seventeenth and eighteenth. In particular, there has been a long tradition among historians and (still more) in the social sciences, of associating European dynamism with an awakening from the long quiescence of 'the middle ages' – a tradition which has been increasingly at odds with the growing appreciation of specialists in these centuries of the immense vigour and creativity of those who struggled not only to survive but to build. In reality it begins here in the eleventh and twelfth centuries, with the birth of Europe itself, and in the inner and outer struggles which shaped the urgent ambitions of the first Europeans. It is true, especially when we look beyond the valleys of the Loire, the Seine, the Meuse, the Rhine and the Thames, that it is not always easy to distinguish clearly between the expansionary movements of the ninth and tenth centuries, which were part of the common experience of extending city-supporting society throughout the Eurasian periphery, and that of the eleventh and twelfth centuries which was the peculiar outcome of the First European Revolution. Nevertheless, the differences between the two turned out to be of decisive importance. They are directly attributable to the dual system of land-holding and the changes in family structures with which it was inseparably connected that we have traced from the later part of the tenth century, and the consequences that flowed from it. Taken together, these were the changes which ultimately imparted, for better and for worse, and for the first time, a common and distinctive character to the territories which their results embraced, despite all that separated them – a character which can only be described by acknowledging that in combination they constituted the first *European* revolution.

Table of Dates

*c.*1060	Peter Damiani, *de parentelae gradibus*	——	Marriage of Heloise and Abelard
1060–91	Norman conquest of Sicily	——?	introduction of abacus to English exchequer
1066	Battle of Hastings		
1070	Demand for a commune at Le Mans	1121	Condemnation of Abelard at Soissons
1071	Battle of Manzikert	1122	Concordat of Worms
1072	Fall of Palermo to Robert Guiscard	——?	Abelard, *Sic et non*
		1123	First Lateran Council
1073–85	Pontificate of Gregory VII	1124–53	Reign of David I of Scotland
1077	Canossa	*c.*1125–1135	Sculpture of Gisebertus at Autun
——	Demand for a commune at Cambrai	1127	Murder of Charles the Good, Count of Flanders
1081	Consuls chosen at Pisa		
——	Grant of customs to St Quentin	1130	Beginning of papal schism
1085	Fall of Toledo to Alfonso VI of Castile	——	Coronation of Roger II of Sicily
1086–7	Domesday Survey		
1086–1127	Reign of William IX of Aquitaine	*c.*1131	Abelard, *Historia calamitatum*
1088–1135	Construction of Cluny III	*c.*1135–44	Rebuilding of St. Denis
*c.*1093	Anselm of Canterbury, *Cur deus homo?*	1135	John of Salisbury reaches Paris
1093–*c.*1130	Construction of Durham Cathedral	1139	Second Lateran Council
1095	Council of Clermont	1140	Council of Sens
1098	Foundation of Citeaux	*c.*1140	'Gratian', *Concordia discordantium canonum*
*c.*1098	Abelard arrives at Paris		
1099	Fall of Jerusalem	1143	dualist heretics burned at Cologne
*c.*1100	Foundation of Fontevrault	1147	Fall of Lisbon to Alfonso I of Portugal
1100–35	Reign of Henry I of England	——	preaching of Second Crusade
1106	Battle of Tinchebrai		
1108–37	Reign of Louis VI of France	1148	Council of Reims
		1148–94	Reign of Raymond V of Toulouse
1115	*Monodiae* ('Memoirs') of Guibert of Nogent	*c.*1150	Thomas of Monmouth, *Life of St. William of Norwich*
1116	Henry of Lausanne at le Mans		
1118	Foundation of Knights Templar	1152–90	Reign of Frederick Barbarossa

1152	Marriage of Henry of Anjou and Eleanor of Aquitaine	1194–1222	Reign of Raymond VI of Toulouse
1153	Death of Bernard of Clairvaux	1198–1216	Pontificate of Innocent III
1154–89	Reign of Henry II of England	1198–1250	Reign of Frederick II
1159–81	Pontificate of Alexander III	1200	Charter of University of Paris
1159	John of Salisbury, *Policraticus, Metalogicon*	1204	Sack of Constantinople
		———	Fall of Normandy to Philip Augustus
1163	Council of Tours	1209–29	Albigensian Crusade and conquest of Languedoc
1163–82	Construction of Notre Dame, Paris	1213	Battle of Muret
1166	Constitutions of Clarendon	1213–76	Reign of James I of Aragon
1170	Murder of Becket	1214	Battle of Bouvines
*c.*1170–*c.*1190	Chretien de Troyes, *Arthurian Romances*	———	Statutes of University of Oxford
1176	Battle of Legnano	1215	Fourth Lateran Council
1178	Papal mission to Toulouse	———	Magna Carta
		———	Statutes of University of Paris
1179	Third Lateran Council	1219	Statutes of University of Bologna
1180–1220	Reign of Philip II (Augustus) of France	1224	Foundation of Teutonic Knights
1184	Council of Verona: bull *ad abolendam*	1226–70	Reign of Louis IX
		1233	Appointment of Dominican inquisitors at Toulouse
1187	Battle of Hattin; Saladin recaptures Jerusalem	1265–73	Thomas Aquinas, *Summa theologiae*
1189	Third Crusade		
1194	Rebuilding of Chartres begun		

Notes

Abbreviations

The following abbreviations are used in the Notes and Bibliography:

AHR	*American Historical Review*
ASOB	*Acta sanctorum ordinis sancti Benedicti*
Bouquet	*Receuil des historiens de Gaule et de la France*
CCM	*Cahiers de civilisation médiévale*
EHR	*English Historical Review*
Mansi	G. D. Mansi *Sacrorum conciliorum nova et amplissima collectio*
MGH	*Monumenta Germaniae Historica*
	Epist. *Epistolae*
	SS *Scriptores*
PL	J. P. Migne, *Patrologia Latina*
P&P	*Past and Present*
RS	Rolls Series
TRHS	*Transactions of the Royal Historical Society*

Introduction

1 Quoted by Geary, *Phantoms of Remembrance*, p. 8.
2 Childe, *What Happened in History*, pp. 97–120.
3 Barthélemy, *Comté de Vendôme, La mutation de l'an mil*, 'Le paix de dieu', *L'an mil*; c.f. Bisson, 'Feudal Revolution', *debate* by Barthelemy and others, P&p, nos 152, 155. Barthélemy had not yet developed his critique of 'mutationism' in his admirable brief survey of the period, *L'ordre seigneurial, XIe–XIIe siècle* (Nouvelle histoire de la France médiévale, vol. 3, (Paris, 1990). Duby is more thoroughgoing in his assertion of revolution in *The Three Orders* than in his earlier work, perhaps under the influence of subsequent research, notably that of Bonassie and Poly. For 'mutation' see Poly and Bournazel, *La mutation féodale*. This 'feudal revolution' or 'mutation' is

not, it must be emphasized, the revolution referred to in the title of this book, whose thesis is not necessarily incompatible with Barthélemy's views: see below pp. 185–9, 196–8.

4 'On the Eve of the First European Revolution', *Gregorian Revolution and Beyond*, pp. 1–19.

5 The phrase and thesis are those of Charles H. Radding, *A World Made by Men*, but especially in recent years there have been numerous assertions of more or less profound and rapid change in mentalities and modes of thought directly associated with the transformation of social structures and solidarities, notably in relation to conceptions of time and space (Le Goff, *Purgatory, Medieval Imagination*), literacy (Clanchy, *Memory to Written Record*, Stock, *Implications of Literacy*), memory (Geary, *Phantoms of Remembrance*, Fentress and Wickham, *Social Memory*, Spiegel, *Romancing the Past*).

6 Southern, *Making of the Middle Ages*, p. 13.

7 *Cligés*, 1. 30–44, here as quoted by Southern.

8 E.g. Reuter and Wickham in Barthélemy and others, 'Debate', *P&P* 155.

9 Theda Skocpol, *States and Social Revolutions* (Cambridge, 1979), p. 3.

1   The Approach of the Millennium

1 Letaldus of Micy, *Delatio corporis sancti Juniani*, col. 824–5.

2 Mansi, 19, col. 89–90.

3 Mansi 19, col. 103–4.

4 Mansi 19, col. 101–2.

5 *Translatio sancti Viviani episcopi*, p. 263.

6 Ed. France, p. 195.

7 Listed by Goetz in Head and Landes, pp. 262–3.

8 *De diversis casibus coenobii Dervensis et mircula S. Bercharii*, quoted by Head and Landes, p. 6.

9 Ed. France, pp. 194–7.

10 Augustine, *De civitate dei* (*The City of God*), Bk. xix, ch. xiii.

11 Mansi 19, col. 2, 3, 5, 22. The account of the canons of this council comes from Ademar of Chabannes. Since the first canon is undoubtedly fictitious, part of Ademar's campaign to have the patron of his monastery, St Martial of Limoges, proclaimed an apostle (Landes, *Relics, Apocalypse*, pp. 3, 7 and *passim*) it is possible that the rest is too. Even in that case, however, it would still illustrate the point being made here, which is about how 'reformers' wanted the world to be, rather than the extent to which their vision was, as yet, being realized.

12 J. M. H. Corbett in *Cambridge Medieval History* V, pp. 507ff.

13 Herlihy, 'Church Property on the European Continent, 701–1200', *Speculum* 36 (1961), 81–105.

14 See Morris, *Papal Monarchy*, pp. 387–416.

15 Damiani, *Vita Romualdi*, ch. xxxiii. I am grateful for Henrietta Leyser's permission to use her translation.

16 *Vita Norberti* ch. 9, *MGH SS* 12, 678–9, quoted by Little, *Benedictine Maledictions*, pp. 235–6.

17 Barthélemy, 'Le paix de dieu dans son contexte', *CCM* 40 (1997), correctly insists on the rhetorical construction of reports of the Peace Councils like those quoted in section 1 ('Glad Confident Morning') above, and on the interest of the church in representing itself as the recipient of popular enthusiasm. However, Radulfus Glaber and his contemporaries were not in this respect exceptional. Collective enthusiasm for religious or what appeared as religious causes was readily available throughout the tenth and eleventh centuries, and often to a greater degree than churchmen found welcome – for reasons which are fundamental to the argument of this book: see below, pp. 23–9.

18 Morris, *Papal Monarchy*, pp. 93–4.

19 Schevill, *History of Florence*, pp. 46ff.

20 Cowdrey, Epistolae vagantes, pp. 27, 15.

21 *Chron. S. Andreae castri cameracesii*, 543; *Registrum* I, 328–9.

22 Leyser, *Hermits and the New Monasticism*, p. 75.

23 Cf. Peter Brown, 'Society and the Supernatural: a Medieval Change' in *Society and the Holy*, pp. 302–32.

24 Sigebert of Gembloux, *MGH Libelli* ii, 438, quoted by Karl Leyser, 'The Polemics of the Papal Revolution', p. 42.

25 *PL* 171, col. 1484.

26 *Acta Sanctorum* June I, 832–3, trans. Moore, *Birth of Popular Heresy*, pp. 28–31.

27 Moore, *Origins of European Dissent*, pp. 83–90. Henry is often called Henry the Monk. The authority for the two epithets is the same – St Bernard, in the letter cited below – but 'of Lausanne' is less misleading if wrong.

28 Bernard, ep. 241, *PL* 182 col. 434, trans. Scott James pp. 388–9.

29 See further below, pp. 107–9.

30 *Gesta pontificum cenomannensium*, trans. Moore, *Birth of Popular Heresy*, pp. 33–8.

31 Rubellin, 'Au temps où Valdès n'était pas hérétique'.

32 *PL* 185, col. 410.

33 Moore, *Origins of European Dissent*, pp. 115–38.

34 The quotation is from Brown, 'The Rise and Function of the Holy Man in Late Antiquity', *Society and the Holy*, pp. 103–52, at pp. 139–40; see also Brown, 'Relics and Social Status', ibid., pp. 222–50.

35 Gregory of Tours, *Gesta martyrum 5*, quoted by Van Dam, *Leadership and Community*, p. 190.

36 See Geary, *Furta Sacra*, pp. 40–50.

37 Guibert, *de pignoribus sanctorum PL* 156, col. 624, but Guibert was not, as was once thought, a precocious sceptic: he wrote his book to sustain the claims of his own local relic, the holy tooth of Laon, and the authority of the clergy, as opposed to the people, to confer such respectability on relics: see Stock, *Implications of Literacy*, pp. 244–52 and below, p. 147.

38 Einhard, *De translatio et miracula sanctorum Marcellini et Petri*, Bk. 4, trans. Dutton, pp. 111–30.
39 *Book of Ste. Foy* 3.1, p. 144.
40 Bernhard Töpfer, 'The Cult of Relics in Burgundy and Aquitaine at the Time of the Monastic Reform', in Head and Landes, *Peace of God*, pp. 41–58, at p. 44.
41 Examples from Töpfer, above, pp. 45–7.
42 *Book of Ste. Foy* 2.4, pp. 120–1.
43 *Vita Hugonis, PL* 159, col. 881.
44 In particular, Little, *Benedictine Maledictions* and Koziol, *Begging Pardon and Favor*.
45 Little, *Benedictine Maledictions*, pp. 137–8.
46 Foreville and Weir, *Book of St. Gilbert*, p. 95.
47 *Book of Ste. Foy*, p. 111.
48 Atto, *Vita B. Gualberti, PL* 146, col. 780–1, 687–8; Odo, *Vita Geraldi, PL*, 133, col. 648; Damian, *Vita Romualdi, PL*, 144, col. 993–4, 1005; *Vita Hugonis, P. L.* 159, col. 873–4. All of these are commonplace examples of the standard repertoire of miracles *in vita*, which could be multiplied scores of times: that is their point.
49 Evans-Pritchard, *Witchcraft, Oracles and Magic*, abridged edition, p. 18: cf. Moore, 'Between Sanctity and Superstition', upon which the present discussion draws heavily.
50 See especially, with differing interpretations of the nature and functions of such beliefs and the attitudes of churchmen to them, but with agreement on their currency, Gurevich, *Medieval Popular Culture*, esp. pp. 39–77; Kieckhefer, *Magic in the Middle Ages*, pp. 56–94; Flint, *The Rise of Magic*, esp. pp. 254–328.
51 Cf. Brown, *The Making of Late Antiquity*, p. 19: 'Men believed in both "miracles" and "magic"...not because their credulity was boundless ...but so that they should feel free to exercise a choice as to which wielder of supernatural power they would acclaim as a holy man and which they would dismiss as a sorcerer.'
52 Max Manitius, *Geschichte der lateinischen Literatur des Mittelalters* (3 vols, Berlin, 1911–14), 2. 414, quoted by Töpfer in Head and Landes, *Peace of God*, p. 52n.
53 Odo, *V Geraldi*, p. 93; *PL*, 133, col. 642.
54 John of Salerno, *V. Odonis*, 1.14, trans. Sitwell p. 16.
55 *Book of Ste. Foy*, p. 55.
56 *Book of Ste. Foy*, 2.12, pp. 137–8.
57 Luchaire, *Social France at the time of Philip Augustus*, p. 28.
58 Flint, *The Rise of Magic*, e.g. at pp. 396–9.
59 *V. Romualdi*, col. 965.
60 On the limited influence of hermits in the *Reich* see Reuter, *Germany in the Early Middle Ages*, pp. 242–3.

2 The Powerful and the Poor

1 Russell, 'Population', pp. 37–41.
2 Paul Bairoch etc., *La population des villes européennes*. It must be emphasized that this compilation merely assembles previously published estimates of urban population, from whatever source, without making any attempt – it would have been impossible – to assess their reliability or to compare the bases on which they were arrived at. Its usefulness even for illustrative purposes is therefore severely limited – it offers, for example, no estimate before 1200 for Milan, almost certainly the largest city in Christian Europe – and no individual estimate should be accepted uncritically; nevertheless, without it this overview could not have been attempted.
3 Nicholas, *Growth*, pp. 34–5; Randsborg, *First Millennium*, pp. 83–90.
4 Sawyer, 'Wealth of England'; Fleming, 'Rural Elites'.
5 Cf. Jacobs, *The Economy of Cities*, to which Constantin Fasolt drew my attention.
6 Fernandez Armesto, *Barcelona* pp. 6–20; on minting, Bonnassie, *La Catalogne*, pp. 186–7.
7 Bonnassie, 'Une famille'; Domenec, 'Urban Origins of Barcelona'.
8 Derville, *St. Omer*, pp. 48–82.
9 Gimpel, *The Cathedral Builders*, p. 1.
10 Orderic Vitalis v, 294–7.
11 Dereine, 'La spiritualité "apostolique"'.
12 Fossier, *Peasant Life*, pp. 50–1, 67–70.
13 Montanari, *Food*, pp. 47–51.
14 *Didascalicon*, 2.25, trans. Taylor, p. 99.
15 Montanari, *Food*, p. 38; on use of woodland, Fichtenau, *Tenth Century*, p. 338ff.
16 Ganshof, *Communities*, pp. 26–7, 90–1.
17 *Miracula S. Hucberti, Acta Sanctorum* Nov. 1, pp. 819–20, quoted by Nelson, *Charles the Bald*, on which this paragraph is largely based, at p. 24.
18 Bonnassie, *Slavery*, pp. 122–3.
19 *Annales regni francorum*, trans. Scholz, p. 83.
20 Reuter, 'Plunder and Tribute'.
21 Sahlins, *Stone-Age Economics*, pp. 1–39.
22 Herlihy, 'Agrarian Revolution in Southern France and Italy', p. 33.
23 Brun, *Bellum saxonicum* c. 25, p. 29, quoted by Leyser, 'From Saxon freedoms to the Freedom of Saxony', *Gregorian Revolution*, p. 60.
24 *Les structures du Latium médiévale*, pp. 303–68.
25 Chris Wickham, 'Property ownership and seignorial power in twelfth-century Tuscany' in Davies and Fouracre, *Property and Power*, pp. 221–44, at pp. 229–30.
26 *V. Romualdi*, col. 965.
27 *Life* ii. 34, trans. Sitwell, pp. 159–60.
28 Bange, *'L'ager et la villa'*.

29 Bourrin-Derrau, *Villages médiévaux en Bas-Languedoc*, 2, 145–80.

30 E.g. Fournier, *Basse-Auvergne*, pp. 366–72; Toubert, *Latium*, pp. 330–1.

31 *Book of Ste. Foy* 2.5, p. 127.

32 Poly, Provence, p. 127; Lauranson Rosaz, *L'Auvergne et ses marges*, pp. 370–1; Bonnassie, *La Catalogne*, pp. 263–313; Debord, 'The Castellan Revolution and the Peace of God in Aquitaine', Head and Landes, pp. 135–64, at pp. 142–8; Chédeville, *Chartres et ses campagnes*, p. 268; similarly in the Languedoc Biterrois: Bourrin-Darruau, *Villages*, 1.77; Poly and Bournazel, *Feudal Transformation*, pp. 26–8.

33 Bachrach, 'The Angevin Strategy of Castle Building'; Poly, *Provence*, pp. 127–8.

34 Glick, *From Muslim Fortress to Christian Castle*, pp. 105–13.

35 In Head and Landes, pp. 147–8.

36 Chédeville, *Chartres et ses campagnes*, pp. 289–90; Bonnassie, *La Catalogne*, p. 441.

37 For forceful statements of arguments developed with increasing vigour through Bonnassie's published work since the 1970s and of Barthélemy's since *c.*1992, see respectively *Slavery to Feudalism* and *La mutation féodale, a-t-elle eu lieu?*

38 Fossier, *Peasant Life*, p. 153.

39 Fossier, *Enfance de'Europe*, p. 299; Marc Bloch, 'Avènement et conquêtes du moulin à eau', *Mélanges Historiques* 2, pp. 800–22, at 814–19.

40 Anselm of Liège in Moore, *Birth of Popular Heresy*, p. 21; cf. Fichtenau, *Heretics and Scholars*, pp. 27–8.

41 Rollason, 'Miracles of St. Benedict', in Mayr-Harting and Moore (eds), pp. 73–90; Koziol, *Begging Pardon and Favor*, p. 202.

42 Examples from Van Dam, *Leadership and Community*, p. 286.

43 *Book of Ste. Foy*, p. 80; Sumption, *Pilgrimage*, p. 85.

44 *PL* 133, col. 656–7.

45 Ibid. col. 660.

46 Van Dam, *Leadership and Community*, pp. 277–300.

47 Cf. Goetz in Head and Landes, pp. 267–70, 327.

48 Cf. Nelson, 'Literacy in Carolingian Government'.

49 Fossier, *Enfance de l'Europe*, pp. 347–58.

50 Brentano, *Two Churches*, pp. 70–1.

51 Gluckman, *Politics, Law and Ritual*, pp. 104–7.

52 Murray, *Reason and Society*, p. 400; Stephen of Fougères, *Vita B. Vitalis*, p. 32.

53 Dalarun, *L'impossible sainteté*, pp. 154–75; 'La veritable fin de Robert d'Arbrissel'.

54 *V. Romualdi*, ch. xiii.

55 Fournier, *Le peuplement rurale*, p. 455; Musset, 'Cimiterium ad refugium tantum vivorum non ad sepulturam mortuorum'; Fossier, *Enfance de l'Europe*, pp. 357–8.

56 Fossier, *Chartes de coutume*, p. 26.

57 Duby, *La société maconnaise* p. 613; Bonnassie, *La Catalogne* pp. 339–41; Beech, *A Rural Society*, p. 27.

58   Bede, *Historia ecclesiastica*, ii. 13, ed. Plummer, pp. 111–12; Flint, *Rise of Magic*, pp. 203–53, 355–75 etc.
59   Orderic, III, ii, ed. Chibnall, II p. 159.
60   Mayr-Harting, 'Functions of a twelfth-century recluse'.
61   Moore, 'Family, Cult and Community'; Wallace-Hadrill, *The Frankish Church*, p. 288.
62   Campbell, 'The Church in Anglo-Saxon Towns', p. 149.
63   Life of Wulfric, ch. 74.
64   Davies, *Small Worlds*, pp. 101–2.
65   *De translatione S. Hunegundi*, PL 137, col. 63–72; Moore, *Origins of European Dissent*, pp. 187–94.

3   Sex and the Social Order

1   Bresc in Bourgière et al., (eds), *History of the Family* I, 461–4.
2   Dameron, *Episcopal Power and Florentine Society*, pp. 26–7.
3   Hughes, 'Urban Growth and Family Structure'.
4   Duby, *The Three Orders*, p. 154.
5   Reynolds, *Fiefs and Vassals, passim*, but see especially pp. 215–57.
6   Duby, 'Lineage, nobility and knighthood', *The Chivalrous Society*, pp. 59–80 (originally 'Lignage, noblesse et chevalrie au xiie. siècle dans la region maconnaise: une revision,' *Annales ESC* (1972)).
7   Ibid., pp. 100, 144; see also E. Bournazel 'Mémoire et parenté', in Delort, *La France de l'an mil*, pp. 114–24.
8   Lewis, *Royal Succession in Capetian France*, pp. 28–32.
9   Bouchard, 'Origins of the French Nobility'.
10   Orderic's main account of the foundation and early history of St Evroul, greatly simplified in what follows, is in Book III of his *Ecclesiastical History* (ed. Chibnall, II, 2–189), placed skilfully in context by Chibnall, *The World of Orderic Vitalis*, pp. 17–28. The operations and strategies of the Giroies and their rivals are brilliantly analysed by Searle, *Predatory Kinship*, especially pp. 179–89 and, more briefly, by Barthélemy, 'The Aristocratic Households of Feudal France' in Ariès and Duby, *Private Life*, pp. 96–105.
11   Orderic, III, ii. 18, ed. Chibnall, II, 17, 31–2.
12   Ibid., pp. 29.
13   Geary, *Phantoms of Remembrance*, pp. 48–80.
14   E.g. Barthélemy, above n. 10.
15   Martin de Viciana, *Chronica de la Inclita e Coronada Ciudad de Valencia* (1564), ii, 38, quoted by Casey, *History of the Family*, p. 32.
16   *Medieval Marriage*, pp. 11–12.
17   Rosenwein, *Neighbor of St. Peter*, p. 16 (table 2).
18   Eric John, 'The King and the Monks in the Tenth Century Reformation' in *Orbis Britanniae*, pp. 154–80; Fleming, 'Monastic Lands and England's Defence'.
19   Below, pp. 184–5.

20 Leyser, *Rule and Conflict*, pp. 63–73.
21 Cowdrey, *The Cluniacs and the Gregorian Reform*, pp. 3–22.
22 Rosenwein, *Neighbor of St. Peter*, pp. 179–94; 'Family Politics of Berengar I'.
23 Dameron, *Episcopal Power*, p. 25.
24 *Grosser Historische Weltatlas*, Map 80.
25 Cf. Constable, *Reformation*, pp. 174–9.
26 For Cluny in the eleventh and twelfth centuries see Iogna-Prat, *Ordonner et exclure*, pp. 33–99.
27 Dameron, *Episcopal Power*, pp. 24–37.
28 *Vita B. Gualberti*, col. 1105.
29 Dameron, *Episcopal Power*, pp. 33–6.
30 See above, p. 14.
31 Gernet, *Chinese Civilization*, pp. 294–6; Lambton, *Landlord and Peasant*, pp. 27–8; Morris, 'The Powerful and the Poor', p. 13.
32 Kulke and Rothermund, *History of India*, pp. 136–8.
33 Orderic, iii, ed. Chibnall, p. 11.
34 Duby, *Peasants and Warriors*, pp. 232–4.
35 Duby, *Société maconnaise*, p. 57–65, 272–7; cf. Bouchard, *Sword, Miter and Cloister*, pp. 225–54, and Bull, *Knightly Piety*, pp. 155–203.
36 Rosenwein, *Neighbor of St. Peter*, pp. 49–68: n.b. the map and chart at pp. 50–1. For another example, involving nine of the twelve leading families among the donors of La Trinité, Vendome, over several generations see Johnson, *Prayer and Patronage*, pp. 91ff.
37 Rosenwein, *Neighbor of St. Peter*, pp. 125–43, and for other indications and aspects of the less absolute conception of ownership and of property rights underlying these traditional attitudes, see White, *Custom, Kinship passim*.
38 *Life*, trans. Sitwell, pp. 118–19. We may wonder whether this view of Gerald's would have survived if Abbot Odilo, rather than Odo, had been entrusted with his biography.
39 Herlihy, 'Agrarian Revolution in Southern France and Italy'.
40 Iogna-Prat, *Agni immaculati*, pp. 305–57.
41 Chronicle of St. Pierre du Puy, Devic and Vaissette, *Histoire du Languedoc* V, col. 15; Moore, 'Peace of God', pp. 311–18.
42 Toubert, 'The Carolingian Moment', pp. 396–406.
43 Duby, *The Knight, the Lady and the Priest*, pp. 321, 203–6.
44 Cf. Morey and Brooke, *Gilbert Foliot and His Letters*, pp. 112–16.
45 Cowdrey, 'Papacy, Patarenes', pp. 26–7.
46 Venarde, *Women's Monasticism*, p. 10.
47 Fletcher, *Conversion of Europe*, pp. 280–4.
48 Goody, *Family and Marriage*, pp. 134–46, with a usefully differentiated discussion of the change; Herlihy, *Medieval Households*, pp. 82–8; Duby, *The Knight, the Lady and the Priest*, pp. 35–6.
49 Cf. Fox, *The Red Lamp of Incest*, pp. 144–65.
50 Ibid., p. 76. Goody, *Family and Marriage*, chap. 6 ('Church, land and family in the West') points to the mutual interest of the church and the

eldest son in reducing the rights of kin, and to the extension of the prohibited decrees as contributing to its achievement.

51 Bloch, 'De la cour royale à la cour de Rome: le procès des serfs de Rosny-sur-Bois', *Mélanges Historiques* 1, 452–61.

52 John of Salisbury, *Historia Pontificalis*, p. 61. John describes Eugenius acting similarly in another case, ibid., p. 81.

53 'Youth in Aristocratic Society', in Duby, *Chivalrous Society*, pp. 112–22.

54 Crouch, *William Marshal* offers an account based on a wider range of sources, as well as a more sceptical reading of them, than Duby, *William the Marshal*; Painter, *William Marshal*, is still worth consulting.

55 Barthélemy, 'Qu'est-ce que la chevalrie?' questioning in this and other respects the received account as given by Duby, Keen etc.

56 Orderic, III, ed. Chibnall, pp. 98–100, pp. 44–63.

57 The phrase, and the examples which follow, are from Robert Bartlett's fine discussion, *The Making of Europe*, pp. 24–59.

58 See, in addition to Duby, Bartlett, *Making of Europe*, pp. 60–3; Keen, *Chivalry*, pp. 23–7.

59 Clanchy, *Peter Abelard*, pp. 47ff.

60 Hibberd, 'Origins of the Medieval Town Patriciate'; Lestocquoy, *Les villes*, pp. 41–56.

61 Duby, *Chivalrous Society*, p. 117. I am grateful to Professor Keith Hopkins for pointing out to me the difficulty of accepting this at face-value.

62 Searle, *Predatory Kinship, passim*.

63 Cf. Murray, *Reason and Society*, pp. 341–9, who sees his examples as evidence of altruistic piety.

64 Weinstein and Bell, *Saints and Society*, p. 74.

65 Bouchard, 'Lords of Seignelay'.

66 John of Salerno, *Life of Odo*. 1.18.

67 Robinson, 'Gregory VII and the Soldiers of Christ'; Keen, *Chivalry*, pp. 44–77.

68 Seidel, *Songs of Glory*, pp. 58–9 and pl. 53; 68–9.

69 Duby, 'Lineage, nobility and knighthood' in *Chivalrous Society*, pp. 76–9; Barthélemy, *Vendôme*, pp. 361–3.

70 Quoted by Duby, *The Knight, the Lady and the Priest*, p. 44.

71 Hincmar *PL* 125, col. 791; Gerald, *PL* 142, col. 1295; Bullough, 'Burial, Community and Belief', p. 201; Fossier, *Enfance de l'Europe*, pp. 334–5.

72 Poly, *Provence*, p. 170; Bates, *Normandy*, p. 116; Duby, *La société maconnaise*, p. 288.

73 Somerville, 'Council of Beauvais', p. 503.

74 Leyser, *Rule and Conflict*, pp. 49–73; Geary, *Phantoms of Remembrance*, pp. 51–73.

75 King, 'Records of the Hotot Family', pp. 18, 47, 53–4; Stenton, *Early Charters*, p. 66; Dean, 'Lost Churches', 18, 53–4. I am grateful for these references to Edmund King, who is not responsible for the use to which I have put them.

76 Duby, *Medieval Marriage* p. 88.

77   Damiani, *vita Romualdi*, ch. 38; *vita B. Wulstani, MGH SS*, ix, 402; *vita B. Gualberti*, col. 1080; Guibert, *Monodiae*, I, 10, ed. Labande, pp. 60–1.

78   Orderic, viii 26, quoted by Constable, *Monastic Tithes*, p. 138; *Exordium parvum* trans. Matarasso, pp. 6–7.

79   Ademar, *Chronicon*, p. 194; Daniel F. Callahan, 'The Cult of the Saints in Aquitaine' in Head and Landes, *Peace of God*, pp. 164–84, at pp. 172–4.

80   Bonnassie and Landes, 'Une nouvelle hérésie'; the editors, in my view mistakenly, take the comment on Arians as a reference to popular heresy.

81   Ademar, *Chronicon*, p. 173.

82   Landes, *Relics, Apocalypse*, pp. 228–50.

83   Magnou-Nortier, 'The Enemies of the Peace'.

84   Mansi, xix, col. 103–4.

85   I owe this point to Stephen D. White.

86   Lauranson-Rosaz, *L'Auvergne et ses marges*, p. 421.

87   Poly and Bournazel, *Feudal Transformation*, p. 36, from P. Duparc, 'La commendise ou commende personelle', *Bibliothèque de l'École de Chartes* 119 (1961).

88   Rosenwein, *Neighbor of St. Peter*, pp. 87–8, 163–70.

89   Landes, *Relics, Apocalypse* pp. 67–9, 175–6.

90   Suger, *de administratione*, xxv, trans. Panofsky, p. 43; at greater length, *de consecratione*, c. ii, ibid., pp. 87–9.

91   Gimpel, *Cathedral Builders*, p. 38.

92   Fichtenau, *Heretics and Scholars*, p. 22.

93   Landes, *Wealth and Poverty of Nations*, p. 22n.

94   Peter the Venerable, *contra petrobrusianos*, p. 5.

95   Ibid. p. 162.

96   Moore, *Birth of Popular Heresy*, pp. 59–60, cf. Zerner, *Inventer l'hérésie?*, p. 129; Lauwers. '*Dicunt vivorum*'.

97   *Inventer l'hérésie?*, pp. 119–56; Zerner shows that the text edited by Raoul Manselli as the debate between Henry and William is in fact a much later treatise against the Waldensian heretics – possibly Valdès himself – which incorporates a version of William's work, but also edits, rearranges and greatly expands it.

98   See above, p. 16.

99   Moore, *Birth of Popular Heresy*, p. 36.

100 Ibid., p. 30.

101 Ibid., p. 49. These sections are first and last in the original treatise as identified by Zerner, not that of the more familiar, later and much enlarged version edited by Manselli.

102 Ep. ccxli, *PL* 182, col. 434.

4   The Ruling Culture

1   'Personal Letters', ed. Muckle, p. 68, trans. Radice (quoted and cited below), p. 109.

2   I do not re-enter the long-standing controversy on the authenticity of the letters. Every alternative that has been proposed strains probability

considerably more than the hypothesis that Abelard wrote the letters attributed to Abelard, and Heloise those attributed to Heloise: they have been thoroughly considered by Luscombe, 'From Paris to the Paraclete', and now, decisively, by Mews, *The Lost Letters*, especially at pp. 37–55.

3   Trans. Radice, p. 117.
4   A *regula mercatorum* was composed for Toulouse by a Dominican named Gui, *c*.1311: Mundy, *Society and Government*, p. 113.
5   Andreas, *Art of Love*, trans. Parry, pp. 106–7; the clerk shouldn't, of course, but if he must he should behave according to the rank of his parents.
6   I place 'Gratian' in inverted commas because Anders Winroth, in *The Making of Gratian's* Decretum, has recently shown that the *Corpus iuris canonici* which immortalizes the name is a second recension, completed by the early 1150s, of a work composed during the 1130s: see further below, p. 119.
7   Baldwin, *Masters, Princes and Merchants*, i, 93–7, ii, 93–5.
8   *Autobiographie*, ed. Labande I, v, pp. 32–3, quoted in Benton's translation.
9   Ibid., I, vi, pp. 38–41.
10 *Metalogicon*, I. 24, trans. McGarry, p. 68.
11 Trans Radice, p. 58.
12 *Metalogicon*, II. 5, trans. McGarry, p. 98; the priest, *Policraticus*, II. 28. On Otto and John as students in Paris, see Southern, *Scholastic Humanism*, vol. I, pp. 208–12, 214–21.
13 *Metalogicon* I, 5, trans. McGarry, pp. 21–2.
14 In this I am persuaded by Benton, *Self and Society*, pp. 229–33, but many still prefer 1053, as suggested by Mabillon.
15 Guibert, *Autobiographie*, I. iii, pp. 18–19, v, pp. 30–1.
16 Bautier, 'Paris au temps d'Abelard', pp. 57–62.
17 Southern, *Scholastic Humanism*, vol. I, p. 225.
18 Ibid., p. 316.
19 See above, n. 6.
20 Southern, 'From Schools to University'.
21 Le Goff, *Intellectuals*, pp. 138–53.
22 Finucane, *Miracles and Pilgrims*, pp. 130–72.
23 Fichtenau, *Heretics and Scholars*, pp. 286–93.
24 Stock, *Literacy*, pp. 273–315.
25 Cowdrey, *Gregory VII*, pp. 496–502.
26 Helpful introductions to an immense literature include Morris, *Papal Monarchy*, pp. 358–78; Clanchy, *Abelard*, pp. 65–118, 264–325; Stock, *Literacy*, pp. 362–403.
27 Baldwin, *Philip Augustus*, esp. pp. 106–36.
28 Leyser, *Communications and Power*, p. 145.
29 Poly and Bournazel, *Feudal Transformation*, pp. 187–92; for servile ancestry among the retinues of great lords in the Berry, Flanders and Champagne as well as the Paris region Duby, *Chivalrous Society*, p. 105, citing P. Petot, 'Observations sur les ministeriales en France', in *Revue historique de droit français et étranger* (1960).

30 Trans. Garmonsway, p. 216.
31 *Autobiographie*, ed. Labande, iii. 7, pp. 322–5, 330–1.
32 Galbraith, *Making of Domesday Book* esp. pp. 28–54; for Samson, Galbraith, *Domesday Book*, pp. 50–1.
33 William of Malmesbury, *Gesta Regum*, iv. 1, here from Giles p. 336; for a modern account see R. W. Southern, 'Ranulf Flambard', and 'Henry I', *Medieval Humanism*, pp. 183–205, 205–33, from which the discussion which follows is very largely derived.
34 *Gesta Regum*, iv. 1.
35 Walter Map, *de nug*, pp. 450–1.
36 But see Hollister, 'The Strange Death of William Rufus'; Barlow, *William Rufus*, pp. 420–6.
37 Map, *de nug*, v. 6, pp. 470–3.
38 Stubbs, *Historical Introductions*, pp. 43–9; C. Johnson, introduction to *Fitznigel*, Dialogus pp. xiv–xv.
39 Southern, *St. Anselm*, pp. 239–40; Smalley, *Becket Conflict*, pp. 59–108 and *passim*; Barlow, *Becket*, pp. 130–4.
40 Barrow, 'Cathedrals, Provosts and Prebends'; 'Education and Recruitment'.
41 Leyser, 'Frederick Barbarossa: Court and Country', in *Communications and Power* 2, at pp. 146–8.
42 Barrow, 'German Cathedrals'.
43 Map, *de nug*, pp. 2–3.
44 Ibid. pp. 493–4; for Walter's life, Brooke's introduction, ibid., pp. xiii–xix.
45 Turner, *Judiciary*, pp. 88–107.
46 Clanchy, *Memory to Written Record*, pp. 224–52; Nigel Longchamps is quoted at p. 226.
47 Jaeger, *Origins of Courtliness*, pp. 25–53; *The Envy of Angels*, pp. 53–117.
48 Southern, 'Henry I', *Medieval Humanism*, pp. 224–5.
49 On Geoffrey's life, Thorpe, *Geoffrey of Monmouth*, pp. 9–12; William of Newburgh is quoted at p. 17.
50 Gillingham, 'Beginnings of English Imperialism'.
51 Chrétien de Troyes, *Yvain*, ll. 124–35, trans. Kibler, p. 296.
52 *Cligès*, ll. 112–15, trans. Kibler, p. 124.
53 The Archpoet's *Confession*, here from Adcock, *Hugh Primas and the Archpoet*, p. 115.
54 Quoted by Southern, *Medieval Humanism*, p. 220.
55 Polycraticus, vii.20, trans. Dickinson p. 307.
56 Talbot, *Life*, p. 67.
57 Map, *de nug*, pp. 416–9; the story may be based on the suppression of Leominster Abbey after the abbess was seduced by Godwine's son Swein.
58 Ibid., v. 6, pp. 470–3.
59 Ibid, p. 222.
60 Fitznigel, *Dialogus*, p. 3.
61 Glanvill, p. 3.
62 Ibid., pp. 167–8.
63 Fitznigel, Dialogus, pp. 18, 35–6.

64 Leo IX to the Patriarch of Constantinople, *PL* 143, col. 761, quoted by Southern, *Western Society and the Church*, p. 71.

65 Guibert, *De Sanctis et eorum pignoribus* 1.1, *PL* 156, col. 614. cf. Smith, 'Oral and Written', pp. 309–10.

66 *Historia calamitatum* trans. Radice pp. 94–5. Abelard, famously, was himself a Breton, but the area near Nantes where he grew up was French-speaking, culturally and economically part of the Loire valley rather than of Brittany.

67 Gillingham, 'Beginnings of English Imperialism'.

68 Trans. O'Meara, pp. 101–2, 106.

69 Southern, *Scholastic Humanism*, vol. I, pp. 61–101.

70 Adelard of *Bath, Questions naturales*, ed. Burnett, *Conversations*, pp. 102–3.

71 *contra sectam sive haeresim saracenorum*, ed. Kritzek, *Peter the Venerable*, p. 226; see also ibid., p. 141.

72 Tolan, *Petrus Alfonsi*, pp. 9–11, 98–9.

73 Trans. Matarasso, *Cistercian World*, pp. 11–12.

74 Chazan, *Medieval Stereotypes*, pp. 1–2, 141–2 notes 3, 4.

75 Stow, *Alienated Minority*, p. 99.

76 Ibid, pp. 65–94, 139–42.

77 Smalley, *Study of the Bible*, p. 55.

78 Southern, *St. Anselm*, pp. 198–202.

79 Abulafia, *Christians and Jews*, pp. 63–93.

80 Lipton, *Images of Intolerance*, pp. 71–4.

81 Cohen, 'The Jews as the killers of Christ'.

82 Tolan, *Petrus Alfonsi*, pp. 19–22.

83 Moore, 'Guibert of Nogent and his World'.

84 Little, *Religious Poverty*, pp. 42–57; Lipton, *Images of Intolerance*, pp. 31–40.

85 Langmuir, 'Thomas of Monmouth, Detector of Ritual Murder', in *Anti-semitism*, pp. 209–36.

86 Smalley, *Study of the Bible*, p. 121; cf. John Mundy's conclusion that 'in numbers and cultural wealth western European jewry reached its peak in the late twelfth and early thirteenth centuries... Both in the north and in Mediterranean Europe Jews flourished as never before.' *High Middle Ages*, p. 81.

87 Thomas of Monmouth, p. 24.

88 Varoqueaux, 'Découvertes'.

89 Chazan, *Medieval Jewry*, pp. 56–9, 69–70.

90 McCulloh, 'Jewish Ritual Murder'.

91 Abelard, *Dialogus* p. 51, trans. Payer, p. 31.

92 Iogna-Prat, *Ordonner et exclure*, p. 279.

93 Chazan, *Medieval Jewry*, p. 75.

94 Iogna-Prat, *Ordonner et exclure*, *passim*; n.b., pp. 103–23, 253–71.

95 Cf. Langmuir, 'Peter the Venerable: Defense against Doubts', *Antisemitism*, pp. 197–208.

96 Douglas, *Purity and Danger*, pp. 140–58.

97 Little, *Religious Poverty*, pp. 52–5.
98 Weber, *Religion of China*, p. 237.
99 Cf. Stock, *Implications of Literacy*, pp. 24–51; Murray, *Reason and Society*, pp. 234–44.
100 Shakespeare, *The Merchant of Venice*, I. 3.
101 Cf. Abulafia, *Christians and Jews*, pp. 63–93.
102 Bernard, ep. 188, trans. Scott James, 238, p. 316.
103 Langmuir, *Antisemitism*, p. 204.

5 Order Restored

1 William of Newburgh, *Historia rerum Anglicarum*, II. xiii, ed. Howlett, vol. i, pp. 131–4. For a fuller version of the following discussion, with full references, see Moore, 'A la naissance'.
2 Mansi, xxi, col. 843; the women sunk in sin, 2 Tim iii: 6.
3 Mansi, xxi, col. 1178.
4 Bouquet, XV, pp. 790, 792, 799.
5 Stubbs, *Select Charters*, p. 173.
6 Bouquet, XIII, 140.
7 *PL* 204, col. 236.
8 Moore, *Origins of European Dissent*, pp. 168–204; Lambert, *Cathars*, pp. 19–44.
9 Mundy, *Liberty and Political Power*, pp. 50–8.
10 Maisonneuve, *Etudes*, pp. 121–41; Biget, 'Les Albigeois'.
11 Given, *Inqusition*, on the technology of documentation, esp. at pp. 25–51.
12 Gottfried von Strassburg, *Tristan*, ch. 23, trans. Hatto, pp. 246–8.
13 Southern, *Making of the Middle Ages*, p. 103.
14 'Society and the Supernatural: a Medieval Change', in Brown, *Society and the Holy*, pp. 302–32.
15 See above, pp. 13–19.
16 Kemp, *Canonisation and Authority*, pp. 82–106; Morris, *Papal Monarchy*, pp. 219, 501–2.
17 Moore, 'Popular Heresy and Popular Violence, 1022–1179'.
18 Mansi, xxii, col. 157–68; Roger of Hoveden, Chronica, ii, pp. 150–60.
19 Moore, *Origins of European Dissent*, p. 13.
20 Barber, 'Catharism and the Occitan Nobility'.
21 See above, pp. 16, 101; Moore, 'Family, Community and Cult'.
22 *PL* 172, col. 1399.
23 Zerner, *Inventer l'hérésie?* pp. 71–2, 133–4, 212–4, 245–7.
24 Robinson, *The Papacy*, pp. 244–91.
25 Leyser, *Communications and Power* 2, pp. 145ff.
26 Given, *Inquisition*, p. 18; Mundy, *Society and Government*, pp. 238–44.
27 Stock, *Implications of Literacy*, pp. 244–52.
28 Oxford, Corpus Christi MS 157 (the chronicle of John of Worcester), illustrated in King, *Medieval England*, pp. 34–5.
29 Moore, *Persecuting Society*, pp. 50–60, 73–80.

30 Ibid., pp. 60–5, 88–99.
31 Clanchy, *Memory to Written Record*, pp. 35–6.
32 Spiegel, *Romancing the Past*.
33 Duby, *The Three Orders*; on the several variants of the theory in circulation up to the twelfth century see especially Iogna-Prat, *Ordonner et exclure*, pp. 23–8, and Constable, 'The Orders of Society', in *Three Studies*, pp. 279ff.
34 Duby, *The Three Orders*, pp. 271–307.
35 Andreas, trans. Parry, pp. 149–50.
36 Ibid., pp. 53–9; Duby, *The Three Orders*, p. 342.
37 Ibid., pp. 346–53.
38 Stafford, *Unification and Conquest*, p. 212.
39 Quoted by Barlett, *Making of Europe*, p. 8.
40 Ibid., pp. 14–15.
41 Cf. Hodges, *Anglo-Saxon Achievement*, pp. 150–85 ('The First English Industrial Revolution').
42 Skocpol, *States and Social Revolutions*, p. 3; see above, p. 5.
43 Fletcher, *Conversion of Europe*, pp. 407–9.
44 Sawyer, *Christianization of Scandinavia*, p. 83.
45 Cowdrey, *Gregory VII*, pp. 443–52.
46 Gellner, *Nations and Nationalism*, pp. 9–13.
47 Lewis, 'The Significance of Heresy in Islam'.
48 Chamberlain, *Knowledge and Social Practice*, especially at pp. 69–90.
49 ibid., pp. 69–90, contrary to the often quoted views of Makdisi, *Rise of Colleges*.
50 Abu Bakr al-Razi, *Ahkam al'Qur'an* (Istanbul, 1335–8), vol. 2, pp. 35–6; I owe this reference and translation to the kindness of Michael Cook.
51 Mottahedeh, *Mantle of the Prophet*, pp. 198–200.
52 Huang, *1587*, pp. 130–55, at p. 146.
53 Southern *Scholastic Humanism*, vol. I, pp. 178–9.
54 Leyser, *Communications and Power*, 2, p. 145.
55 Beattie, *Land and Lineage*, pp. 17–19; Ho, *Ladder of Success*, p. 256.
56 Ebrey, *Family and Property in Sung China*, pp. 15–17; Chang, *Income of the Chinese Gentry*, pp. 197–8.
57 Ho, *Ladder of Success*, pp. 92–125.
58 Beattie, *Land and Lineage*, pp. 57–87.
59 Hymes, *Statesmen and Gentlemen*, esp. pp. 62–81.
60 Magdalino, 'Enlightenment and Repression', p.372.
61 Wickham in 'Debate', *P&P* 155, p. 198.

Bibliography

Where the edition referred to is not in the language of the original, the place and date of first publication are also given; a second and earlier date of publication is that of the original publication of a work cited here in translation.

Abelard, Peter, *Historia Calamitatum*, ed. J. T. Muckle, 'Abelard's Letter of Consolation to a Friend', *Mediaeval Studies* 12 (1950); trans. Betty Radice, *The Letters of Abelard and Heloise* (Harmondsworth, 1974), pp. 57–106.
——, 'The Personal Letters between Abelard and Héloise', ed. J. T. Muckle, *Mediaeval Studies* 15 (1953), 47–94, 163–213, trans. Betty Radice, *The Letters of Abelard and Heloise* (Harmondsworth, 1974), pp. 109–56.
——, *Dialogus inter philosophum, Iudaeum et Christianum*, ed. R. Thomas (Stuttgart, 1970), trans. P. J. Payer, *A Dialogue of a Philosopher with a Jew and a Christian* (Toronto, 1970).
Abulafia, Anna Sapir. *Christians and Jews in the Twelfth Century Renaissance* (London, 1995).
Acta synodi atrebatensis, PL 142, col. 1271–1312.
Adelard of Bath, ed. and trans. Charles Burnett, *Conversations with his Nephew* (Cambridge, 1998)
Ademar of Chabannes, *Chronicon*, ed. J. Chavanon (Paris, 1897).
Andreas Capellanus, The Art of Courtly Love, trans. J. J. Parry (New York, 1941).
Anglo-Saxon Chronicle, trans. G. N. Garmonsway (London, 1953).
Archpoet, ed. and trans. Fleur Adcock, *Hugh Primas and the Archpoet* (Cambridge, 1994).
Ariès P. and G. Duby (eds), *A History of Private Life, volume ii – Revelations of the Medieval World* (Cambridge, MA, 1988; 1985).
Bachrach, Bernard, 'The Angevin Strategy of Castle Building', *AHR* 88 (1983), 533–60.
Bairoch, Paul, Jean Batou and Pierre Chèvre, *La population des villes européennes de 800 à 1800* (Geneva, 1988).

Baldwin, John W., *Masters, Princes and Merchants* (2 vols; Princeton, 1970).
——, *The Government of Philip Augustus* (Berkeley, 1986).
Bange, François, 'L'*ager* et la *villa*: structures du paysage et du peuplement dans la région maconnaise à la fin du Haut Moyen Age (ixe.–xie. siècles)', *Annales* 39, 3 (1984), 529–69.
Barber, Malcolm, 'Catharism and the Occitan Nobility: The Lordships of Cabaret, Minerve and Termes', in C. Harper-Bill and R. Harvey (eds), *The Ideals and Practice of Medieval Knighthood* (Woodbridge, 1986), pp. 1–19.
Barlow, Frank, *William Rufus* (London, 1982).
——, *Thomas Becket* (London, 1986).
Barrow, Julia, 'Cathedrals, Provosts and Prebends', *Journal of Ecclesiastical History* 37 (1986), 536–64.
——, 'Education and the Recruitment of Cathedral Canons in England and Germany, 1100–1225' *Viator* 20 (1989), 117–38.
——, 'German Cathedrals and the Monetary Economy', *Journal of Medieval History* 16 (1990), 13–38.
Barthélemy, Dominique, *L'ordre seigneurial, XIe–XIIe siècle* (Paris, 1990).
——, *La société dans le comté de Vendôme de l'an mil au XIVe siècle* (Paris, 1993).
——, *La mutation de l'an mil, a-t-elle eu lieu?: servage et chevalerie dans la France des Xe et XIe siecles* (Paris, 1997).
——, 'Le paix de dieu dans son contexte', *CCM* 40 (1997).
——, and others, 'Debate: The Feudal Revolution', *P&P* 152 (1996), 155 (1997).
Bartlett, Robert, *The Making of Europe: Conquest, Colonization and Cultural Change, 950–1350* (London, 1993).
Bates, David, *Normandy Before 1066* (London, 1982).
Bautier, R-H., 'Paris au temps d'Abélard', in Jean Jolivet (ed.), *Abélard en son temps* (Paris, 1981), pp. 21–77.
Beattie, Hilary J., *Land and Lineage in China* (Cambridge, 1979).
Bede, *Historia ecclesiastica gentis anglorum*, ed. Charles Plummer (Oxford, 1896).
Beech, George T., *A Rural Society in Medieval France: the Gâtine of Poitou in the Eleventh and Twelfth Centuries* (Baltimore, 1964).
Benson, Robert L. and Giles Constable (eds), *Renaissance and Renewal in the Twelfth Century* (Cambridge, MA, 1982).
Bernard of Clairvaux, *Letters*, trans. Bruno Scott James (London, 1953).
Biget, J-L, '"Les Albigeois": remarques sur une dénomination', in Zerner, *Inventer l'hérésie?*, pp. 219–55.
Bisson, Thomas N., 'The Organised Peace in Southern France and Catalonia, *c.*1140–*c.*1233', *AHR* (1977), 290–311.
——, 'The Feudal Revolution', *P&P* 142 (1994), 6–42
Bloch, Marc, *Mélanges Historiques* (2 vols; Paris, 1963).
Bonnassie, Pierre, 'Une famille de la campagne barcelonaise et ses activités économiques aux alentours de l'An Mil', *Annales du Midi* 76 (1964).
——, *La Catalogne au tournant de l'an Mil* (Paris, 1993).
——, *From Slavery to Feudalism in South-Western Europe* (Cambridge, 1991).

——, and R. Landes, 'Une nouvelle hérésie est née dans le monde' in M. Zimmerman (ed.), *Les sociétés méridionales autour de l'an mil* (Paris, 1992), pp. 435–59.

The Book of Ste. Foy, trans. Pamela Sheingorn (Philadelphia, 1995).

Bouchard, Constance M., 'The Structure of a Twelfth-Century Family: The Lords of Seignelay', *Viator* 10 (1979).

——, 'The Origins of the French Nobility: a Reassessment', *AHR* 86 (1981).

——, *Sword, Miter and Cloister: Nobility and the Church in Burgundy, 980–1198* (Ithaca, 1987).

Bourrin-Derruau, Monique, *Villages médiévaux en Bas-Languedoc: Genèse d'une sociabilité* (2 vols; Paris, 1987).

Bourgière, André et al. (eds), *A History of the Family* (2 vols; Oxford, 1996, 1986).

Brentano, Robert, *Two Churches: England and Italy in the Thirteenth Century* (Princeton, 1968; Berkeley, 1988 edn).

Brown, Peter, *The Making of Late Antiquity* (Cambridge, MA, 1978).

——, *The Cult of Saints: its Rise and Function in Late Antiquity* (Chicago, 1981).

——, *Society and the Holy in Late Antiquity* (Chicago, 1981).

——, *The Rise of Western Christendom* (Oxford, 1996).

Bull, Marcus, *Knightly Piety and the Lay Response to the First Crusade: The Limousin and Gascony, c.970–c.1130* (Oxford, 1993).

Bullough, Donald A., 'Burial, Community and Belief in the Early Medieval West', in Patrick Wormald et al. (eds), *Ideal and Reality in Frankish and Anglo-Saxon Society: Studies presented to J. M. Wallace-Hadrill* (Oxford, 1983), pp. 177–201.

Campbell, James 'The Church in Anglo-Saxon Towns', *Studies in Church History* 16 (1979).

Casey, James, *The History of the Family* (Oxford, 1989).

Chamberlain, Michael, *Knowledge and Social Practice in Medieval Damascus, 1190–1350* (Cambridge, 1994).

Chang Chung-li, *The Income of the Chinese Gentry* (Seattle, 1962).

Chazan, Robert, *Medieval Jewry in Northern France* (Baltimore, 1973).

——, *Medieval Stereotypes and Modern Antisemitism* (Berkeley, 1997).

Chédeville, André, *Chartres et ses campagnes, xie.–xiiie. siècles* (Paris, 1973).

——, 'De la cité à la ville' in G. Duby, ed., *Histoire de la France urbaine 2: La ville médiévale* (Paris, 1980), pp. 36–181.

Chibnall, Marjorie, *The World of Ordericus Vitalis* (Oxford, 1984).

Childe, V. Gordon, *What Happened in History* (London, 1942).

Chrétien de Troyes, *Ouevres complètes*, ed. D. Poirion (Paris 1994), trans. William W. Kibler, *Arthurian Romances* (Harmondsworth, 1991).

Chronicon Sancti Andreae castri cameracesii, ed. D. L. C. Bethmann, *MGH SS* 7.

Clanchy, Michael, *From Memory to Written Record* (London, 1979).

——, *Abelard: A Medieval Life* (Oxford, 1997).

Cohen, Jeremy, 'The Jews as the killers of Christ in the Latin tradition, from Augustine to the Friars', *Traditio* 39 (1983), 1–27.

Constable, Giles, *Monastic Tithes, from their origins to the twelfth century* (Cambridge, 1964).

——, *Three Studies in Medieval Religious and Social Thought* (Cambridge, 1995).

——, *The Reformation of the Twelfth Century* (Cambridge, 1996).

Cowdrey, H. E. J., 'The Papacy, the Patarenes and the Church of Milan', *TRHS* 5/18 (1968), 25–48.

——, *The Cluniacs and the Gregorian Reform* (Oxford, 1970).

——, *The* epistolae vagantes *of Gregory VII* (Oxford, 1972).

——, *Pope Gregory VII, 1073–1085* (Oxford, 1998).

Crouch, David, *William Marshal* (London, 1990).

Dalarun, Jacques, *L'impossible sainteté: la vie retrouvée de Robert d'Arbrissel (v. 1045– 1116), fondateur de Fontevraud* (Paris, 1985).

——, 'La veritable fin de Robert d'Arbrissel (d'aprés une pièce inconnue du dossier hagiographique)' *CCM* 27 (1984), 303–13.

Damiani, Petrus, *Vita B. Romualdi, PL* 144.

——, *de parentelae gradibus.*

Dameron, George W., *Episcopal Power and Florentine Society, 1000–1320* (Cambridge, MA, 1991).

Davies, Wendy, *Small Worlds: The Village Community in Early Medieval Brittany* (London, 1988).

——, and Paul Fouracre (eds), *Property and Power in the Early Middle Ages* (Cambridge, 1995).

Dean, Mary A., 'Lost Churches of the Nene Valley and the Rediscovery of St. Peter's Clopton', *Northamptonshire Past and Present* 7, 2 (1984).

Debord, André, 'The Castellan Revolution and the Peace of God in Aquitaine', in Head and Landes, *Peace of God*, pp. 135–64.

De diversis casibus coenobii Dervensis et mircula S. Bercharii, ASOB II 859.

Delort, Robert (ed.), *La France de l'an Mil* (Paris, 1990).

Dereine, C, 'La spiritualité "apostolique" des premiers fondateurs d'Affligem (1083–1100)', *Revue d'histoire écclésiastique* 54 (1959), 41–65.

Derville, Alain, *St. Omer des origines au début du xive. siecle* (Lille, 1995).

Devic, C. and J. Vaissette, *Histoire général du Languedoc* V (Toulouse, 1875).

Domenec, J. E. R., 'The Urban Origins of Barcelona', *Speculum* 52 (1977).

Douglas, Mary, *Purity and Danger* (London, 1966).

Dutton, P. E., *Charlemagne's Courtier: the Complete Einhard* (Peterborough, Ontario, 1998).

Duby, Georges, *La société aux xie. et xiie. siècles dans la région maconnaise* (Paris, 1953).

——, *The Early Growth of the European Economy* (London, 1974).

——, *The Chivalrous Society* (London, 1977).

——, *Medieval Marriage: Two Models from Twelfth-Century France* (Baltimore, 1978).

——, *William Marshal* (London, 1986).

——, *The Three Orders: Feudal Society Imagined* (Chicago, 1980; 1978).

——, *The Legend of Bouvines* (Cambridge, 1990; 1973).

Eadmer, *Historia Novorum in Anglia*, ed. M. Rule (RS London, 1884), trans. Geoffrey Bosanquet, *Eadmer's History of Recent Events in England* (London, 1964).

Ebrey, Patricia B., *Family and Property in Sung China: Yuan Tsai's Precepts for Social Life* (Princeton, 1984).

Evans-Pritchard, E. E., *Witchcraft, Oracles and Magic among the Azande* (Oxford 1937, abridged edition, Oxford, 1976).

Fairbank, J. K., *China: A New History* (Cambridge, MA, 1992).

Fentress, James and Chris Wickham, *Social Memory* (Oxford, 1992).

Fernandez Armesto, Felipe, *Barcelona* (Oxford, 1992).

Fichtenau, Heinrich, *Living in the Tenth Century* (Chicago, 1991; 1984).

——, *Heretics and Scholars in the High Middle Ages*, trans. D. A. Kaiser (Philadelphia 1998; 1992).

Finucane, Ronald C., *Miracles and Pilgrims: Popular Beliefs in Medieval England* (London, 1977).

Fitznigel, Richard, ed. Charles Johnson, *The* Dialogus de scaccario (London, 1950).

Fleming, Robin, 'Monastic Lands and England's Defence in the Viking Age', *EHR* 100 (1985), 247–65.

——, 'Rural elites and urban communities in Late Saxon England', *P&P* 141 (1993), 13–37.

Fletcher, Richard, *The Conversion of Europe: from Paganism to Christianity, 371–1386 AD* (London, 1997).

Flint, Valerie I. J., *The Rise of Magic in Early Medieval Europe* (Oxford, 1991).

Foreville R. and G. Weir, *The Book of St. Gilbert* (Oxford, 1987).

Fossier, R. *Chartes de coutume en Picardie (XIe.–XIIIe. siècles)* (Paris, 1975).

——, *Enfance de l'Europe, Xe.–XIIe siècle: aspects économiques et sociaux* (2 vols; Paris, 1982).

——, *Peasant Life in the Middle Ages* (Oxford, 1988; 1984).

Fournier, Gabriel, *Le peuplement rural en Basse-Auvergne durant le haut moyen age* (Paris, 1962).

Fox, Robin, *The Red Lamp of Incest* (London, 1980).

France, John, Nithard Bulst and Paul Reynolds, *Rodulfus Glaber Opera* (Oxford, 1989).

Galbraith, V. H., *The Making of Domesday Book* (Oxford, 1961).

——, *Domesday Book; its Place in Administrative History* (Oxford, 1974).

Ganshof, F. L., *Rural Communities in the Medieval West* (Baltimore, 1990).

Geary, Patrick, *Furta sacra: Thefts of Relics in the Central Middle Ages* (Princeton, 1978).

——, *Living with the Dead in the Middle Ages* (Ithaca, 1994).

——, *Phantoms of Remembrance* (Princeton, 1994).

Gellner, Ernest, *Nations and Nationalism* (Oxford, 1983).

Geoffrey of Monmouth, trans. Lewis Thorpe, *History of the Kings of Britain* (Harmondsworth, 1966).

Gerald of Wales, trans. J. J. O'Meara, *The History and Topography of Ireland* (Harmondsworth, 1982).

Gesta pontificum cenomannensium, Bouquet XII, 547–51.

Gernet, Jean, *A History of Chinese Civilization* (Cambridge, 1982; 1972).

Gillingham, John 'The Beginnings of English Imperialism', *Journal of Historical Sociology* 5/4 (1992), 392–409.

Gimpel, Jean, *The Cathedral Builders* (London, 1983; 1980).

Given, James, *State and Society in Medieval Europe: Gwynedd and Languedoc under Outside Rule* (Ithaca, 1990).

——, *Inquisition and Medieval Society: Power, Discipline and Resistance in Languedoc* (Ithaca, 1997).

Glanvill, *Tractatus de legibus et consuetudinibus regni Anglie qui Glanvilla vocatur*, ed. and trans. G. D. G. Hall (London, 1965).

Glick, Thomas F. *From Muslim Fortress to Christian Castle* (Manchester, 1995).

Gluckman, Max, *Politics, Law and Ritual in Tribal Society* (Oxford, 1965).

Goody, Jack, *The Development of the Family and Marriage in Europe* (Cambridge, 1983).

Gouttebroze, J. C. 'Le duc, le comte et le peuple: remarques sur une sédition des paysans de Normandie autour de l'an mil', *Le Moyen Age* 101 (1995).

Gregory VII *Registrum*, ed. E. Caspar, *MGH Epist.* II.

Grosser Historische Weltatlas: vol. – ii Mittelalter, ed. Josef Engel (Munich, 1970).

Guibert de Nogent, *Autobiographie*, ed. and trans. E. R. Labande (Paris, 1981); trans. John F. Benton, *Self and Society in Medieval France: the Memoirs of Abbot Guibert of Nogent (1064?–c.1125)* (New York, 1970).

——, *De sanctis et eorum pignoribus*, PL 156, col. 607–80.

Gurevich, Aaron, *Medieval Popular Culture: Problems of Belief and Perception* (Cambridge, 1988).

Harding, Stephen, *monitum*, trans P. Matarasso, *The Cistercian World* (Harmondsworth, 1993).

Head, Thomas, *Hagiography and the Cult of Saints: The Diocese of Orléans, 800–1200* (Cambridge, 1990).

——, and Richard Landes (eds) *The Peace of God: Social Violence and Religious Response around the Year 1000* (Ithaca, 1992).

Heloise, 'The Personal Letters between Abelard and Héloise', ed. J. T. Muckle, *Mediaeval Studies* 15 (1953), 47–94.

Herlihy, David, 'The Agrarian Revolution in Southern France and Italy, 850–1100', *Speculum* 31 (1956).

——, 'Church Property of the European Continent, 701–1200', *Speculum* 36 (1961).

——, *Medieval Households* (Cambridge, MA, 1985).

Hibberd, A. B., 'The Origins of the Medieval Town Patriciate', *P&P* 3 (1953), 15–27.

Ho Ping-ti, *The Ladder of Success in Imperial China: Aspects of Social Mobility 1368–1911* (New York and London, 1962).

Hodges, Richard, *The Anglo-Saxon Achievement* (London, 1989).

Huang, Ray, *1587. A Year of No Significance: the Ming Dynasty in Decline* (New Haven, 1981).

Hugh of St. Victor, *Didascalicon*, trans. Jerome Taylor (New York, 1961).

Hughes, Diane Owen, 'Urban Growth and Family Structure in Medieval Genoa', *P&P* 66 (1975), 3–28.

Hymes, Robert P., *Statesmen and Gentlemen: The Elite of Fou- chou, Chiang-hsi, in Northern and Southern Sung* (Cambridge, 1986).

Iogna-Prat, Dominic Agni immaculati: *Recherches sur les sources hagiographiques relatives à Saint Maieul de Cluny (954–994)* (Paris, 1988).

——, *Ordonner et exclure: Cluny et la société chrétienne face à l'hérésie, au judaïsme, à l'Islam 1000–1150* (Paris, 1998).

Jacobs, Jane. *The Economy of Cities* (New York, 1970).

Jaeger, C. Stephen, *The Origins of Courtliness: Civilizing Trends and the Formation of Courtly Ideals, 930–1210* (Philadelphia, 1985).

——, *The Envy of Angels: Cathedral Schools and Social Ideals in Medieval Europe, 950–1200* (Philadelphia, 1994).

John, Eric, *Orbis Britanniae* (Leicester, 1966).

John of Ford, *Life of Wulfric of Haslebury*, trans. Matarasso, *Cistercian World*, pp. 235–73.

John of Salerno, *Vita Odonis*, PL 133, col. 639–704.

John of Salisbury, *Metalogicon*, trans. Daniel D. McGarry (Berkeley, 1955).

——, *Policraticus* Books 4, 5, 6, parts of 7, 8, trans. J. Dickinson, *The Statesman's Book of John of Salisbury* (New York, 1927).

——, *Historia Pontificalis*, ed. Marjorie Chibnall (Edinburgh, 1956).

Johnson, Penelope, D., *Prayer, Patronage, and Power: the Abbey of La Trinité, Vendôme 1032–1187* (New York, 1981).

Keen, Maurice, *Chivalry* (New Haven and London, 1984).

Kemp, E. W., *Canonisation and Authority in the Western Church* (Oxford, 1948).

Kieckhefer, Richard, *Magic in the Middle Ages* (Cambridge, 1989).

King, Edmund (ed.), 'Estate Records of the Hotot Family of Northamptonshire', *A Northamptonshire Miscellany*, Northants Record Society xxxii (1983).

——, *Medieval England* (London, 1988).

Koziol, Geoffrey, *Begging Pardon and Favor: Ritual and Political Order in Early Medieval France* (Ithaca and London, 1992).

Kritzek, James, *Peter the Venerable and Islam* (Princeton, 1964).

Kulke, Hermann and Dietmar Rothermund, *History of India* (London, 1986).

Lambert, Malcolm, *The Cathars* (Oxford, 1998).

Landes, David, *The Wealth and Poverty of Nations* (New York, 1998).

Landes, Richard, *Relics, Apocalypse and the Deceits of History: Adedmar of Chabannes, 989–1034* (Cambridge MA, 1995).

Langmuir, Gavin, *Toward a Definition of Antisemitism* (Berkeley, 1990).

Lauranson-Rosaz, Christian, *L'Auvergne et ses marges (Velay, Gévaudan) du viiie. au xie. siècle* (Le Puy en Velay, 1987).

Lauwers, Michel, '*Dicunt vivorum beneficere nihil prodesse defunctis*. Histoire d'une thème polémique, XIe–XIIe siècles' in Zerner (ed.), *Inventer l'hérésie?*, pp. 157–92.

Le Goff, Jacques, *Intellectuals in the Middle Ages* (Oxford, 1993; 1957).

——, *Time, Work and Culture in the Middle Ages* (Chicago, 1980; 1977).

——, *The Birth of Purgatory* (Chicago, 1984; 1981).

——, *The Medieval Imagination* (Chicago, 1988).

Lestocquoy, J., *Les villes de Flandres et d'Italie sous le gouvernement des patriciens* (Paris, 1952).

Letaldus of Micy, *Delatio corporis sancti Juniani in synodem Carrofensem*, PL 137.

Lewis, Andrew W., *Royal Succession in Capetian France: Studies in Familial Order and the State* (Cambridge, MA, 1982).

Lewis, Bernard, 'The Significance of Heresy in Islam', *Studia Islamica* I (1955), 43–63, also in Lewis, *Islam in History* (London, 1973).

Leyser, Henrietta, *Hermits and the New Monasticism* (London, 1984).

Leyser, Karl, 'The Polemics of the Papal Revolution', in B. Smalley (ed.), *Trends in Medieval Political Thought* (Oxford, 1965).

——, *Rule and Conflict in an Early Medieval Society: Ottonian Saxony* (London, 1975).

——, *Medieval Germany and its Neighbours* (London, 1982).

——, *Communications and Power in Medieval Europe: volume 1, The Carolingian and Ottonian Centuries; volume 2, The Gregorian Revolution and Beyond* (London, 1994).

Lipton, Sara, *Images of Intolerance: the Representation of Jews and Judaism in the* Bible moralisée (Berkeley, 1999).

Little, Lester K., *Religious Poverty and the Profit Economy in Medieval Europe* (Ithaca, 1978).

——, *Benedictine Maledictions: liturgical cursing in Romanesque France* (Ithaca and London, 1993).

Lo, Winston, *An Introduction to the Civil Service of Sung China* (Honolulu, 1987).

Luchaire, Achille, *Social France at the time of Philip Augustus* (trans. Edward B. Krehbiel, New York, n.d)

Luscombe, D. E., 'From Paris to the Paraclete: the correspondence of Abelard and Heloise', *Proceedings of the British Academy* 74 (1988), 247–83.

Magdalino, Paul, 'Enlightenment and Repression in Twelfth-century Byzantium: the evidence of the canonists' in N. Oikonomides, ed. *Byzantium in the Twelfth Century: Canon Law, State and Society* (Athens, 1991), pp. 359–73.

Maisonnneuve, Henri, *Etudes sur les origines de l'inquisition* (second edn; Paris, 1960).

Makdisi, George, *The Rise of Colleges: institutions of learning in Islam and the West* (Edinburgh, 1981).

Map, Walter, *de nugis curialium*, ed. and trans. M. R. James, C. N. L. Brooke and R. A. B. Mynors (Oxford, 1983).

Marbod of Rennes, *ep.* vi, PL 171, col. 1483–5.

Mayr-Harting, Henry, 'Functions of a twelfth-century recluse', *History* 60 (1975), 337–52.

——, and Moore R. I. (eds.), *Studies in Medieval History Presented to R. H. C. Davis* (London, 1985).

McCulloh, John M., 'Jewish Ritual Murder: William of Norwich, Thomas of Monmouth, and the Early Dissemination of the Myth', *Speculum* 72/3 (1997), 698–740.

Mews, Constant, *The Lost Letters of Heloise and Abelard* (New York, 1999).
Miracula S. Hucberti, AASS Nov. 1.
Montanari, Massimo, *The Culture of Food* (Oxford 1994; 1993).
Moore, R. I., *The Birth of Popular Heresy* (London, 1975).
——, *The Origins of European Dissent* (London, 1977).
——, 'Family, Community and Cult on the Eve of the Gregorian Reform', *TRHS* 5/30 (1980), 49–69.
——, 'Popular Heresy and Popular Violence, 1022–1179', in *Studies in Church History 21*, ed. W. J. *Sheils, Toleration and Persecution* (Oxford, 1984), 43–50.
——, 'Guibert of Nogent and his World', in Mayr-Harting and Moore (eds), *Studies in Medieval History Presented to R. H. C. Davis*, pp. 107–17.
——, *The Formation of a Persecuting Society: Power and Deviance in Western Europe, 950–1250* (Oxford, 1987).
——, 'Anti-semitism and the Birth of Europe', in *Studies in Church History* 29, ed. Diana Wood, *Christianity and Judaism* (Oxford, 1992).
——, 'Postscript: The Peace and the Social Revolution', in Head and Landes (eds), *The Peace of God*, pp. 308–26.
——, 'A la naissance de la société persécutrice: les clercs, les cathares et la formation de l'Europe' in *La persécution du catharisme: Actes de la 6e. session d'histoire médiévale organisée par la Centre d'Etudes Cathares* (Toulouse, 1996), pp. 11–37.
——, 'Between Sanctity and Superstition: Saints and their Miracles in the Age of Revolution', in Miri Rubin (ed.), *The Work of Jacques le Goff and the Challenges of Medieval History* (Woodbridge, 1997).
Morey, Adrian and C. N. L. Brooke, *Gilbert Foliot and his Letters* (Cambridge, 1965).
Morris, Colin, *The Papal Monarchy: the Western Church from 1050 to 1250* (Oxford, 1989).
Morris, Rosemary, 'The Powerful and the Poor in Tenth-Century Byzantium: Law and Reality', *P&P* 73 (1976), 3–27.
Mottahedeh, Roy, *The Mantle of the Prophet* (London, 1985).
Mundy, John H., *Liberty and Political Power in Toulouse 1050–1230* (New York, 1954).
——, *Europe in the High Middle Ages* (second edn; London, 1991).
——, *Society and Government at Toulouse in the Age of the* Cathars (Toronto, 1997).
Murray, Alexander, *Reason and Society in the Middle Ages* (Oxford, 1978).
Musset, Lucien, '*Cimiterium ad refugium tantum vivorum non ad sepulturam mortuorum*', *Revue du moyen age latin* 4 (1948).
Nelson, Janet L., 'Literacy in Carolingian Government', in R. McKitterick (ed.), *The Uses of Literacy in Early Medieval Europe* (Cambridge, 1990), pp. 258–96.
——, *Charles the Bald* (London, 1992).
Nicholas, David M., *The Growth of the Medieval City* (London, 1997).
Odo of Cluny, *Vita Geraldi, PL* 133, col. 641–704.
Orderic Vitalis, *Ecclesiastical History*, ed. Marjorie Chibnall (6 vols; Oxford, 1968–80).

Painter, Sidney, *William Marshal* (Baltimore, 1933).

Panofsky, E., *Abbot Suger on the Abbey Church of St. Denis and its Art Treasures*, ed. G. Panofsky Soergel (second edition; Princeton, 1976).

Peter the Venerable, *Tractatus contra petrobrusianos*, ed. James Fearns, *Corpus Christianorum, Continuatio mediaevalis X* (Turnholt, 1968).

——, *Liber contra sectam sive haeresim saracenorum*, ed. James Kritzek, *Peter the Venerable and Islam* (Princeton, 1964).

Poly, J-P., *La Provence et la société féodale, 879–1166* (Paris, 1976).

——, and Bournazel, E., *La mutation féodale, x*ᵉ*–xiii*ᵉ *siècles* (Paris, 1981; trans. C. Higgitt, *The Feudal Transformation 900–1200*) (New York, 1991).

Radding, Charles M., *A World Made by Men: cognition and society, 400–1200* (Chapel Hill and London, 1985).

Ramseyer, Valerie, *Ecclesiastical Power and the Reconstruction of Society in Eleventh-Century Salerno* unpublished Ph.D. dissertation, University of Chicago, 1996.

Randsborg, Klaus, *The First Millennium* AD *in Europe and the Mediterranean* (Cambridge, 1991).

Reuter, T. A. (ed.), *The Medieval Nobility* (Amsterdam, 1978).

——, 'Plunder and Tribute in the Carolingian Empire', *TRHS* 5/35 (1985) 75–94.

——, *Germany in the Early Middle Ages* (London, 1991).

Reynolds, Susan, *Kingdoms and Communities in Western Europe, 900–1300* (Oxford, 1984).

——, *Fiefs and Vassals: The Medieval Evidence Reinterpreted* (Oxford, 1994).

Robinson, I. R., 'Gregory VII and the Soldiers of Christ', *History* 58 (1973), 179–92.

——, *The Papacy, 1073–1198* (Cambridge, 1990).

Roger of Hoveden, *Chronica*, ed. W. Stubbs (2 vols; RS London, 1867).

Rollason, David W., 'The Miracles of St. Benedict: A Window on Early Medieval France' in Mayr-Harting and Moore (eds), *Studies in Medieval History Presented to R. H. C. Davis*, pp. 73–90.

Rosenwein, Barbara, *To Be the Neighbor of St. Peter: The Social Meaning of Cluny's Property, 909–1049* (Ithaca and London, 1989).

——, 'The Family Politics of Berengar I, King of Italy (888–924)', *Speculum* 71 (1991).

Rubellin, Michel, 'Au temps où Valdès n'était pas hérétique: hypothèse sur la rôle de Valdès à Lyon', in Zerner, *Inventer l'hérésie?*, pp. 193–218.

Russell, J. C., 'Population in Europe, 500–1500', in Carlo M. Cipolla (ed.), *The Fontana Economic History of Europe*: Volume I, *The Middle Ages* (London, 1972), pp. 25–70.

Sahlins, Marshall, *Stone Age Economics* (Chicago, 1972).

Sawyer, Birgit, P. Sawyer and I. N. Wood (eds), *The Christianization of Scandinavia* (Alingsås, 1987).

Sawyer, P. H., 'The Wealth of England', *TRHS* 5/15 (1965), 145–64.

Schevill, F. C., *History of Florence* (New York, 1961).

Scholz, B. W., *Carolingian Chronicles* (Ann Arbor, 1970).

Searle, Eleanor, *Predatory Kinship and the Creation of Norman Power, 840–1066* (Berkeley, 1988).

Seidel, Linda, *Songs of Glory: The Romanesque Façades of Aquitaine* (Chicago, 1981).

Sitwell, T., *St. Odo of Cluny* (London, 1958).

Skocpol, Theda, *States and Social Revolutions* (Cambridge, 1979).

Smalley, Beryl, *The Study of the Bible in the Middle Ages* (Oxford, 1941).

——, *The Becket Conflict and the Schools* (Oxford, 1973).

——, (ed.), *Trends in Medieval Political Thought* (Oxford, 1965).

Smith, Julia M. H. 'Oral and Written: Saints, Miracles and Relics in Brittany, *c.*850–1250', *Speculum* 65 (1990), 309–43.

Somerville, Robert, 'The Council of Beauvais, 1114', *Traditio* 24 (1968).

Southern, R. W., *The Making of the Middle Ages* (London, 1951).

——, *Western Society and the Church in the Middle Ages* (Harmondsworth, 1970).

——, *Medieval Humanism and Other Studies* (Oxford, 1970).

——, *St. Anselm: A Portrait in a Landscape* (Cambridge, 1990).

——, 'From Schools to University', in J. I. Catto (ed.), *The History of the University of Oxford*, volume I (Oxford, 1984), pp. 1–36.

——, *Scholastic Humanism and the Unification of Europe: volume I, Foundations* (Oxford, 1995).

Spiegel, Gabrielle, *Romancing the Past* (Berkeley and London, 1993).

Stafford, Pauline, *Unification and Conquest* (London, 1989).

Stenton, F. M. (ed.), *Facsimiles of Early Charters from Northamptonshire Collections*, Northants Record Society iv (1930).

Stock, Brian, *The Implications of Literacy* (Princeton, 1983).

Stow, Kenneth R., *Alienated Minority: the Jews of Medieval Latin Europe* (Cambridge, MA, 1992).

Stubbs, William, *Historical Introductions to the Rolls Series*, ed. A. Hassall (London, 1902).

——, *Select Charters*, 9th edn, by H. W. C. Davis (Oxford, 1913).

Sumption, Jonathan, *Pilgrimage: An Image of Mediaeval Religion* (London, 1975).

Talbot, C. H. (ed.), *The Life of Christina of Markyate* (Oxford, 1959).

Thomas of Monmouth, *The Life and Miracles of William of Norwich*, ed. and trans. A. Jessopp and M. R. James (Cambridge, 1896).

Tolan, John, *Petrus Alfonsi and his Medieval Readers* (Gainsville, 1993).

Toubert, Pierre, *Les structures du Latium médiévale: le Latium méridional et la Sabine du ixe. siècle à la fin du xiie. siècle* (Rome, 1973).

——, 'The Carolingian Moment', in André Bourguière et al. (eds), *History of the Family*, I, pp. 379–406.

Translatio sancti viviani episcopi, Analaecta Bollandiana viii (1889), 256–77.

Turner, Ralph V., *The English Judiciary in the Age of Glanvill and Bracton, c.1176–1235* (Cambridge, 1985).

Van Dam, Raymond, *Leadership and Community in Late Antique Gaul* (Berkeley and Los Angeles, 1985).

Varoqueaux, C., 'Découvertes de vestiges médiévaux à Rouen, Rue aux Juifs', in R. Foreville (ed.), *Les mutations socio-culturelles au tournant du xie.–xiie. siècles* (Paris, 1984).

Venarde, Bruce, *Women's Monasticism in Medieval Society: Nunneries in France and England, 890–1215* (Ithaca and London, 1997).

Violante, Cinzio, *La società Milanese nell'età pre-comunale* (Bari, 1953).

Vita Hugonis auctore Hildeberto Cenomnanensis Episcopo PL 159.

Vita Sancti Iohannis Gualberti auctore Andrea abbate Strumensi, ed. F. Baethgen *MGH SS* 30, ii.

Vita Norberti, ed. R. Wilmans, *MGH SS* 12.

Vita S. Stephani Obazinensis: Vie de Saint Etienne d'Obazine, ed. Michel Aubrun (Clermont-Ferrand, 1970).

Vita B. Vitalis Saviniacensis, ed. E. P. Sauvage (Brussels, 1882).

Wallace-Hadrill, J. M., *The Frankish Church* (Oxford, 1983).

Weber, Max, *The Religion of China* (Glencoe, 1951).

Wickham, Chris, 'Property ownership and seignorial power in twelfth-century Tuscany' in Wendy Davies and Paul Fouracre (eds), *Property and Power in the Early Middle Ages* (Cambridge, 1995), pp. 221–44.

White, Stephen D., *Custom, Kinship and Gifts to Saints* (Ithaca, 1988).

William of Malmesbury ed. W. Stubbs, *Gesta Regum Anglorum* (2 vols; RS London, 1887–9), trans. J. A. Giles, *Chronicle of the Kings of England* (London, 1847).

William of Newburgh, *Historia rerum Anglicarum*, ed. R. Howlett, *Chronicles of the Reign of Stephen etc.* (2 vols; RS London, 1884–5).

Winroth, Anders, *The Making of Gratian's* Decretum (Cambridge, 2000).

Zerner, Monique (ed.), *Inventer l'hérésie? Discours polémiques et pouvoirs avant l'inquisition* (Nice, 1998).

Index